Blood and Religion

Blood and Religion

The Unmasking of the Jewish and Democratic State

Jonathan Cook

First published 2006 by Pluto Press
345 Archway Road, London N6 5AA
and 839 Greene Street, Ann Arbor, MI 48106

www.plutobooks.com

British Library Cataloguing in Publication Data
A catalogue record for this book is available from the British Library

ISBN 978 0 7453 2555 2 Paperback
ISBN 978 0 7453 2556 9 Hardback
ISBN 978 1 8496 4326 9 PDF
ISBN 978 1 7837 1589 3 EPUB
ISBN 978 1 7837 1590 9 Kindle

Library of Congress Cataloging in Publication Data applied for

10 9 8 7 6 5 4 3 2 1

Designed and produced for Pluto Press by
Chase Publishing Services Ltd, Fortescue, Sidmouth, EX10 9QG, England
Typeset from disk by Stanford DTP Services, Northampton, England
Printed and bound by CPI Group (UK) Ltd, Croydon, CR0 4YY

For Sally, Ziad, Maha and all the other "Israeli Arabs" who fight for the right to identify themselves as Palestinians

Contents

Preface

Few tasks are more challenging than writing about Israel. For those trying to report or comment intelligently on events in the Israeli-Palestinian conflict, the effort can sometimes seem futile. Israel's apologists have succeeded in excising from the debate about the Jewish state the language of universal human rights and justice, values by which we judge other problematic conflicts. In the case of Israel, the culture of apology is now deeply rooted in the West, particularly among European and American Jewry.

The apologist has a well-tested strategy. Whenever a critic of Israel makes his case by citing an incident or example, the apologist will provide a counter-example or counter-incident, however irrelevant, to suggest either his "opponent" is unfamiliar with the material or that his motives are suspect, the anti-Semitism canard. Challenges of this kind may do nothing to blunt the thrust of the original argument but they are a very successful ploy. The critic's credibility can be dented with readers and, more damagingly, with commissioning editors, the media's gatekeepers, who decide whether a news report or comment article will be published. Critical writers who wish to contribute to the mainstream media must either accept a bland, diluted terminology acceptable to the apologists or devote endless amounts of time, energy and valuable space trying to second-guess how the information they include will be distorted. As a consequence, much of the debate about Israel is weighed down with trivia, pedantry and obscurantism.

I have tried to avoid these pitfalls. In doing so, I am sure to antagonise some readers. Doubtless I also risk accusations of anti-Semitism. Wherever possible, therefore, I have cited senior Israeli politicians and officials to support my arguments and quoted from Israeli publications, even if they are simply confirming my own observations and experiences as a reporter. A majority of my endnotes refer to articles and interviews in the *Ha'aretz* and *Jerusalem Post* newspapers. I have largely neglected non-Israeli and Arab sources not because I doubt their credibility but because they will be less convincing to those who seek to reject my argument.

Choice of language is problematic too when writing about Israel: certain words are deemed to signify where you stand in a debate.

For example, I could have described the barrier built around the West Bank as a "wall", seen as the pro-Palestinian label, or a "fence", viewed as the pro-Israeli one, or as a "barrier", the anaemic language of neutrality. I have chosen to vary the terminology, not least because I do not think there is a correct answer in this semantic debate. Both fences and walls aim to demarcate boundaries and to prevent movement, but walls are usually preferred over fences to shield from view unwanted or troublesome things. The West Bank barrier achieves all three goals. In the places where most Palestinians experience their physical separation from Israel and other Palestinians, in cities like Jerusalem, Qalqilya and Tulkaram, the barrier is most definitely a wall rather than a fence.

As for the members of the population group that this study mainly concerns, I have variously called them Israeli Arabs, Palestinian or Arab citizens of Israel, and the Palestinian or Arab minority. Language difficulties arise here too. The Israeli Arabs are often seen as having an identity crisis, because they belong to the Israeli state but identify with the Palestinian people; or, put another way, they have Israeli citizenship but Palestinian nationality. I have not taken a rigidly ideological view. I do not believe most Arab citizens of Israel have a cut-and-dried identity, either as Israelis or as Palestinians. They manoeuvre between these two identities – and others, including ethnic, religious, tribal, social and class affiliations – attracted more to one or the other in some respects and at certain times.

The elasticity of the Palestinian citizens' identity was illustrated to me in stark fashion during a conversation with a middle-aged Druze shopkeeper in the mixed Arab town of Shafa'amr. We spoke in August 2005, shortly after a 19-year-old Jewish soldier, Eden Natan Zada, had shot dead four local residents – Muslims and Christians – on a bus close by his shop. Impassively my Druze interviewee said he had witnessed Zada being beaten to death by the crowds who stormed the bus when Zada ran out of ammo. The shopkeeper then announced proudly that he too was a soldier, a member of the Golani Brigade, an elite military unit with a notorious record of using violence against Palestinians in the occupied territories. (Druze men, uniquely among the Palestinian minority, are drafted into the Israeli army, serving alongside Jews.) Next, he denounced Zada as a terrorist. "Soldiers don't kill other soldiers," he said, presumably referring to the fact that Zada had opened fire in a Druze neighbourhood, even if no Druze had been killed in the attack. Finally, he added that, although he had just received his call-up for reserve duty in Gaza helping with the disengagement, he had torn up the papers. He was refusing to go in protest at Zada's "racist attack".

In other words, Arab identity in Israel is rarely a straightforward matter, even for citizens like the Druze who are seen as unwaveringly loyal. A proportion of Arab citizens prefer the label "Israeli Arab", the term the state of Israel uses whenever referring to them and wants them to use when they refer to themselves. Israel has its reasons, which this book explores: not least its interest in severing the Arab citizens' ideological and historical ties to the land of Palestine-Israel. The Israeli Arabs are the sole remnants of the expelled indigenous Palestinian people living on their land inside Israel, and as such the state has worked tirelessly over many decades since its establishment to "de-Palestinianise" them. It has wanted the question of their rights separated from those of the Palestinians of the occupied territories and the millions of refugees. It has striven to eradicate the Arab minority's national and cultural memories, to turn them into identity-starved "Arabs".

But it is also true that Israel has almost certainly failed to achieve its objective. (In fact, as this book discusses, the security establishment appears to have abandoned this goal and is now publicly recharacterising the minority as a "fifth column" of the Palestinians, as a population group that can have no future inside a Jewish state.) Among the younger generation of Arab citizens, there has been a resurgence of "Palestinian-ness", particularly since the outbreak of the second intifada. This has been encouraged – inadvertently or otherwise – in two ways by Israel. First, the minority's growing perception that Israel is not really interested in creating a viable Palestinian state in the occupied territories has forced many Arab citizens to conclude that there will never be peace in the region and that they will always be seen as proven or potential traitors. Second, Israel's continuing insistence on conflating the Israeli and Jewish national identities has failed to offer the Palestinian minority a national or civic identity inside Israel.

Despite simplistic Israeli assertions about the disloyalty of its Arab citizens, the trend of "Palestinianisation" has not been straightforward. Since the Palestine Liberation Organisation recognised Israel in the late 1980s, its leaders have consistently ignored the political consequences of their decisions on Israel's Arab minority, especially the establishment under the Oslo Accords of a Palestinian state-in-the-making next door in the occupied territories. Most Arab citizens may not see themselves as fully Israeli but equally they do not see any welcome for them in a future Palestinian state.

Today, the revival of a Palestinian identity among the Arab minority exists mainly as a cultural rather than a political phenomenon. Surveys consistently show that, while many Israeli Arabs want cultural autonomy, very few want to be included in a future Palestine – partly, no doubt, because of their assessment that Israel will continue controlling such a state in a detrimental fashion. Citizenship of Israel, a state in which they have some rights protected by the courts, is preferable to citizenship in Palestine, a state where their rights will be entirely subservient to Israel's own national goals. Israeli Arabs are therefore seeking solutions within the framework of their continuing Israeli citizenship. The overwhelming majority believe that decades of discrimination against their communities cannot be reversed without major political reforms. The priority for most is directed less at the development of their Palestinian identity and more at the reinvention of the state of Israel, from a Jewish state to a democratic state representing all its citizens.

A brief note on the book's structure. The introduction argues that Israel's image as a benevolent, democratic state has faced an unprecedented threat in the past few years from the political dissent of its Palestinian citizens and their relentless growth in numbers. The first two chapters examine how, in response, Israel has developed and reinforced an image of the minority as an irredentist population group, an enemy trying to subvert the Jewish state from within on behalf of the Palestinians in the occupied territories. It crafted this image both by dramatically overreacting and violently crushing protests inside Israel that coincided with the outbreak of the intifada, and by then skewing the agenda of a state-appointed inquiry that investigated those events. Chapters 3 and 4 explore the consequences of Israel's new approach: first, its development of policies to limit the demographic influence of Palestinians in general and its own Palestinian population in particular; and second, the belated decision to fix the borders of an expanded Jewish state in such a way as to include as many Jewish settlers as possible while seeking to exclude as many Palestinian citizens as possible. The final chapter argues that Israel is creating a new Jewish consensus against the Other, its Palestinian citizens, to legitimise its policies. My general argument – the thread connecting each chapter – is that Israel is beginning a long, slow process of ethnic cleansing both of Palestinian non-citizens from parts of the occupied territories it has long coveted for its expanded Jewish state and of Palestinian citizens from inside its internationally recognised borders.

Finally, I ought briefly to refer to political events unfolding in Israel as I write this. Trade union leader Amir Peretz unexpectedly snatched the leadership of the Labor party from elder statesman Shimon Peres in mid-November 2005 and bolted the national unity government. Backed into a corner by Labor's action and a looming rebellion among hawks in his own party, Prime Minister Ariel Sharon dissolved the Knesset, quit the ruling Likud party, which he helped to found, and set up a new centrist party to run in a general election due in late March 2006. Despite much talk of seismic shifts in the Israeli political landscape, as well as conjecture about new opportunities and dangers for the peace process, I can find no reason to reassess the conclusions I reach in the book about the future direction of the Middle East conflict, or my judgment that Israel is committed to completing a policy of unilateral separation designed to create a "Jewish fortress". My view, as stated elsewhere in the book, is that what are commonly seen as Sharon's personal policy initiatives – the West Bank wall and the Gaza disengagement – were actually being advocated long ago by the country's establishment left, including previous prime ministers Yitzhak Rabin and Ehud Barak and many in the senior army command. Unlike others who have written about the second intifada, I do not believe Sharon has broken with the trend of Israeli "peace"-making since Oslo, though his style has often been more confrontational than his recent predecessors. Sharon's decision to sever ties with the diehard hawks in the Likud party and create a new centrist party is a sign that he is firmly committed to a realignment of Israeli politics to build a Jewish consensus behind the idea of fixing once and for all the borders of the Jewish state.

* * *

Many thanks go to the following friends and colleagues who in their different ways helped to clarify the issues that really matter when thinking about Israel, Palestine and what separates them, Zionism: Hassan Jabareen, Marwan Dalal, Orna Kohn, Rina Rosenberg and the staff of Adalah; Mohammed Zeidan, Tariq Ibrahim, Souhair Ailabouni and the staff of the Arab Association for Human Rights; Ziad Awaisi; Maha Qupty; Tareq Shihadi; Isabelle Humphries; Susan Nathan; Khalil Suleiman; Dr Nakhleh Bishara; Wahbe Bidarni; Ali and Terese Zbeidat; Elias and Martina Shama; Richard Ratcliffe;

Hatim Kanaaneh; Jafar Farah; Khuloud Bedawi; Tirza Ulanovsky; Benoit Challand; Claire Perez; Gavin O'Toole; Alexander Key; Peter Lagerquist; and Ian Douglas.

I would also like to thank the following interviewees who gave generously of their time: Dr Ilan Pappe; Prof. Ramzi Suleiman; Prof. As'ad Ghanem; Dr Uri Davis; Dr Dan Rabinowitz; Dr Yaron Ezrahi; Dr Adel Manna; Dr Said Zidane; Prof. Nadim Rouhana; Nimr Sultany; Ameer Makhoul; Mohammed Abu el-Haija; Eitan Bronstein; Dr Sammy Smooha; Dr Saleh Abdel Jawad; Prof. Ali Jerbawi; Dr George Giacaman; Hana Sweid; Prof. Arnon Sofer; Dr Dan Shueftan. Not all of them will like my conclusions; a few will vehemently disagree with them.

This book has gained substantially from the advice and encouragement of my editor at Pluto, Roger van Zwanenberg. Draft sections of the manuscript were read by Marwan Dalal, Nur Masalha and Gary Sussman, though, of course, responsibility for any remaining faults is entirely mine.

I owe a debt of gratitude to the inhabitants of Nazareth who have supported me as I made a new home in the city. Those who offered me generous hospitality and guided me through the minefield of potential cultural misunderstandings include the Muslimani, Suleiman and Jandeli families, as well of course as my in-laws from the Awad and Azzam families.

Finally, the biggest thanks go to my own family: my mother, father, Clea, Richard, Sue, Aliona and Joe for their support and indulgence of my passions. As for my wife Sally – researcher, translator, friend and confidante – she knows thanks are not enough.

Jonathan Cook
Nazareth
November 2005

0
10
20
30
Kilometres
LEBANON
Kiryat Shmona
GOLAN
Safad
Acre
Karmiel
Haifa
Sakhnin
Arrabe
Sea of Galilee
Tiberias
Shafa'amr
Mediterranean Sea
GALILEE
Nazareth
Afula
Umm al-Fahm
Hadera
Jenin
Jatt
River Jordan
Netanya
Tulkaram
Nablus
Herzliya
Qalqilya
Kafr Qassem
Ariel
Tel Aviv
JORDAN
WEST BANK
Lod
Ramle
Ramallah
Jericho
Ma'ale Adumim
Jerusalem
Ashkelon
ISRAEL
Bethlehem
Gaza City
Dead Sea
Hebron
GAZA
Rafah
Be'ersheva
N
EGYPT
NEGEV
© Keith Cook

Introduction
The Glass Wall

For a country so reluctant to define the extent of its sovereignty – to establish its borders – Israel has a peculiar fondness for erecting barriers. Across the Holy Land there are now walls and fences carving up territory and living space.

Israel began building its most famous wall, a series of interconnecting barriers of concrete, steel and razor wire, in the West Bank in the summer of 2002 to encircle most of the territory's 2.3 million inhabitants. The mammoth structure – when finished it is expected to measure nearly 700 km in length – was named the "security fence" and later the "anti-terror fence", titles that helped to persuade many observers its sole purpose was the protection of Israeli civilians. In truth, the security aspects of the barrier seemed a secondary consideration: its immediate impact was to transform the Palestinian towns and villages of the West Bank into a series of ghettos, cutting them off from their farmland and wells, and – together with hundreds of army checkpoints on the territory's main roads – severing their ties to neighbouring Palestinian communities, which served them with jobs, schools, universities, hospitals and markets. As the wall marched across the landscape of the West Bank, it ate up ancient olive groves, destroyed pastures and greenhouses, and made well-established roads impassable. After the wall's completion in each area, an Israeli army commander would issue a military order confiscating sections of Palestinian farmland or a well that could no longer be reached.

A PREFERENCE FOR DECEPTIVE BORDERS

According to a common Western perception, the wall created an absolute border of the kind that satisfied Israel's security needs, even if it was one that many believed was being built in the wrong place and to the detriment of the Palestinian people. In relation to the way Palestinians experienced the wall, this perception had some truth. Although it deviated substantially from the Green Line – the 1949 armistice line that much of the world considers the most feasible border for a future Palestinian state – the wall did create a clearly demarcated boundary that Palestinians could not cross. For Israelis, on the other hand, the wall was something much less solid and tangible. It was a soft, permeable border that the Israeli army, settlers and their visitors could cross at will in either direction. The wall created a sealed border for the Palestinians while leaving the border open for Israelis.

This difference in Israeli and Palestinian experiences of the barrier extended to the way it appeared to an observer on either side. For example, as the wall skirted homes and businesses in the Palestinian city of Tulkaram, close to the Green Line, its concrete surface towered eight metres above the ground, with Israeli soldiers in gun-towers watching over the inhabitants. On the Israeli side, however, the wall was all but invisible. Most Israeli drivers and tourists who passed close by Tulkaram on the busy four-lane Trans-Israel Highway did not realise that the concrete structure was just a few metres away. They saw only a landscaped embankment, planted with cactuses, tall grasses and bushes. In other areas, sections of the wall were painted with murals on the Israeli side, reimagining the view that was now missing while making sure that it was empty of the Palestinian villages that could be seen before its construction.[1]

Nearly a decade earlier Israel had built a similar barrier that established a border in one direction only. In 1994 more than one million Palestinians were sealed in behind an electronic fence erected around Gaza, a strip of land measuring just 28 miles long by six wide on the Mediterranean coast. Again the official excuse was security. But, even after the fence was finished, several thousand Jewish settlers were able to live inside the Strip in communities separate from the Palestinians. For the settlers the fence was no barrier; it was not even an inconvenience. Whereas Palestinians could not leave Gaza without a permit from the Israeli military authorities, the settlers could drive straight into Israel via a series of special roads separated from Gazans by razor wire, tanks and soldiers. Thus protected, the settlers plundered the Strip's limited resources of farmland and water for their domestic and commercial benefit, while poverty and unemployment rocketed among Palestinians.[2]

Finally in the summer of 2005 Israel dismantled the Gaza settlements. The unilateral move, known as "disengagement", was sold to the world as the end of the Strip's occupation. In a speech in April 2005 President George W Bush sanctioned such an interpretation, claiming the evacuation would provide an opportunity to create "a democratic state in Gaza".[3] The widely shared assumption was that the Israeli prime minister, Ariel Sharon, had decided – or been forced under pressure from Washington – to take the first historic step in establishing the borders of a Palestinian state.

Critics suspected more cynical motives on Sharon's part: that he hoped to use the disengagement as a distraction while he consolidated his grip on the West Bank, fortifying large settlements like Ariel, Ma'ale Adumim and the Gush Etzion bloc. Though doubtless true, the explanation missed an equally important reason why Israel needed to leave Gaza. For some years Israeli professors of demography, the gurus of population trends, had been warning the government that a critical point was about to be reached when there would be parity between the number of Jews and Arabs living in the land between the Mediterranean Sea and the River Jordan – the area comprising Israel and the occupied territories that Israelis call "Greater Israel" and Palestinians know as historic Palestine. The Israeli government, finally confronted by its own fears that the world would soon see a minority of Jews ruling over a majority of Arabs and call it apartheid, was cornered into disengaging from Gaza's large Palestinian population.

After the settlers and the soldiers had withdrawn, Gaza's Palestinians found themselves still prisoners. On three sides they faced the perimeter fence, and dug in behind it the Israeli and Egyptian armies, and on the fourth the Israeli navy patrolling the coast. There was even talk of building an "underwater wall" to ensure no Palestinian swimmers, rafts or boats could leave Gaza.[4] The Strip's air space was entirely Israeli-controlled too. The disengagement simply removed the prison guards from view.

TWO PHILOSOPHIES: THE IRON WALL vs THE GLASS WALL

The West Bank and Gaza's walls gave physical expression to the philosophy of an early Zionist movement led by Vladimir Jabotinsky known as Revisionism,[5] the intellectual inheritance of today's ruling Likud party in Israel. In 1923 Jabotinsky laid down the group's core principles in an article entitled *The Iron Wall*. He concluded that Zionists who believed a Jewish state could be created on the Palestinian homeland through compromise – whether by reaching an agreement, buying the land or duping the natives – were deluding only themselves. The indigenous Palestinian population would never agree to its own dispossession. As there were too many Arabs to expel them all, he argued, a policy of unremitting force was needed to cow them into submission. His "iron wall" was a metaphor for might makes right.

> It is my hope and belief that we will then offer them [the Arabs] guarantees that will satisfy them and that both peoples will live in peace as good neighbours. But the sole way to such an agreement is through the iron wall, that is to say, the establishment in Palestine of a force that will in no way be influenced by Arab pressure.[6]

Belatedly, 80 years after publication of *The Iron Wall*, Jabotinsky's philosophy of forceful unilateralism found solid and permanent form in the concrete and steel erected around the West Bank and Gaza.

These walls and fences, however, are not the only barriers Israel has built to contain Palestinians. Another group, rarely mentioned in discussions of the Israeli–Palestinian conflict, is similarly trapped. The 1.3 million Palestinian citizens of Israel, commonly referred to as "Israeli Arabs" and comprising nearly a fifth of the country's population,[7] are separated from the Jewish majority by a glass wall,[8] an invisible barrier that for them is as unyielding and solid as the walls around the West Bank and Gaza are for their own Palestinians. The purpose of the glass wall is much the same as that of the concrete and steel ones around the occupied territories: to imprison a Palestinian population and force it into submission, while shielding its oppression from view.

Given international sensitivities, Israel has justified building its physical barriers in the West Bank and Gaza with two different, if related, arguments. To the world, it says the walls are needed for Israel's physical security, to prevent Palestinian attacks that harm Israelis. But to its own Jewish public, it says the walls are needed to defend a much broader idea of security, a physical and demographic security. Not only does Israel need protecting from attacks but also from two demographic threats facing the Jewishness of the state: the far higher birth rates of Palestinians, which one day soon will lead to a Palestinian majority in the region; and the continuing Palestinian demand for a right of return of the hundreds of thousands of Palestinians, and millions of their descendants, who were expelled from the country in 1948. On both fronts, says Israel, its "security" is at risk. This enlarged concept of security effectively blurs the threats facing Israel so that physical and demographic dangers cannot easily be distinguished.

So far Israel has not been required to make a defence of its glass wall. Most of the world believes such a wall does not exist because they cannot see it. Inside its own borders, Israel is assumed to be what is usually termed a "Western-style democracy". As Noam Chomsky once observed of American liberal commentary: "There is admiration of Israel's secularism and equitable treatment of its Arab minority. Such general acclaim is matched only by the no less general ignorance of the facts."[9]

BEHIND THE 'BENEVOLENT' GLASS WALL

This book questions the basis of Western assumptions, suggesting that Israel's glass wall is an even greater obstacle to a Middle East peace than its walls of concrete and steel. The glass wall – like the "iron wall" – is designed to intimidate and silence its captive Palestinian population; but unlike the iron wall it conceals the nature of the subjugation in such a way that it is seen as necessary, even benevolent. By understanding the glass wall, we can know what really matters to Israel: not just the use of unrelenting force to guarantee its control of the region and its Palestinian inhabitants, but also the protection of its image as an island of enlightened democracy in the Middle East. The glass wall is more effective than its concrete cousin because it masks the nature of the separation it embodies: as will become clear, the glass wall is essentially a deception, one that prevents observers from comprehending what they see.

The glass wall is not simply a metaphor. In the spring of 2001, hearings began in front of a state-appointed inquiry into the deaths of 13 unarmed Palestinians – 12 Israeli Arabs and one Gazan – killed by the security forces during a brief outbreak of protests inside Israel that coincided with the start of the intifada. The inquiry, named the Or Commission, was a unique event: for the first time a senior judge was in a position to examine authoritatively and in public the state of relations between Israel's Jewish majority and its Palestinian minority, and thereby also shine a spotlight on the Zionist foundations of the Jewish state. Justice Theodor Or questioned police commanders and senior politicians, including the prime minister of the day, Ehud Barak, on the country's long-standing policies of discrimination, on the nature of its security agenda in relation to "Arabs" and on the decision-making that lay behind the police's use of rubber bullets and live ammunition as a first method of crowd control against unarmed civilians. By Israel's standards of dealing with its Palestinian minority, it was an opportunity for unparalleled self-scrutiny and self-criticism.

And yet within weeks, the hearings at the Supreme Court building in Jerusalem had descended into chaos, bitterness and recriminations. The families of the 13 dead watched helplessly as police officers involved in the shootings calmly recounted, often unchallenged, events of that period before claiming memory loss at the crucial moment when a relative was killed. At the end of each day, many of the families angrily denounced the proceedings to the media as a whitewash, arguing that the inquiry's three panel members were not subjecting the police to rigorous cross-examination and that their own lawyers were being prevented from presenting evidence. On separate occasions, the fathers of two young men who had been killed launched themselves from their chairs in the public gallery to lash out at a policeman in the witness stand whose testimony suggested that he had killed their son. Recommending both fathers be prosecuted for assault, Justice Or ordered a halt to the proceedings while he considered how to restore order. Several solutions were proposed, including using a larger room to separate the families from the witnesses and making the families sit in a separate hall where they could watch the proceedings on closed-circuit television.[10]

But Justice Or devised another solution: he demanded that a glass partition be built between the public gallery, where the Palestinian families sat, and the rest of the courtroom.[11] It was a very Israeli solution. During the rest of the hearings, which lasted another year and a half, the judges, inquiry officials and state witnesses were to be found on one side of the wall and the families on the other. On the TV news and in newspaper photographs, however, it looked as if all the participants to the inquiry were sitting in the same room. The inquiry appeared to be treating all the parties equally when in reality its Arab participants were outsiders, excluded and largely ignored.

Israel's Palestinian citizens are not alone in having lived behind a glass wall. Until Israel began building its concrete and steel barriers in the occupied territories, its economic management and exploitation of the West Bank and Gaza were quietly achieved for several decades through the use of exactly the same kind of invisible walls. Just as at the Or Commission hearings the Arab families appeared to be in the courtroom but in truth were helpless outsiders watching events they could not influence, so the Palestinians of the West Bank and Gaza long appeared to inhabit the same space as their Jewish "neighbours" in the settlements while in fact being powerless to drive alongside them on their roads, to enter Israel freely like them to live and work, or to prevent their land and water being taken for the benefit of Jews.

Traditionally, the glass wall has been a useful way of projecting an image of Palestinian life under benevolent Israeli rule that bears no resemblance to reality. That policy has faltered in the occupied territories over more recent years, under the strains imposed by the Palestinians' refusal to have their image managed by Israel. It is a sign of Israel's strategic desperation that it has been forced to convert the glass walls in the occupied territories into tangible ones. As a result Israel has had to reinvent the conflict, downplaying the historic and diplomatic narrative of the occupied territories as "disputed" land, and accentuating Palestinian terrorism and the Jewish state's need for security.

* * *

DECADES OF SILENT OPPRESSION

The glass wall, however unnoticed it is by the international community, is more than apparent to Israel's Palestinian citizens. In the country's first two decades, when the world was extolling the virtues of the only democracy in the Middle East, praising its socialist economy and inspired by the idea of its kibbutz farming communes, the Arab minority was living apart from the Jewish majority, under a highly repressive Israeli military regime. True, the 150,000 Palestinians remaining inside the borders of the new Jewish state after the 1948 war received formal citizenship – a passport and the right to vote in the country's parliamentary elections – but in every other respect they were non-citizens, stripped of the rights associated with a democracy. They needed a permit from the local military governor to work outside their town or village, or to visit relatives or friends living in other parts of the country; independent newspapers, and political parties and gatherings were banned; Arab teachers were vetted by the Shin Bet secret service (as they were until very recently); coercion and torture were used routinely to pressurise Arabs to turn informant for the security services; and political dissidents were deported from the country.[12]

Arab life was considered cheap too. In 1956, in the build-up to the Suez campaign, the army killed 48 men, women and children from the rural community of Kafr Qassem after a 5 pm curfew was imposed on the village at short notice. As workers returned home, they were shot dead at a checkpoint at the entrance to the village. For two months no mention of the massacre was allowed in the media. At a cabinet meeting held in the meantime, ministers worried about the bad publicity if a trial was not held quickly. Golda Meir, then foreign minister, is recorded as saying: "There's no doubt that it cannot be hidden for very long. I don't know how much time is needed for the completion of the trial. Maybe it's possible to keep this unpublished and then go public with the verdict."[13] Eleven soldiers and officers were prosecuted but, as the *Ha'aretz* newspaper reported, they

> all received a 50 per cent increase in their salaries ... The accused mingle freely with the spectators; the officers smile at them and pat them on the back; some of them shake hands with them. It is obvious that these people, whether they will be found innocent or guilty, are not treated as criminals but as heroes.[14]

The commander responsible, Issachar Shadmi, was found guilty of an "administrative error" and given the symbolic punishment of a one penny fine.[15]

Even when the military government was phased out in 1966, the state continued to treat the minority as a hostile and alien element inside the Jewish state. The fields and fertile valleys belonging to Arab communities were frequently declared "closed military zones" (an ominous echo of a phrase now commonly heard by Palestinians in the occupied territories), making it impossible for local residents to access them. In some cases, the army planted fields with mines to further dissuade their owners from tending the land. After a few years of lying fallow, the land reverted to state ownership under ancient Ottoman laws revived by Israel; it could then safely be passed on to Jewish communities, like the kibbutzim and moshavim, for their exclusive development as part of the national project of building a Jewish state. When the Palestinian minority staged its first general strike in 1976 to protest against the continuing mass confiscation of land, the security forces shot dead six unarmed protesters in the Galilean town of Sakhnin.[16] Today, the battle for control of the land is largely finished: 93 per cent of the territory inside Israel is effectively nationalised, held on behalf of Israeli Jews and in trust for the Jewish people around the world rather than for all the country's citizens.

Outside Israel, little more was heard of the Palestinian minority for many years. There was a brief flurry of interest in March 2000 when an Arab family, the Ka'adans, won a five-year legal battle in the Supreme Court forcing an exclusive Jewish community called Katzir to consider their application to live there. At the time, the ruling was hailed, not a little prematurely, as the end of land segregation in Israel. Earlier, the president of the court, Justice Aharon Barak, had urged the two parties to reach a settlement out of court, describing the case as "one of the most difficult and complex judicial decisions that I have ever come across".[17] Only when Katzir continued to refuse to consider the Arab family, did Justice Barak finally intervene. But in practice the Ka'adan ruling changed nothing. Katzir's vetting committee, like those of hundreds of other Jewish communities, still refused to consider an Arab family for membership, and the court never enforced its decision. Local Jewish leaders suggested publicly that the Ka'adans were not acting on their own initiative. Katzir's mayor, Dov Sandrov, for example, told Israeli radio: "I wouldn't be surprised if one day it is revealed that the ones standing behind this affair are the Palestinian Authority and the funds are from Iranian and Saudi sources."[18]

Only a handful of Arab families were turning to the courts asking to be given access to Jewish communities. Most Palestinian citizens chose a different path: rather than trying to flee their own communities, they demanded an end to the discrimination in budgets and resources that kept their towns and villages poor, miserable and overcrowded places.[19] These dire problems have been compounded by the state's refusal to establish a single new Arab community since 1948.[20]

In the late 1990s an Arab Member of the Knesset and a former philosophy professor, Azmi Bishara, offered the Palestinian minority a new political slogan: he called for Israel's reinvention from a Jewish state into a "state of all its citizens".[21] An idea that had until then remained largely an obscure academic talking point quickly became a rallying cry for the minority.[22] Decades of privileges for Jewish citizens had to end, Bishara and others demanded, and a common bond of Israeli citizenship for Jews and Arabs be forged instead. Land and budgets should be allocated on the basis of need instead of ethnic belonging, a long-standing discriminatory policy of house demolitions enforced only against Arab homeowners should be halted, control of Arab education and culture should be placed in the hands of Arab institutions, and racist employment practices that excluded Palestinian citizens from large sections of the Israeli economy should be made illegal.

A HISTORY OF ARAB QUIESCENCE

Until its call for a state of all its citizens, the Palestinian minority had maintained a position of political quiescence. In the mid-1980s Shmuel Toledano, the adviser on Arab affairs to three prime ministers, Levi Eshkol, Golda Meir and Yitzhak Rabin, observed: "Sometimes I am amazed, from the pure security point of view, at how 600,000 Arabs [the minority's total number then] – with intellectuals, with people suffering, with people thinking that they're second class – have such quiet behaviour." He added that the unwavering loyalty of the minority permitted the discrimination to continue. All three prime ministers, he said, "didn't care about the Arabs. This problem didn't bother them, the general problem of the Arabs of Israel. Everything was quiet, everything went smoothly. The problem of the Arabs of Israel was not pressing."[23] When the first uprising in the occupied territories erupted in late 1987, and lasted another five years, Palestinian citizens offered neither physical nor ideological support. They kept silent and remained on the sidelines.

There were several important historic reasons for the minority's political inactivity. During the 1948 war Palestine had been almost entirely emptied of its urban elites, leaving behind only the inhabitants of poor, often isolated rural communities. As the historian Rashid Khalidi has noted, the early refugees from Palestine in 1948, were those with "the highest levels of literacy, skills, wealth and education".[24] After the war there was no Palestinian leadership remaining to develop and articulate a political programme, or mobilise the minority. The absence of an Arab leadership was perpetuated, as we have seen, during Israel's first two decades, when the Jewish state established a highly repressive military government to intimidate and silence what was left of the population, using a rigid system of control to prevent all expression of dissent. The aim was to strip Palestinian citizens of their national identity, sever them from their compatriots in the occupied territories and the Middle East's refugee camps, and turn them into "Israeli Arabs", an unthinking and loyal minority. Finally, a continuing lack of clarity in the vision of the Palestine Liberation Organisation about the Palestinian people's future has left the minority rudderless. Should Israel's Palestinian citizens be campaigning for a one-state or two-state solution in their historic homeland? Should they see themselves as part of the Palestinian nation's future, or as a discrete population that will one day be absorbed properly into Israel? They have been offered few answers.

Israeli anthropologist Dan Rabinowitz has referred to Palestinian citizens as a "trapped minority", arguing that they are marginalised twice over: first by their state, Israel, and then by their mother nation, the Palestinian people. "Seen from the Arab world, the Palestinian citizens of Israel emerge as an ambiguous and problematic element whose status in the national arena is yet to be determined, and whose loyalty to the Palestinian nation might still be suspect." Caught in political and cultural limbo, the minority has traditionally found itself riven by chronic internal ideological and political divisions, says Rabinowitz. "These divisions are related to the tension and confusion associated with their structural position between host state and mother nation."[25]

In practice such discord has been manifest in sectarian differences promoted by Israel between the Muslim, Christian and Druze communities. A confidential document written in 1949 by the director of the Religious Affairs Ministry, for example, urges the Education Ministry to "emphasize and develop the contradictions" between each of the religious communities, Muslim, Christian and Druze, to diminish their Arab identity. "By this way they will forget that they are Arabs and will recognise that they are Israelis of several kinds."[26] Today, divisive sectarian ideologies among the Arab population are dressed up as political programmes, especially evident in the dramatic growth in support for the Islamic Movement over the past two decades and Christian attempts to prevent the encroachment of political Islam, first through the Communist party and more recently through a platform of secular cultural nationalism.[27]

Although such divisions have paralysed the Palestinian minority politically for most of its history, developments associated with the Oslo peace process began to effect a change in the mid-1990s. When Yasser Arafat and his PLO exiles in Tunis were finally allowed to return to the occupied territories in 1994, the general assumption was that there would eventually be territorial separation between Jews and Palestinians and the creation of a Palestinian state in the West Bank and Gaza. For the first time Israel's Palestinian citizens were forced to consider more seriously their future inside Israel. Most aspired to be genuine Israeli citizens: surveys showed more than 80 per cent did not want to move to a future Palestinian state.[28] Although such polls baffled Israeli commentators, the responses were not difficult to understand. Why would a Palestinian citizen of Israel choose to move to a Palestinian state, to become a voluntary refugee from his town or village? Why would he want to live in another state where he would most likely continue to be considered suspect, this time by his own Palestinian kin? And finally, and most importantly, why would he choose to become a citizen of a weak, dependent Palestinian state, the only kind of state he knew Israel had in mind for the Palestinian people?

THE THREAT OF A STATE OF ALL ITS CITIZENS

But if most Palestinian citizens refused to contemplate transferring their homes or their citizenship, they also rejected the inferior status conferred by belonging to a self-declared Jewish state, instead demanding the redefinition of Israel in non-ethnic and non-discriminatory terms. In calling for a state of all its citizens, Azmi Bishara had given the minority a unifying political platform for the first time in its history. Palestinian citizens demanded a genuine democratisation of Israeli society. And it caused howls of outrage from Israeli Jews.

Israel's defenders had long suggested that the Jewish state was comparable to Western liberal democracies, even if some admitted it contained a stronger "ethnic element" than most.[29] Ruth Gavison, a professor specialising in human rights law at Hebrew University in Jerusalem, averred: "There is no inherent disagreement between the Jewish identity of the state and its liberal-democratic nature." She justified her position on the grounds that Israel simply represented the aspirations for self-determination of its national majority, Jews. A "neutral state", she claimed, would fail to protect Jewish public culture; on the other hand, as long as minority rights were protected for Arabs, it was legitimate that "state lands, immigrations, and the defense of the civilian population are all in the hands of a Jewish government".[30]

Aware of the extent of the discrimination inside Israel, however, other Israeli academics developed the model of "ethnic democracy", a supposedly rare species of democratic state in which power was exclusively exercised by the ethnic majority to ensure that the rights of the minority were subordinate to those of the majority, but which nonetheless still operated within the parameters of democratic behaviour.[31] Only belatedly, in the late 1990s, did dissident Israeli intellectuals begin challenging this comforting picture. Most notably, Oren Yiftachel, a political geographer from Ben Gurion University in the Negev, referred to Israel as an "ethnocracy", arguing that Israel's continuing repression of the Palestinian minority, its policy of Judaising all public space, its undefined borders and inclusion of extra-territorial Jewish settlers within its body politic, the enduring influence of the Jewish diaspora and international Zionist organisations inside Israel, and its lack of laws ensuring equality and protection of minority rights disqualified Israel from being a democracy. Ethnocracies, he noted, "are neither authoritarian nor democratic. Such regimes are states which maintain a relatively open government, yet facilitate a non-democratic seizure of the country and polity by one ethnic group ... Ethnocracies, despite exhibiting several democratic features, lack a democratic structure."[32]

It had taken nearly half a century for the Palestinian minority to move from political quiescence to assertiveness. Its leaders began arguing that the discrimination Arab citizens suffered was not comparable to the racism faced by other minority, usually immigrant, communities in Europe and America. However much Arab citizens tried to be good, they were always Arabs first – and in Israel, "Arab" was synonymous with "enemy". In a Jewish state, the glass wall meant that an Arab could never really belong, never be equal to a Jew. Bishara himself characterised the status of the Palestinian minority in the following terms: "Jewish democracy can tolerate Arab citizens as guests so long as they respect the rules of hospitality. In other words, Israel can tolerate the presence of those Israeli-Arabs who agree to remain on the margins of both Arab society and Israeli society."[33] Elsewhere he argued that the problem was "not discrimination but something else – exclusion".[34]

Increasingly in the late 1990s Israeli Arab leaders began to speak of their treatment in a Jewish state as mirroring other indigenous peoples who had suffered at the hands of colonial settler regimes, from the Native Americans and Aborigines of Australia to the black population in apartheid South Africa.[35] Israel, they believed, had shown no intention of integrating, let alone assimilating, its Arab citizens. It was interested only in keeping them separate and weak so that they could be neglected or exploited. Asked if Israel was Jewish and democratic, an Arab Knesset member, Ahmed Tibi, retorted: Yes, it is "democratic towards Jews and Jewish towards Arabs".[36]

This realisation has yet to filter through to most Israeli academics or their colleagues outside Israel. Even progressive commentators on the Middle East usually characterise the Israeli Arabs as "second-class citizens", as though a few years of affirmative action programmes and race relations campaigns could equalise their status with Jews. But this is a serious misconception. Discrimination in Israel against the Arab population is not equivalent to the discrimination practised against blacks, Asians or Muslims in Europe and America.[37] Whatever the problems of institutionalised racism in the West, and there are many, state officials and companies in Europe and America are usually breaking the law when they discriminate against weaker groups by using ethnic criteria in reaching their decisions; they are violating their institution's public codes and legal obligations. The same is far from true in Israel: institutionalised discrimination is not a reflection of the bad faith of individual officials (although it may be that too), but a reflection of the bad faith of organisations and the state structures within which they operate. The racism is inherent in the state's ideology; it is entwined with the very concept of Israel as a Jewish state.

* * *

The glass wall is effectively a perceptual sleight of hand, like the glass partition in Justice Or's courtroom, needed to cloak the contradictions inherent in the concept of Israel as a "Jewish and democratic" state. It is the distorting lens through which the world is presented with the democratic elements of Israel, the way it relates to its Jewish citizens, while missing the racist elements, the way it relates to its Arab citizens.

The deception was advanced most famously by a former chief justice of Israel, Meir Shamgar, when he observed: "The existence of the state of Israel as the state of the Jewish people does not negate its democratic character, just as the Frenchness of France does not negate its democratic character."[38] Given a moment's thought, however, the comparison is patently absurd: a country's being Jewish is not the equivalent of its being French. In Shamgar's formulation, "Jewish" might be being used in either a religious or an ethnic sense, but neither is the same as "French". The difference between a Jewish state and a French state is obvious the moment we try to imagine how one could naturalise as a Jew without converting to Judaism.[39] No one, after all, is required to convert to being French. In truth, the conception of a "Jewish state" can be understood in either theocratic terms or ethnic terms. But identifying such a state as democratic makes no more sense than calling a self-declared Roman Catholic state or Afrikaner state democratic.

Shamgar and other Zionists counter this argument by claiming that it is anti-Semitic to refuse to acknowledge that "Jewish" can refer to a national identity as well as a religious or ethnic one. They rely instead on another deception: that the establishment of Israel allowed the Jews to normalise, to become "a nation like other nations". But what exactly is the nation of Israel? In other countries, the answer is relatively simple: the French nation, for example, is the collection of people who hold French citizenship; it is, in other words, the sum of French citizens. But the Israeli nation is something different. According to Israel's founding laws, the state belongs not just to the people who live in Israel, to its citizens (one in five of whom is ethnically Arab), but to the Jewish people wherever they live around the world and whatever other nationalities – American, French, British, Argentinian – they consider themselves to be. As the Israeli sociologist Baruch Kimmerling points out: "The state is not defined as belonging to its citizens, but to the entire Jewish people."[40]

SEPARATE NATIONALITIES, UNEQUAL CITIZENS

The murkiness of Israel's self-definition is underscored by the privileged status various international Zionist organisations, including the Jewish Agency and the Jewish National Fund, enjoy in Israeli law. They have a semi-governmental status, including owning vast tracts of Israeli land, even though their charters require them to act exclusively in the interests of world Jewry.

As a consequence, Arab citizens' exclusion from the Israeli and Jewish nation has very concrete effects both on their social position in Israel and the possibility of developing a civic identity. For example, there are some 137 possible nationalities that can be recorded on Israeli identity cards: from Jew, Georgian, Russian and Hebrew through to Arab, Druze, Abkhazi, Assyrian and Samaritan. Everything, in fact, apart from Israeli.[41] This is because the state refuses to acknowledge that the Israeli nation can be separated from the Jewish nation. The two are seen as identical, meaning that non-Jews in Israel, including the population of more than one million Palestinians, are effectively citizens without a nationality; they are more akin to permanent residents. The state's approach suggests that it regards the nation of Israel as *including* potentially millions of Jews who do not live in Israel and do not have Israeli citizenship and as *excluding* the more than one million Palestinians who do live in Israel and do have Israeli citizenship.

The courts have consistently upheld this position. In 1971, for example, when an Israeli Jew petitioned the Supreme Court to have his nationality changed from Jewish to Israeli in public records, Chief Justice Shimon Agranat rejected the application, arguing:

> If there is in the country today – just 23 years after the establishment of the state – a bunch of people, or even more, who ask to separate themselves from the Jewish people and to achieve for themselves the status of a distinct Israeli nation, then such a separatist approach should not be seen as a legitimate approach.[42]

Agranat's ruling was confirmed by the courts again in early 2004.

The difficulty facing the Israeli legal system is that to recognise a common Israeli nationality – to recognise in effect a shared bond of citizenship between Jews and Arabs inside Israel – would negate the intentions of the country's founding fathers, who premised their state on the principle that it was a haven-in-waiting for the whole Jewish people, wherever they lived. In this sense the legal concept of Israeli nationality is unlike that found on the statute books anywhere else in the world. Jews and Arabs may share the same label of "Israeli" but they are different kinds of nationals and citizens: the former are included in the notion of a common national good, while the latter are excluded.

Consider just one example of the racist implications of this view of Israeli nationality, sanctioned by both the state and the courts. Although almost all land in Israel is nationalised, the state publicly admits that it does not hold it for the benefit of the country's citizens. It is held, in trust, on behalf of Jewish people around the world. The land of Israel is the property not of the Israeli people but of the Jewish nation, of Jews everywhere and for all time. As a result, Arab citizens have no rights to most of the country's territory, and legally can be excluded from the communities built on that territory. A Jew from Brooklyn and his or her children and unborn children enjoy absolute and eternal rights in Israel (even if they choose not to realise those rights), while a Palestinian citizen living in Nazareth or Haifa, whose family has lived on the land now called Israel for many generations, does not. In 2002 Prime Minister Ariel Sharon explained the difference during a Knesset debate when he observed that while Arab citizens enjoyed "rights *in* the land" – they had tenants' rights – "all rights *over* the Land of Israel are Jewish rights".[43] In short, the state considers the Jewish people as the landlords of Israel.

The difference in the nature of the nationality enjoyed by Jews and Arabs is embodied at the most basic level in an early piece of immigration legislation called the Law of Return. Passed in 1950, two years after the establishment of the state, the Law of Return was designed to ensure that the demographic ghost of the Palestinian homeland on which the Jewish state was built never return to haunt it. It gives a right to every Jew in the world to migrate to Israel and receive automatic citizenship while barring the return of Palestinians exiled by the 1948 war. The legislation skews the demographic realities in Israel so that Jewish numerical dominance can be maintained in perpetuity. It has eased the passage of some three million Jews to Israel, and disinherited the 750,000 Palestinians who were either expelled or terrorised out of the country under cover of war, and millions of their descendants. The consequence of the Law of Return – if not its purpose – has been to ensure that inside Israel the Jewish population maintains an unassailable numerical majority over what remains of the Palestinian population.

THE JEWISH STATE DEFINED

The Jewish identity of the state, and the permanent marginalisation of the Palestinian citizens it was forced to inherit in 1948, was enshrined in the country's founding document, the Declaration of Independence, which mentions only the history, culture and collective memory of the Jewish people.[44] It speaks not on behalf of the country's citizens but on behalf of the representatives of the Jewish people, as well as the Zionist movements, including the Jewish Agency and the Jewish National Fund.[45] These organisations, which enjoy a legal right to discriminate in favour of Jews, control social, political and economic benefits for Jews only.

Despite a pledge in the Declaration of Independence to produce a constitution within six months of the establishment of the state, no document has yet been drawn up. One of the insuperable obstacles facing the drafters has been how to embody the ethnic and religious values of a Jewish state without resorting to clearly discriminatory language.[46] A flavour, however, of what values the courts think a "Jewish state" embodies have been provided by the current chief justice, Aharon Barak, considered one of the most progressive and secular voices in Israel:

> [The] Jewish state is the state of the Jewish people ... it is a state in which every Jew has the right to return ... it is a state where the language is Hebrew and most of its holidays represent its national rebirth ... a Jewish state is

> a state which developed a Jewish culture, Jewish education and a loving Jewish people ... a Jewish state derives its values from its religious heritage, the Bible is the basic of its books and Israel's prophets are the basis of its morality. A Jewish state is also a state where the Jewish Law fulfills a significant role ... a Jewish state is a state in which the values of Israel, Torah, Jewish heritage and the values of the Jewish *halacha* [religious law] are the bases of its values.[47]

Instead of a constitution, Israel has 11 Basic Laws, none of which guarantees freedom of speech, freedom of religion or, most importantly, equality. The Basic Law on Human Dignity and Liberty, passed in 1992 and the nearest thing Israel has to a Bill of Rights, fails to include equality among the rights it enumerates, instead emphasising the values of the state as "Jewish and democratic". As a result, state-organised discrimination cannot easily be challenged in the courts. Repeated attempts by Arab Knesset members to introduce an amendment to the Basic Law on Human Dignity and Liberty incorporating the principle of equality have been rejected by an overwhelming majority of Jewish MKs.[48] (In any case, since the 1948 war Israel has never revoked a state of emergency that allows gross violations of human rights inside Israel.)[49]

ISRAEL'S PACT BETWEEN THE RELIGIOUS AND SECULAR

The veiling of the religious and ethnic discrimination at the heart of Israel has been partly achieved through the seemingly unimportant decision of its founding fathers to remove the state from all matters of personal status. Each religious community has been left to regulate issues relating to its members' births, deaths and marriages. In these core matters in each citizen's life there are no civil institutions or courts to which he or she can turn. It is neither possible to register as an atheist or agnostic, nor formally to bring up one's children as secular citizens. Instead, the leaderships of each of the main religious communities – Jew, Muslim, Christian and Druze – have been given exclusive powers to deal with their own members. Anyone belonging to the Arab Christian community of the Greek Orthodox faith, for example, must seek a divorce in a Greek Orthodox religious court before a panel of clergy in proceedings possibly carried out in Greek, with translation for the Arab participants, and according to Byzantine laws dating back to the fourteenth century.[50] Similarly, no civil marriage is possible in Israel, forcing citizens from different religious communities to marry abroad.

Rather than encouraging diversity, Israel has used the "subcontracting out" of personal status matters as a way to create a series of ethnic and communal partitions. There is no room for civil society to flourish when the state has abandoned its citizen to their religious ghettos, and the arbitrary decisions of their religious leaders. Instead individual citizens have been left to fight lonely battles to establish their rights in the most private areas of their lives, without the help or protection of civil institutions and laws. By refusing to offer an alternative, secular identity to its citizens in addition to that offered by the religious authorities, or to arbitrate in disputes between individuals and their confessional group, the state leaves citizens prey to anachronistic traditions and the whims of bigots. In Israel, the most lively public debates concentrate on arcane personal status issues, such as the battles to ease marriage restrictions, allow public venues to open on the Sabbath, and end the Jewish Orthodox's iron grip on conversion. There is no room to adopt a more critical civil discourse, one that questions the huge budgetary requirements of Israel's military or the economic policies that have opened up huge disparities in wealth and employment.

The authority wielded by the various religious leaderships, rather than equalising the status of the different religions before the law, has served to entrench an especially privileged place for Judaism in Israel, as the religion of the majority. The Hebrew calendar and the Jewish religious holidays are the only ones recognised; offices, banks, institutions and public transport shut down for the Jewish Sabbath only; restaurants, factories and public institutions are obligated to follow only the hygiene practices of Jews; only Jewish holy sites are recognised and protected by law; almost the entire budget of the Religious Affairs Ministry is reserved for Jewish places of worship, cemeteries, seminaries and religious institutions;[51] and Jewish religious schools receive resources far outstripping those given to state-run Jewish and Arab education.[52]

Conversion, which would at least offer a route, if a problematic one, to inter-confessional marriage inside Israel and lower the barriers between religious communities, has been made all but impossible in the case of Judaism. In an agreement forged in the earliest days of the Jewish state, control over personal status matters was passed exclusively to rabbis representing Orthodoxy, a fundamentalist stream of Judaism and the least progressive of its major movements.

As well as insisting on a purist definition of who is registered as a Jew (only those born to a Jewish mother), the Orthodox rabbinate in Israel approves only a handful of conversions to the Jewish faith each year, requiring that converts accept a fundamentalist interpretation of Judaism, including observance of *halacha* (Judaism's equivalent of sharia law). Conversions performed in Israel by rabbis belonging to other streams, such as the Conservative and Reform movements, are not recognised by the state.

This pact between the state and Orthodoxy has averted any threat, however improbable, of Palestinian citizens converting en masse to Judaism and thereby ending their exclusion from the centres of power. But it has also caused collateral damage, making life extremely difficult for Jews living in Israel who are not considered Jewish by the Orthodox rabbinate, including more than a quarter of a million immigrants who arrived in the last 15 years following the collapse of the Soviet Union.[53] Because they are the non-Jewish spouses of returning Jews, or the offspring of such marriages, they find themselves unable to wed in Israel,[54] to be buried in Jewish cemeteries, or to be registered as a Jew on their identity cards. Their children inherit this flaw.

Religious control over personal status matters has erected impenetrable barriers between Jews and Arabs in both the communal and the individual sphere. The policy has undermined any awareness of shared interests between Israel's different confessions; instead, communal groups must battle for resources that benefit their members alone rather than forging alliances that might unite groups on other bases. The arrangements put in place by the state have forced citizens to remain in a sectarian, tribal formation – as Jews, Muslims, Christians and Druze – vying for resources and privileges.

In this hierarchy of citizenship, given the state's definition as a Jewish state, the Jewish majority is always the winner by some considerable margin;[55] lagging a great distance behind are the Christian Arab denominations, which, because of their historic links to the global Churches, have enjoyed better opportunities for education and travel;[56] next comes the small Druze community, treated by the state as a national minority separate from the Arab population whose members are obligated in law to perform military service alongside Jews; and in last place is to be found the large Muslim population, comprising 80 per cent of the country's Palestinian minority, which has been entirely marginalised.

THE EMPTY SYMBOLISM OF THE ARAB VOTE

To many outsiders, however, the formula of a "Jewish and democratic" state sounds meaningful simply because Israel has universal suffrage, making no distinction between Jewish and Arab citizens in voting rights. This view ignores two key factors ensuring that political power in Israel is retained solely in Jewish hands and used exclusively for the benefit of the Jewish population. The first is that Arab parties, including the one small Jewish and Arab coexistence party,[57] have been excluded from every government coalition and every major decision-making body in Israel's history. Given the demographic superiority of Jews, enforced by the Law of Return, Arab citizen's entitlement to vote is little more than symbolic, never threatening the dominance of the electoral system by Jewish voters.[58] Because, as we have seen, Israel ensures Jewish political, social and economic concerns are entirely separate from Arab concerns, there are no shared interests on which Israelis could vote; instead they vote tribally.

There is only one exception to the symbolic nature of the Israeli Arab vote. On rare occasions, when Jewish opinion is profoundly and equally divided, Arab participation in the political system may influence the result. Jewish politicians, however, regard such outcomes as improper – and say so publicly.[59]

Consider an example from February 2005, when Ariel Sharon presented to a Knesset committee his financial package to compensate the settlers in Gaza, who were due to be evacuated later that year. Half the committee's Jewish members opposed the disengagement and hoped to scupper the plan by blocking the compensation package. Muhammad Barakeh, the sole Arab MK on the committee, therefore found himself with the casting vote. He backed the compensation offer and thereby also ensured a key element of the disengagement legislation passed a critical parliamentary stage. The response from the opponents of the disengagement was immediate: Barakeh's involvement was roundly condemned, including by Education Minister Limor Livnat, who called his role "illegitimate".[60] In the end Sharon was forced to intervene, untypically, to remind his party that Arabs were citizens too – or at least they were when it served his purposes.

The second factor is that all the political parties participating in national elections must pledge their loyalty and commitment to the Zionist conception of Israel as a "Jewish and democratic" state.[61] In this sense, therefore, even when Israeli Arabs have an influence in the political process, they do not contribute to shaping the public agenda. The framework within which the Arab MKs operate in the Knesset is an entirely Jewish, Zionist one. To continue the example above, Barakeh was publicly opposed to the way the disengagement was being implemented – unilaterally, without consultation with the Palestinians – and therefore had to choose between two alternatives he did not care for: a continuation of the occupation in Gaza or a withdrawal that was effectively a redeployment of the army to the perimeters of the Strip.

As Baruch Kimmerling has noted:

> A vote for an "Arab party" is in fact lost because generally a law passed with a majority based on such votes, or a government based on their support, is considered illegitimate. This derives from the constitutional definition of the state as "Jewish and democratic".[62]

Because Arab parties, like Jewish parties, must pledge a commitment to the "Jewish and democratic state", all of them skate close to illegality with their platform demanding Israel's democratisation as a "state of all its citizens". The constant threat of disqualification, and prosecution, of the minority's politicians has been an effective way to rein in free speech and silence dissent. In the years following the outbreak of the intifada, Israel launched investigations of all but one of the Arab parties' MKs.[63] The country's two most influential Arab leaders, Azmi Bishara of the National Democratic Assembly[64] and Sheikh Raed Salah of the Islamic Movement, were both prosecuted in cases that later largely collapsed because of a lack of evidence but which did grave damage to their reputations and that of Arab citizens generally.[65]

* * *

It is worth noting that a glass wall is primarily an instrument for deceiving onlookers and third parties, less so the participants themselves. Justice Or and the Arab families at his inquiry hearings both knew that the glass partition separated them and that its purpose was to exclude the Arabs. Only to outsiders did it appear as though state officials and the families were in one room together. Nonetheless, it is possible for the dominant group to slip into forms of self-delusion, believing that no separation exists or forgetting that there are two groups present, insiders and outsiders. Precisely because of the rigid segregation in Israel between Jew and Arab – in terms of citizenship, personal status, geography, work, leisure activities and opportunities – Jews who never or rarely meet an Israeli Arab are often barely aware that they exist, let alone that they suffer discrimination.[66]

Thus, many Israeli Jews were able to forget about the Palestinian minority and its problems until its presence could no longer safely be ignored. That moment arrived with the revolutionary new thinking of Arab citizens expressed in the slogan "a state of all its citizens", which raised the minority's profile among Israeli Jews in a dramatic and entirely negative fashion. The concept of a state of all its citizens, a demand for democratisation, harmless though it may sound to Western ears, was profoundly troubling to the Jewish majority on several levels. First, it exposed as hollow the cherished notion of a "Jewish and democratic" state by highlighting just how meaningless the democratic element of the equation was. Second, it challenged Israel's ideological foundations: Zionism's presumption that the Jewish state was an exclusive haven for a persecuted people. In a state of all its citizens, Arab citizens would be as entitled as Jews to demand that family members living in exile – in their case in Lebanon, Syria and Jordan – be given the right to "return" to Israel. Third, and most dangerously of all, the state of all its citizens roused from its lair a demographic monster that could devour the Jewish state almost overnight. If Israel did not end its occupation of the West Bank and Gaza and the substantial Palestinian populations that came with these territories, democratisation would mean only one thing: a Palestinian majority in Greater Israel and the end of the Jewish state.

DEMOCRATISATION AS SEDITION

Israeli Jews, aware that a detailed explanation of their reasons for rejecting a state of all its citizens might hint at the racist logic at the heart of the "Jewish and democratic" project, have remained coy about engaging directly in such debates. A state of all its citizens is dismissed, mystifyingly to outsiders, as a "threat to Israel's existence", "incitement" or even as part of the "ideology of terror". One must read between the lines, decoding what is meant when Israelis deploy these terms.

An example is the tortuous writing of Matti Golan, a former editor-in-chief of the *Ha'aretz* newspaper and now a regular media commentator. In one typical column he implies that Azmi Bishara was not the true author of the state of all its citizens programme: it was devised instead, he suggests, by Israel's arch-enemy, the Palestinian leader Yasser Arafat.

> Israeli Arabs like Bishara view the very act of living among us as their contribution to the fight. To the extent they are a fifth column, it is not necessarily by means of extending active help to [Palestinian] terrorists but by living here that gives them influence and makes the fight against terror considerably more difficult ... The declared dream of Israel's Arabs is a Palestinian state – a "state of all its citizens" with the majority, of course, being Palestinian. Which would mean the end of Israel as a Jewish state.[67]

Golan's discussion of Bishara creatively elides Palestinian terrorism, a state of all its citizens, an Israeli Arab "fifth column" and the destruction of Israel. In his conclusion, Golan argues that the citizenship rights of Israeli Arabs may justifiably be revoked because they have been unmasked as terrorists by proxy. It is simply an act of self-defence by the Jewish state.

The adamant refusal by most Israeli Jews to reflect on the nature of their state meant that the Palestinian minority's call for a state of all its citizens could lead in one direction only: to confrontation. By exposing the glass wall, Arab citizens were threatening to shatter it. Israeli Jews would protect it at all costs.

BARAK: PROTESTS WERE 'ON BEHALF OF ARAFAT'

In its popularised form, the democratisation ideology of a state of all its citizens emerged in the late 1990s, shortly before the eruption of the second intifada. Maybe then it is not so surprising that most Israeli Jews regarded the two phenomena as intimately connected. The Arab protests that erupted inside Israel in the immediate wake of the second intifada were interpreted by the Israeli government, the security establishment and the Jewish public as sedition, as part of a nationalist insurrection inspired by the Palestinians of the occupied territories. In dealing with Israel's Arab citizens, therefore, the Israeli security services adopted the same tactics of lethal force used against the occupied Palestinians. Within a few days 13 unarmed Arab demonstrators had been shot dead inside their own communities and hundreds more seriously wounded.

The prime minister of the day, Ehud Barak, and the leader of the Likud opposition, Ariel Sharon, both intimated that the Arab minority's protests were not only illegitimate but subversive, incited by the Israeli Arab leadership on behalf of Yasser Arafat. In Barak's words, the Arab minority was serving as the Palestinians' "spearpoint".[68] He believed the Palestinian president had crafted the state of all its citizens ideology as a ploy to defeat Israel by demographic means, to use Palestinian wombs as well as guns against the Jewish state. In calling for a state of all its citizens the Arab minority was not demanding its legitimate rights but rather was acting as an ideological "fifth column" through which Arafat could infiltrate the Israeli body politic and bring about its demise. In 2002 Barak explained the dangers for Israel if it was reconfigured as a state of all its citizens: "Then [the Palestinians] will push for a binational state and then demography and attrition will lead to a state with a Muslim majority and a Jewish minority ... it would mean the destruction of Israel as a Jewish state."[69]

However improbable it sounds that Arab citizens were acting as a fifth column, the degree to which this scenario resonated with the Jewish public and Israeli media should not be underestimated. In September 2003, the former defence minister Moshe Arens noted

> the rapid rise in subversive activities and incitement against the state that occurred among a part of Israel's Arab community since the Oslo accords. ... [The October 2000 protests] were demonstrations against Israel and in support of Yasser Arafat, and not in demand of greater equality for Israel's Arab citizens.[70]

In August 2005 Yosef Goell, a "moderate" columnist for the *Jerusalem Post* specialising in Jewish–Arab relations, cast his eye back on the events of five years earlier. He concluded that the clashes with the security forces in the Galilee had occurred "in obvious coordination with the eruption of Yasser Arafat's second murderous intifada in the territories".[71] He also noted "the growing and vociferous identification of the Israeli Arab leadership with Arafat and the PLO". Meanwhile, the more stridently rightwing pundit Caroline Glick argued that following the October 2000 events Israel should have acted to arrest the Arab leadership, ban the Islamic Movement and end "PA infiltration into the Arab sector".[72] And what was the evidence of such infiltration and coordination? None of the writers tells us; we are left to infer that the proof is to be found in the minority's demand for a state of all its citizens.

The glass wall, the deception implicit in the idea of a Jewish and democratic state, became visible to the Jewish public only when the country's Arab citizens tried, after many decades of quiescence, to destroy it. As soon as the Palestinian minority challenged the legitimacy of an ethnic state – one that never tired of claiming to be a democracy – Israeli Jews felt their security, both physically and ideologically, was threatened. In demanding a state of all its citizens, the Arab minority had understood that the Jewish state was designed to exclude them from power, even from representation, for ever. In a Jewish state there were no channels available for Arabs to reform the system or – as they found when they took to the streets in October 2000 – to protest.

THE MISSING KEY TO UNDERSTANDING THE CONFLICT

Of the scholars writing about Israel's Palestinian minority, many have chosen to limit their studies to issues of discrimination in resources or to identity politics, the problem facing a group that is Arab by ethnicity, Palestinian by nationality and Israeli by citizenship.[73] That is not the focus of this work; rather, I examine Israel's relationship to its Arab citizens in the context of the Middle East conflict, the conduct of the majority towards the minority, what this reveals about the nature of a Jewish state, and the likely future direction of hostilities. In this sense, the vilification and unstinting abuse of the country's Palestinian citizens reveals a great deal about the wider intentions of the state of Israel, in its view of "the Other", the Arab, and about its claims to be seeking a peaceful and secure place within the Middle East.

It is my contention that the historic and current treatment of Israel's Palestinian citizens is a key to understanding the obstacles that lie in the way of a peaceful resolution of the Israeli–Palestinian conflict. The Israeli state and Jewish public's determined opposition to ending discrimination against Palestinians inside Israel and their resistance to creating a truly democratic state are not passing symptoms of the conflict; they are part of its root cause. Israel cannot democratise – equalise the status of Jews and Arabs – because to do so would require it to begin on the path of atonement for the crimes it committed in 1948: namely, the mass expulsion of the indigenous population and the dispossession of the Palestinian people. It would open the historical record to proper inspection.

Instead surveys have consistently shown over many decades that a clear majority of Israeli Jews want the rights of Israeli Arabs severely curtailed. In recent years, as Arab citizens have begun to demand recognition of their Palestinian identity and the redefinition of their country as a state of all its citizens, there has also been a clear Jewish majority supporting their "transfer", a euphemism for ethnic cleansing, either through the creation of "inducements" for them to emigrate or through enforced removal.[74]

These surveys fit into a much larger picture of Jewish chauvinism and state racism. As will become clear in the following chapters, the modern Zionist conception of Israel – as a state designed to offer and defend by whatever means necessary a privileged space for Jews in the Promised Land – condones the theft of resources from "non-Jews", encourages the use of repressive violence when faced with dissent, sanctions demographic "adjustments" to dispose of population groups that threaten the numerical superiority of Jews, and makes a virtue of misinformation and distortion to advance the idea of a benevolent Jewish state, what Israelis call *hasbara*. Such policies are justified because in the thinking of most Israelis a significant Palestinian presence in itself threatens the interests of the Jewish state as a state that privileges Jews.

In laying bare the plight of Israel's Palestinian citizens, this book seeks to show how the Jewish state has revealed its true hand since 2000 through the increasingly abusive treatment of a largely quiescent Palestinian minority. It examines the two prisms through which Israel views its own Palestinian population: security and demography. Arab citizens are defined and dealt with both as a security threat, because they are perceived to have double loyalties, and as a demographic danger, because their higher birth rates threaten to invalidate the Jewish and democratic conception of the state. The minority's demand for a state of all its citizens – as we will see in Chapters 1 and 2 – simply served to conflate such fears, magnifying them to the point where the Israeli leadership, backed by a Jewish majority, believed action must be taken once and for all against its Palestinian citizens.

* * *

The analysis presented in the following chapters, concerning the Jewish state's view and treatment of its Palestinian minority during the second intifada, suggests that a new kind of strategy is becoming discernible in the Middle East conflict. Israel is seeking to blur the differences of national identity it has always maintained between Palestinians in the occupied territories and "Israeli Arabs". Increasingly the Jewish state is recognising both groups as equally Palestinian. This is not, I believe, a belated sign of Israeli goodwill towards the minority, nor is it intended as the first step towards recognition of its members' historic rights; it is the beginning of a process, already visible, in which Israel wants to separate – unilaterally – from both the occupied Palestinians and from its Arab citizens. Such separation is motivated solely out of a demographic fear that in the near future Israel will no longer be able to protect its image as "Jewish and democratic". It is the contention of this book that Israel is preparing to create a phantom Palestinian state out of the space it leaves behind after disengaging from Gaza and building its series of walls and fences across the West Bank. Once this process is complete, Israel hopes to transfer the citizenship rights of its Palestinian minority to the new state.

Until now, Israel's Arab population has enjoyed the residual rights of democratic citizenship, even if – as we have seen – it is of a very inferior status to Jewish citizenship. Palestinian citizens' individual rights are technically safeguarded in law, but the potential benefits of citizenship – in terms of a civic identity and in the political, social and economic spheres – are severely eroded because Israel recognises only the group rights of its national majority, of Jews. Nonetheless, inferior citizenship is better than no citizenship at all – the effective status of the Palestinians living under occupation in the West Bank and Gaza, whose rights Israel can trample on almost at will. Therefore, the Palestinian minority stands to lose a great deal if its Israeli citizenship is revoked.

A full-frontal assault on the democratic rights of Palestinian citizens threatens to smash the glass wall that has worked so effectively to protect the Jewish state's image for nearly six decades. It would also be a grave breach of international law. So why would Israel risk doing it?

CRAFTING A NEW IMAGE OF BENEVOLENCE

Israel can afford to destroy the glass wall inside Israel (which protects the illusion of a Jewish and democratic state), only because it is planning to resurrect it in the occupied territories (creating the illusion that Palestinians are being given sovereignty in a state of their own). The deception embodied by the glass wall will survive the transition because the image it projects will be inverted: until now the glass wall has been designed to deceive the world into believing that Palestinian citizens are *included* as equal citizens in a Jewish state; in time the glass wall will be used to deceive the world into believing that Palestinian citizens, like those under occupation, are being *excluded* from the Jewish state, so that their rights to "complete citizenship" can be realised. The glass wall will continue to persuade observers of Israel's benevolence by suggesting that the Palestinians are finally masters of their own destiny. With the two populations separated, no questions will be asked about the rights of Palestinian citizens inside a Jewish state, because there will be no Palestinian citizens left. Jewish democracy will be guaranteed, a democracy of Jewish blood and religion.

To breathe life into the deception, Israel needs to establish what appear to be clearly demarcated boundaries for the new state. Then it can argue that within those borders Palestinians are truly realising their citizenship. Paradoxically, the glass wall will camouflage the real purpose of the concrete and steel walls in the West Bank and Gaza: it will provide an appearance of strict separation between nations while protecting Israel's continuing interference in and domination of Palestinian life. Far from ending the occupation, these "borders" will work – as they have done till now – in one direction only, restricting Palestinian movement while enabling Israeli domination. Palestinians will be contained and subdued in what is left of the territories – their new state – without any limits being placed on Israel's military and economic reach. The spaces Israel concedes to a Palestinian state will be little more than open-air prisons, guarded by the Israeli army.

As we shall see in Chapter 4, the principle of unilateral separation – both in the form of disengagement and of wall-building – was not the brainchild of Sharon. The testimonies of senior Israeli officials show that it was the fallback position of both Yitzhak Rabin and Ehud Barak if their respective initiatives – Olso and Camp David – failed. Widespread demographic fears have persuaded most of the central figures in the security and political establishment of the need for physical separation from the Palestinians since the early 1990s.

The Israeli leadership's demographically driven thinking about the conflict was explained by Avi Primor, vice-president of Tel Aviv University, in September 2002. He noted that Sharon and his generation of military generals had always harboured an especial fondness for South Africa's solution to its own demographic problems: the system of fictitious black homelands known as Bantustans. In these homelands, termed "independent states" by white South Africans, the country's black population was supposed to exercise its political and civil rights. Writing three years before the Gaza disengagement, Primor argued that Israel had begun establishing just such homelands for the Palestinians:

> A process is underway establishing a "Palestinian state" limited to the Palestinian cities, a "state" comprised of a number of separate, sovereignless enclaves, with no resources for self-sustenance. The territories of the West Bank and Gaza remain in Israeli hands, and its Palestinian residents are being turned into "citizens" of that "foreign country".

Primor did not comment on the fate of Israel's Palestinian citizens in such a scheme but he did hint at a further lesson from the Bantustans that would supply the excuse for the transfer of Israeli Arabs' rights into a phantom Palestinian state: "All blacks outside these fictitious 'states' [that is, those living in 'white areas'] were arbitrarily assigned citizenship in those [black] states. In other words, they became foreign residents in their own land."[75]

It is my belief that, despite the common perception that a peace process of sorts was being re-established in late 2005, Israel's "disengagement" marked the beginning of a new phase of the conflict, one in which the stakes will be much higher and the fighting far deadlier. It is a period in which the endgame will eventually bind the fate of the Palestinians in the occupied territories to that of Israel's Palestinian citizens. As Israel finally begins to fashion these "borders", Palestinians both inside Israel and in the occupied territories will find themselves in parallel situations, facing mirror images of the same racist policies.

It is futile to believe such an arrangement – rigid ethnic separation on Israel's terms – will bring peace to the region. Instead it will create a staunchly chauvinist Jewish state searching ever more ruthlessly for ways to maintain its ethnic purity and exploit its Palestinian neighbours behind their glass wall.

1
Israel's Fifth Column

What is necessary is cruel and strong reactions. We need precision in time, place, and casualties. If we know the family, [we must] strike mercilessly, women and children included. Otherwise, the reaction is inefficient. At the place of action, there is no need to distinguish between guilty and innocent.

David Ben Gurion (1948)[1]

Our demands should be moderate and balanced, and appear to be reasonable. But in fact they must involve such conditions as to ensure that the enemy rejects them. Then we should manoeuvre and allow him to define his own position, and reject a settlement on the basis of a compromise position. We should then publish his demands as embodying unreasonable extremism.

Yehoshafat Harkabi, former head of Israeli Military Intelligence (1973)[2]

Israel must be like a mad dog, too dangerous to bother.

Moshe Dayan (undated)[3]

Mahmoud Yazbak looked as crumpled as a discarded packet of the cigarettes he smokes obsessively. The Haifa University history lecturer was not only much paler and thinner than I remembered from our last meeting nine months earlier but lacked his previous sharpness of thought and easy charm. Sitting in his home in a suburb of Nazareth, he was a shadow of his former self.

Between our two meetings events in the Middle East had taken a dramatic turn for the worse. On 28 September 2000 the then leader of the opposition Likud party, Ariel Sharon, made a visit to the Old City of Jerusalem and a site sacred to both Jews and Arabs. The visit was designed to be provocative in the extreme: Sharon, a man renowned throughout the Arab world as the general who engineered the invasion of Lebanon in 1982 and whose soldiers oversaw the massacre of thousands of Palestinian civilians by Lebanese Christian militias in Beirut's refugee camps, marched on to a plaza of mosques known as the Haram al-Sharif, or Noble Sanctuary, backed by more than 1,000 armed Israeli security staff and policemen. The backdrop to his photo-call was the impressive golden-topped Dome of the

Rock, reputedly the place where the Prophet Muhammad ascended to heaven on a ladder of light and received God's prayers for his followers to perform.

Although during the Six-Day War of 1967, Israel occupied and later annexed East Jerusalem, including the Old City, it promised to leave control of the mosques under the exclusive authority of Muslim clerics, through a religious endowment known as the *waqf* that had overseen the region's Islamic holy places for hundreds of years. Over the next three decades, however, Israeli leaders asserted with increasing fervour their country's rightful ownership of the site, basing their claim to sovereignty on the presumption that the Noble Sanctuary is built on a small mount that was once home to the First and Second Temples, built respectively by Solomon and Herod. The Second Temple was destroyed 2,000 years ago, and only an original retaining wall known as the Western Wall survives, but the Temple Mount – as it is known to Jews – has become the main symbolic focus of attention of Israeli politicians fighting the Palestinians for control of Jerusalem. They have been demanding that Jews be given access to the Noble Sanctuary's plaza of mosques in violation of centuries of rulings by rabbis that Jews are forbidden by *halacha* (religious law) to step anywhere on the Mount.[4]

The Israeli leadership's motive is mainly political: by playing up the significance of Jewish ownership of the Temple Mount, Israel strengthens its hand in preparation for the day when it may have to negotiate with the Palestinians over the future division of spoils in Jerusalem and the rest of the occupied territories. Israeli politicians have found vociferous support among Israel's growing number of fundamentalist Jews, especially the Messianic movements among the settlers, who want the complex of mosques destroyed to make way for a Third Temple to herald the arrival of the Messiah. Over the years several plots to bomb the Mount have been uncovered by Israeli security organisations.[5] Israel has won further backing for its ambitions in the Old City among the large and powerful community of Christian Zionists in the United States, evangelical fundamentalists who have the ear of President Bush and other senior figures in the Washington Administration.[6]

The Palestinians, mostly confined by Israeli walls, fences, checkpoints and curfews to the towns and villages of the West Bank and Gaza, cannot reach the Old City of Jerusalem, but they desire it, as well as the Muslim and Christian holy places, and the income and prestige they would bring, for the future capital of their state. The

35-acre site has therefore become the most disputed piece of territory in a conflict that is essentially about real estate claims. Both Israelis and Palestinians have turned Jerusalem's Old City into a powerful national symbol, each demanding it as a capital: in Israel's case, of a state of expanded borders that the world so far refuses to recognise; and in the Palestinians' case, of a shrunken state whose birth Israel has consistently blocked.

THE CAMP DAVID STALEMATE OVER JERUSALEM

A chance to end the deadlock was offered in July 2000, when American President Bill Clinton hosted "make-or-break" talks between Israel and the Palestinians at his Camp David retreat. The Israeli prime minister, Ehud Barak, had called for the negotiations as a way to bypass the deadening pace of the Oslo process. He wanted to broker a final-status agreement with the Palestinians on all the major outstanding issues of the conflict, including security, borders, settlements, refugees and Jerusalem. The result, the Palestinians hoped, would be the creation of a Palestinian state. According to many of the participants, however, Israel made control over East Jerusalem, including the Old City, the biggest stumbling block. Barak had hoped that Yasser Arafat would be persuaded to accept Abu Dis, a Palestinian village lying close by Jerusalem, as his capital and rename it al-Quds (the Holy), Jerusalem's title in Arabic. When it became clear he would not, nor would he settle for "functional autonomy" in the Old City – responsibilities for policing and garbage collection – without actual sovereignty, Barak's position hardened. As Martyn Indyk, the US Ambassador to Israel, recalled, the talks soon "got swamped in on the Jerusalem issue".[7]

Fourteen days later, the Camp David talks collapsed. As the two sides walked away empty-handed, the Israelis cast the blame on Arafat. The Palestinian leader, said Barak, had rejected his "generous" offers and had thus been unmasked as no partner for peace. The Americans supported the Israeli accusations. Tensions between the Palestinians, who felt they had been cheated of a state by the more powerful side, and the Israelis, who claimed they had no one to talk to, simmered all summer long.

Contacts between the two sides, however, continued through the autumn, although little progress was made. By December 2000, as Barak faced an imminent election he was expected to lose and Clinton was waiting out the dying days of his presidency, the American team brought the two parties together for one last stab at a peace deal. The US President read out the basis for an agreement, what came to be known as the "Clinton parameters". Again, Barak made Jerusalem a hurdle that could not be surmounted. According to Barak's main adviser on Jerusalem, Dr Moshe Amirav, the Israeli prime minister insisted on describing the whole plaza of the Noble Sanctuary, including the mosque areas, as the "Holy of Holies", a title traditionally reserved by Jews for the small inner sanctum of the temple, whose location is unknown and where only the High Priest was allowed to enter. Barak was the first Israeli leader to use the term in this way. Amirav later observed that, by maintaining his uncompromising position on sovereignty over Temple Mount, Barak had chosen to "blow up" the negotiations.[8]

Sharon's brief and high-profile occupation of the plaza in the wake of the failed Camp David talks was designed to send a message to the Palestinians and the world about who ultimately was master of the sacred site. It also served to demonstrate to the Israeli public that Sharon, unlike Barak, was not prepared to compromise sovereignty of the Mount at any price.[9] "The Temple Mount is the most sacred place, it is the basis of the existence of the Jewish people, and I am not afraid of riots by the Palestinians," Sharon declared.[10]

The response to Sharon's visit from ordinary Palestinians was predictable; in fact, it was so predictable that the Palestinian leadership, including Yasser Arafat, the head of the Jerusalem police, Yair Yitzhaki, and US officials all warned Barak to prevent it.[11] Their advice was ignored. Although there were only small-scale clashes between Palestinians and the Israeli security forces during Sharon's visit, the next day, on 29 September, the violence grew much worse. As Palestinians massed at the Noble Sanctuary for Friday prayers to make a show of strength, Barak and his public security minister, Shlomo Ben Ami, prepared for a showdown. They deployed a huge number of police officers and stationed a special anti-terror sniper unit at a location overlooking the site. When Palestinian youths began throwing stones at the massed ranks of the security forces, the police opened fire with rubber-coated bullets and live ammunition, killing at least four Palestinians and injuring 200 more.[12] Israel's chief of police, Yehuda Wilk, later admitted that snipers had fired into the crowds of demonstrators, a fact confirmed by doctors who reported that three of the dead had been hit by live rounds.[13] The violent clashes were the trigger for an outpouring of Palestinian anger and the eruption of the intifada, a grassroots uprising that was soon sweeping out from Jerusalem towards the West Bank and Gaza – and finally towards Israel itself.

Mahmoud Yazbak's grief sprang from the same source as that of the thousands of other Palestinian families who lost loved ones to Israeli bullets and shells in the days, months and years that followed Sharon's visit. In Yazbak's case, he was mourning his own *shaheed*, his 25-year-old nephew, Wissam, who was killed on the night of 8 October 2000 inside Israel, in the city of Nazareth. Wissam, a builder studying business administration in his spare time, was due to be married a month later.

In the first days of the intifada world attention concentrated on the barbaric events unfolding in the occupied territories, where scores of mostly unarmed Palestinians were dying at the end of Israeli soldiers' gunsights. As figures provided by the Israeli human rights group B'Tselem showed, about three-quarters of the 230 Palestinians killed in the occupied territories by the army in the first two months of the intifada died in clashes that did not involve any Palestinian gunfire.[14] A third of those shot dead were minors. Most of the rest were youths armed only with stones or slingshots facing down snipers, tanks and Apache helicopters operating inside the occupied territories. Just 24 members of the Palestinian security forces were killed during this period. But later, as the death toll continued to mount in Palestinian towns and villages, the confrontations with the Israeli army increasingly sucked in the Palestinian security forces and the armed factions. A wave of Palestinian suicide bomb attacks was launched against Israeli civilian targets from January 2001.[15] All of this created the impression in Israel and abroad that the intifada was a war between two opposed, if very unevenly matched, armies.

The rising death toll on the Israeli side, even if it paled beside the Palestinian one, allowed government spin-doctors to present the intifada as a well-planned assault on the Jewish state, led by the Palestinian security forces under the direction of Yasser Arafat himself. In fact, Israeli officials went further: they argued that the Palestinian leader had been hoping at Camp David to use demographic weapons, most notably an insistence on the right of return of millions of Palestinian refugees, to destroy Israel as a Jewish state and turn the whole area into "Greater Palestine". When he failed, they alleged, he fell back on Plan B, unleashing the armed intifada.[16] Later Barak himself would claim as much. In an interview with the Israeli historian Benny Morris in 2002, he argued that the intifada "was pre-planned, pre-prepared. I don't mean that Arafat knew that on a certain day in September [it would begin] ... It wasn't accurate, like computer engineering. But it was definitely on the level of planning, of a grand plan."[17]

One of the senior American participants at the Camp David negotiations, Robert Malley, President Bill Clinton's special adviser on Arab–Israeli affairs, wrote lengthy articles debunking Israel's account of the talks and its explanation of the intifada.[18] But only very belatedly, nearly four years after the outbreak of the uprising, was the Israeli story – almost universally accepted by the world's media – finally and irreversibly discredited.

GEN. MALKA EXPOSES ISRAEL'S INTIFADA MYTHS

In June 2004 a senior army officer, General Amos Malka, the former head of Israeli Military Intelligence, broke his silence to reveal that the assessments about Arafat's involvement in the intifada endlessly voiced by Israeli politicians and the army had not been based on any intelligence information. They were the personal hunches of Malka's immediate subordinate, Amos Gilad, who had been responsible for intelligence gathering during that period. According to Malka, Gilad had ignored the available intelligence and told the political and military echelons either what he personally believed or what he thought they wanted to hear: that Arafat was not a partner for peace but a terrorist who was planning the destruction of Israel, either through a demographic war or an armed struggle.[19] Malka argued that, in reality, the available intelligence suggested the opposite. Arafat, he said, was ready to reach a compromise with Israel but not on the terms offered. He was forced to ride the unexpected outpouring of Palestinian public anger, the intifada, after the failure of the Camp David talks.

Malka's devastating criticisms of Gilad were supported by Colonel Ephraim Lavie, who had supplied Gilad with his intelligence information about the Palestinian leadership. Lavie noted that "while we warned of the possibility of a clash, we never said before the conflict broke out such unequivocal things as 'Arafat does not want a two-state arrangement but rather the eradication of Israel through demography'." He added: "The prevailing concept about Arafat having only one, absolute goal – establishing 'Greater Palestine' – and deliberately initiating general hostilities, is nowhere to be found in the papers prepared by the research division."[20] Instead, Lavie observed, the intifada "began from below, as a result of rage that had accumulated toward Israel, Arafat and the [Palestinian Authority]. Arafat hitchhiked on it for the sake of his personal needs."[21]

Once Malka and Lavie's revelations burst forth, Mati Steinberg, the chief adviser on Palestinian affairs in the Shin Bet, the country's domestic security service, admitted he had reached the same conclusions. He told *Ha'aretz*: "The intifada did not result from a decision reached up above; it stemmed from a mood that swept through the Palestinian public. The Palestinians felt as though they had reached a dead end due to the failure of the Camp David summit." Steinberg ridiculed Gilad's claims that Arafat had aspired to create a Palestinian state through a demographic war of attrition. "Factually, there is no support for this contention. Had [Arafat] concentrated on demographic factors, he would have had to refrain from the diplomatic process and he would have waited for natural population increase to do its part, and for Israel to self-destruct."

Instead, Steinberg said, Arafat shared the Palestinian public's view that, in agreeing to forgo their claims to most of their historic homeland, they were making a supreme compromise that should be reciprocated by Israel. "The Palestinian way of thinking is this: We are prepared to establish a state on the Gaza Strip and the West Bank, on just 22 percent of the Palestinian homeland. Our consent to the 1967 borders is, for us, an unbearable sacrifice." Arafat had no choice but to insist at Camp David that the proposed Palestinian state have sovereignty over the Noble Sanctuary (Temple Mount), conceded Steinberg.

> Realizing sovereignty rights on the Temple Mount is not just a religious or symbolic matter: it's a matter of survival. A Palestinian state which controls the Temple Mount will be a source of interest, and will attract millions of Palestinians; it will be a magnet for tourism and pilgrimages. There isn't a single Muslim – not even the most selfless altruist – who can accept Israeli sovereignty on the Temple Mount.

Given the enduring nature of Israel's political assessments of the conflict, said Steinberg, he was pessimistic about the future.

> Under conditions of an asymmetric confrontation, one in which Israel is many times stronger than the Palestinians, we have decisive influence on the course of events. Hence, a mistaken assessment on the stronger side's part creates reality; it becomes a self-fulfilling prophecy ... Whoever upholds such a position has concluded that there is no possibility of attaining an

> agreement with the Palestinian side. This approach dictates just one choice to the Palestinians: either they surrender to Israel's dictates, or they rise up against the dictates at all cost ... The Palestinian public has come to feel that it has nothing to lose. That's the background to the emergence of a culture of suicide bombers.[22]

Gilad's unsupported assessments of the situation facing Israel had terrible consequences for the Palestinians, as the commentator Reuven Pedatzur observed:

> This explains why the IDF [Israeli army] began to use such massive firepower when the [Palestinian] uprising broke out in the territories. This also explains why over a million [Israeli] bullets were fired in the first few days, even though there was no operational or professional justification. The intent was to score a winning blow against the Palestinians, and especially against their consciousness. This was not a war on terror, but on the Palestinian people. IDF commanders projected their viewpoint regarding Arafat's intentions on to the entire Palestinian society.[23]

PARALLEL WARS BY ISRAEL'S ARMY AND POLICE

The military onslaught against the Palestinians in the occupied territories in the first days of the intifada overshadowed a much briefer but equally horrifying assault carried out by the police forces inside the borders of Israel. In the first week of October 2000, 12 unarmed Palestinian citizens and a casual labourer from Gaza were shot dead and hundreds more seriously injured by the police in the north of Israel using huge quantities of rubber-coated bullets and live rounds – ammunition that, at least officially, was not intended for use against protesters inside Israel. According to the *Ma'ariv* newspaper of 2 October 2000, the Israeli police had been put on their highest state of alert, "Paam Gimel", effectively on a war footing, in preparation for dealing with demonstrations by Israeli Arabs in the wake of the Temple Mount violence.[24]

Wissam Yazbak was among the 13 dead inside Israel. Most were killed in the first three days of October as they burst on to the streets of their towns and villages to protest against the savagery with which the Israeli army was dealing with the Palestinian uprising. The first Arab demonstrations inside Israel occurred three days after Sharon's visit, on Sunday 1 October, a public holiday marking Rosh Hashanah (the Jewish New Year). The local Arab leadership declared the day a general strike, though given the short notice they had no time to organise, as was customary, a central protest in each region. Instead, communities were left to organise their own demonstrations. On 30 September, the night before the strike, Arab satellite channels broadcast footage of 12-year-old Muhammad al-Durra shivering in fear behind his father as the pair came under a hail of bullets from an Israeli military position in Gaza. Moments later the boy was dead.

When the protesters emerged on to the streets of their communities the next day, they were in bitter mood. In many places they held noisy protest marches; in others they also burnt tyres at the entrances to their towns and villages. The participants, at least in the early stages, included not just angry youths but their parents, community leaders and intellectuals. They all wanted to show solidarity with their people, the Palestinians, and vent their frustration at five decades of ethnic discrimination and oppression inside Israel.

In the view of most Israeli Jews, however, these events looked not like the legitimate protests they largely were but like a nationalist insurrection – an internal intifada – that was shaking the foundations of the Jewish state. As Ehud Barak himself would later describe the events, they were like an "earthquake".[25] Whereas most of the Israeli public were psychologically prepared for Palestinian unrest in the occupied territories, they were not ready to countenance such clear expressions of discontent from Israeli Arabs. As far as the Jewish public was concerned, the way the police chose to react to the protests was proof enough that they were unlawful and that those who had been killed deserved to die.

In many Israeli Arab areas the police responded to the minority's demonstrations not by containing them and waiting for the collective anger to subside, but by storming into the communities armed only with tear gas, rubber-coated bullets and live ammunition. Police units lacked any of the equipment needed for crowd control: riot shields, water cannon, even loudhailers.[26] Their behaviour hinted at a racist logic among Israel's security services and government, one doubtless developed after decades of repressing the Palestinians in the occupied territories. Riot equipment was superfluous to the police armoury because "Arab riots" would need to be dealt with by far harsher means. On this view, Israeli Arabs were capable of understanding only the same kind of force used against their Palestinian kin.

Such a worldview found its most prominent exponent in Moshe Ya'alon, the head of the Israeli army for much of the intifada, who gave an interview to the *Ha'aretz* newspaper in summer 2002. Asked how he would define victory for Israel, he replied:

> The very deep internalization by the Palestinians that terrorism and violence will not defeat us, will not make us fold... If that [lesson] is not burned into the Palestinian and Arab consciousness, there will be no end to their demands of us... That will have an impact not only on those who are engaged in the violent struggle, but also on those who have signed agreements with us and on extremists among the Arabs in Israel. That's why this confrontation is so important. There has not been a more important confrontation since the War of Independence [in 1948, which created Israel on the Palestinian homeland].[27]

The worsening nature of the confrontation between the police and unarmed protesters in October 2000 quickly became self-fulfilling. Arab citizens demonstrating against the violent repression being used against Palestinians by Israeli soldiers in the occupied territories found themselves under attack on the streets of their own communities from Israeli policemen adopting exactly the same methods. Their citizenship, they quickly learnt, offered no protection. They were regarded first and foremost as Arabs and therefore as the enemy. It was a painful lesson, revealing to them both the extent of their inferior status as citizens and the racist thinking of the security forces on both sides of the Green Line that permitted the unleashing of such lethal force with so little provocation.

A CULTURE OF RACISM IN THE SECURITY FORCES

The roots of such racism in the Israeli police are not hard to understand. The police force is far from representative of the communities it serves. Nearly one in five of the Israeli population is Palestinian – more than one million Arab citizens – but they are almost entirely excluded from both the police and the army. In fact, service in the two security forces is intimately connected: policemen are expected to have completed their three-year army draft, to have mastered the use of weapons as a serving soldier and to have imbibed the country's security-conscious culture, including a profound distrust of Arabs.

The law requires that most Jews are conscripted on leaving school, and a proportion chooses afterwards to join the country's enormous security industry, as career soldiers, prison warders, security guards, policemen and officers of the Shin Bet secret service. Alongside them are a number of Druze, a small community that Israel treats as a national group separate from the country's Christian and Muslim populations. Given the high rates of unemployment in their community, many Druze men continue afterwards to serve as lowly policemen and prison warders, roles in which they have earnt a reputation for holding virulently anti-Arab attitudes. No official estimates, however, exist for how many non-Druze Arabs serve in the security forces, although it is known to be very low indeed. One Israeli Arab academic, Rhoda Kanaaneh, who has made a study of this phenomenon, puts the figure at no more than 5,000 serving in the various branches of the security services.[28] The great majority hold junior positions, usually serving inside local Arab communities. Arab representation in decision-making roles in the security forces, such as at the national police headquarters and in the Shin Bet, is virtually non-existent.

As a result there is little to differentiate the "security cultures" of the army and the police. Racist stereotypes encouraged and reinforced at an impressionable age during military service in the occupied territories are not dispelled when most Jews join the police force. Given the fact that, typically, Arab communities can draw on only a third of the policemen available to Jewish areas,[29] most officers encounter Arab citizens only when they are called in as reinforcements to enforce repressive and confrontational policies, such as demolishing homes or dispersing demonstrations. The attitude of ordinary policemen towards the Arab minority therefore largely reflects the Israeli military mindset.

David Ankonina, who led a special police unit that orchestrated the police response in several towns in the north in early October 2000, described his job thus: "I have my warriors, I have my squad commanders, I direct the warfare."[30] As one seasoned Israeli commentator observed:

> Many of the policemen who confronted Arab citizens of Israel in October had no experience in dispersing demonstrations within the Green Line – only in the territories during their military service... [One] cannot escape the impression that some of the ways of dealing with Palestinian demonstrations have crossed the Green Line and become part of the standard procedures of the security forces in Israel. This includes, for example: using snipers; following guidelines for using rubber-coated bullets against "inciters" and people wielding slingshots, even if they do not pose an immediate threat to

> policemen; and firing rubber-coated bullets into a crowd without aiming at a particular target or while running toward the demonstrators.[31]

In one place, by the town of Umm al-Fahm, close to the West Bank, the clashes on the first day of the general strike, 1 October, turned most violent as a small group of Arab youths, some concealing their faces with the Palestinian headscarf, the *Kaffiyah*, threw stones from a hillside at cars driving along the Wadi Ara road below and at police units. Relations between the police and the inhabitants of Umm al-Fahm had been unusually strained since a violent confrontation two years earlier. In September 1998 the police had been called in to enforce a state order confiscating thousands of acres of farmland belonging to Umm al-Fahm in an area known as al-Roha so that it could be incorporated into a military firing range. The creation of firing ranges and closed military zones has been one of the main pretexts used by Israel to confiscate land from Arab communities; typically a short time afterwards, the land is rezoned for development so that exclusive Jewish communities can be established on it. In this way most Arab land in Israel has been transferred to the state and then on to Jewish citizens. During the al-Roha clashes, the police surrounded Umm al-Fahm's high school, firing tear gas and rubber bullets into the buildings, wounding 400 local residents, including many children.

Almost exactly two years later, on 1 October 2000, the police and demonstrators appeared to be carrying on unfinished business. Units that arrived to disperse the youths again quickly resorted to rubber-coated bullets, severely injuring many demonstrators. As more and more youths joined the stand-off with the police, the situation rapidly deteriorated. At one point the youths managed to stop a bus and set it on fire. In reply the police stepped up their firepower. Three demonstrators were shot dead in and around Umm al-Fahm that day and dozens more were injured.[32]

The next day, Monday 2 October, Arab communities staged larger protests, this time over the deaths inside their own communities. The police responded with an even greater show of force – just as they had done at the Noble Sanctuary in Jerusalem a few days earlier. Unknown to the demonstrators, the same unit of anti-terror snipers used in Jerusalem was brought to Umm al-Fahm and Nazareth, the first time in the country's history that such snipers had ever been deployed inside Israel. As the number of casualties among the demonstrators grew rapidly, angry protesters torched petrol stations, banks and any other institutions in their communities they identified with the state. It is these images, captured by Israeli cameramen and photographers, that cast in the minds of the Jewish public the idea that the police had been holding a last desperate line of defence against a dangerous rampaging mob determined to overthrow the state, rather than citizens incensed by the lethal force used against their fellow protesters. By sunset on 2 October six more Palestinian citizens were either dead or dying and hundreds more injured, many seriously.[33] The next day, on Tuesday, as the Arab leaders scrambled to Jerusalem to plead with Barak and Ben Ami to pull back their security forces, another two youths were killed by police fire in the Galilean towns of Kafr Manda and Kafr Kana, and dozens more were wounded.[34]

JEWISH PROTESTS HANDLED DIFFERENTLY

The Palestinian minority was not alone in taking to the streets inside Israel at the start of the intifada. Across the country Jewish citizens began their own violent protests. Although well documented, this phenomenon was little commented on. The Jewish protesters appeared to have a variety of motives: some were angered by what they saw as Arab citizens' disloyalty; others were in shock at the kidnapping of three Israeli soldiers during an incursion by the Lebanese militia Hizbullah in the north under cover of the intifada; and yet more were deeply opposed to recent government decisions they believed were responsible for feeding Palestinian expectations. Confused by Barak's own apparent ambivalence towards the Camp David negotiations, a significant proportion of the Jewish population opposed Israel signing a deal with Palestinian President Yasser Arafat, which they feared might see the settlements abandoned and Jerusalem pass to Palestinian control.

In several areas of Israel, Jewish protesters threw stones and Molotov cocktails, and assaulted police officers who came to restore order. What *Ha'aretz* termed "rampages" by Jews in the towns of Tiberias, Karmiel, Upper Nazareth, Jaffa, Petah Tikva and Bat Yam, included attacks on Arab citizens and their restaurants and businesses. In Bat Yam Jewish youths stabbed two Arabs and threw Molotov cocktails at police when they tried to intervene. Police also faced Molotov cocktails when they tried to stop rioting Jews from burning down a mosque in Tel Aviv.[35] In Karmiel more than 1,000 Jews massed in the streets, attacking their mayor, Adi Eldar, when he tried to intervene.[36] In these Jewish areas, neither rubber bullets nor live ammunition were used. The police were reluctant even to use tear gas. In Tiberias, police were told to leave their guns behind and use only batons against the Jewish protesters.[37]

Tal Etlinger, a woman officer in the Border Police, a paramilitary force that operates both inside Israel and in the occupied territories, was part of units sent to disperse Arab protests in the Old City of Jerusalem and Umm al-Fahm, and, later, Jewish protests in Tiberias. She told the *Yediot Aharonot* newspaper:

> The most difficult event was the riot in Tiberias. Hundreds of violent Jews blocked a highway and threw Molotov cocktails at us. They almost set fire to one of our vehicles, and only sheer luck enabled us to put the flames out in time ... It was just as violent as what happened in Umm al-Fahm. According to the rules of engagement, we can fire when a Molotov cocktail is thrown at us. But we handle Jewish riots differently. When such a demonstration takes place, it is obvious from the start that we do not bring our guns along. Those are our instructions. All we used there [in Tiberias] was tear gas.[38]

In contrast to the handling of Jewish unrest, the police reacted to Israeli Arab protests with the same lethal force being used by the army against the Palestinians in the West Bank and Gaza. The Palestinian minority's citizenship proved irrelevant. Not only were 13 Arab demonstrators left dead, but at least 500 were injured[39] (almost certainly an underestimate as many of the wounded, fearful of arrest if they went to hospital, sought out treatment from private Arab doctors[40]). In many areas, the national ambulance service Magen David Adom refused to enter Arab communities to treat the injured. In the case of Ahmad Siam, who was shot close to his left eye during protests in Umm al-Fahm on 1 October, the ambulance service's refusal to enter the town probably contributed to his death, according to Afu Ajabaria, the local doctor who treated him.[41]

There were also plentiful stories, months after the demonstrations were over, of police assaulting Arab citizens whom they suspected of having participated in the protests. More than 750 Arab citizens were arrested in sweeps by the police that continued until late December.[42] A report from the Israeli prisoner rights organisation the Public Committee Against Torture in Israel found shocking examples of mistreatment of Arab detainees, including children, who were severely beaten with batons and rifle butts, tied in painful positions to chairs, and denied basic legal rights, such as access to lawyers. Relatives of detainees were also attacked. The Committee Against

Torture concluded: "The law enforcement agencies are riddled with institutional racism."[43]

COVER-UP OVER WISSAM YAZBAK'S DEATH

At the time of my second meeting with Mahmoud Yazbak, five months after the "October events", as they were soon called, the circumstances of Wissam's death were still deeply contested. Wissam and another man from Nazareth were shot dead on Sunday 8 October, a week after the initial clashes between police and demonstrators had occurred, when the Arab protests across the Galilee had been subdued into a stunned silence by the police violence. But while Arab citizens were mourning their dead and nursing their wounds, Jewish citizens were growing bolder in their defiance. On the night of 7 October, a group from the Jewish town of Upper Nazareth descended on the eastern margins of neighbouring Nazareth to throw stones at Arab cars and buildings. The next evening, as the Jewish holy day of Yom Kippur (Day of Atonement) began, a much larger contingent of Jews, numbering several hundred, including many bearing guns, gathered by the edge of the Arab town again, throwing stones at cars, threatening to set fire to buildings and chanting "Death to the Arabs".[44] The mosques in Nazareth called out on their loudspeakers for Nazarenes to defend the city, and within a short time a potentially dangerous stand-off developed between the Jewish invaders from Upper Nazareth and the Arab inhabitants of Nazareth. Police arrived to separate the two communities; in the subsequent events Wissam Yazbak and 42-year-old Omar Akawi were killed.

Mahmoud Yazbak had a good idea of what had happened that night, not least because he had been close to his nephew through much of the evening of 8 October on the hillside overlooking Nazareth. When I spoke to him, several months later, no official body had asked him for his account, not the police or the Justice Ministry's special police investigations unit, Mahash. He had been left alone to dwell bitterly on the police behaviour that night, and how it had been misrepresented in the Hebrew media. The official story, repeated by Israeli journalists, was that Wissam Yazbak and Omar Akawi had been killed by gunfire from their own, Arab, side. The two pieces of proof, according to the police, were that they had been shot with live ammunition (the police force was claiming that its officers had not used live fire that night, or at any other time during the October events), and that the pair had been hit in the back. The theory promoted by the police was that the two Nazarenes had been killed, and a handful more seriously wounded, by stray fire from a gunman standing in the crowd behind them.[45]

That was the conclusion reached by an internal police inquiry led by Superintendent David Peel, who, despite an obvious conflict of interest, had been asked by Moshe Waldman, his commanding officer in Nazareth, to investigate the two deaths. Peel did not interview Waldman, even though the latter had directed the operations, and only questioned a small number of the policemen on duty. His investigators waited three days before visiting the site and did not collect any evidence. Shell cases found by local residents were passed on to a forensic expert who did not write up a report and never recorded the fact that at least one of the rounds was live. Peel later explained his decision to ignore Arab testimony. "From my experience, they aren't the most credible [witnesses]. They add all sorts of things to the events. They try to cover up crime scenes. I don't need to say more."[46]

Mahmoud Yazbak had a very different account from the police version, one that would much later be accepted as an accurate description of what took place that evening. Yazbak recalled his shock on the night of 8 October at discovering, as he arrived on the outskirts of Nazareth, that the police were not trying to protect the Arab inhabitants under attack from the Jewish mob, nor were they even taking a neutral stance. They were positioned between the two sides, but with their backs to the Jewish invaders and their guns pointed at the Arab crowd defending their city. The municipal limits of Nazareth and Upper Nazareth are separated by a dual carriageway road. On the edge of the Jewish town is a high, four-storey shopping mall where, according to many witnesses, the police had stationed snipers, with their guns trained on Arab residents. "The police did not look as if they were there to disperse the Jewish mob, or even to prevent a clash," said Yazbak. "It was as though they were holding a line, defending the Jews, some of them armed, who had crossed over the road to attack us."

The police required the Arab inhabitants of Nazareth to leave the area immediately, despite protests from senior local leaders, including Ramez Jeraisi, the mayor of Nazareth, that fairness dictated that the police ensure the Jews who were invading the city leave first. After negotiations, however, the Arab crowd was persuaded to head back towards their homes. Several youths, including Wissam Yazbak, agreed to form a human chain to shepherd the crowd downhill. It was as he and the other volunteers had their backs to the police that a burst of automatic gunfire could be heard from a dirt hill where a group of policemen was stationed. Several witnesses close to the police said they heard an order to open fire in Hebrew.[47] Moments later a handful of youngsters, all hit from behind, were lying on the ground fighting for their lives.

According to Dr Nakhle Bishara, the medical director of Nazareth's Scottish Hospital, so named because of its historic links with the Edinburgh Medical Society, Wissam arrived in the emergency room brain dead. Alongside him were four unconscious youths in a serious condition, including one with no pulse or blood pressure. All had entry wounds to their upper backs, as well as exit wounds, and were saved after major surgery in which all or parts of their lungs were removed. Dr Bishara concluded that they had been hit by live fire. In Wissam's case there was no exit wound; Dr Bishara said he could feel a live round lodged in Wissam's brain.[48] The body was immediately transferred to Rambam Hospital in Haifa, where it was assumed an autopsy would be carried out. In fact, as was the case with most of the other bodies, no post-mortem examination was held. (In contravention of Justice Ministry procedures, autopsies were not carried out on nine of the 13 dead. In the cases of four Arab citizens killed in the Umm al-Fahm area, post-mortems were held but only because lawyers who accompanied the bodies insisted on examinations. Even in these cases, however, the authorities refused to release the reports until required to do so many months later under pressure from a state inquiry.[49])

It is known that the bullet was removed from Wissam's skull by a surgeon in Haifa, but this vital piece of evidence went astray. Yazbak's family and their lawyers could not get an official report from the hospital or the Abu Kabir forensic laboratories in Tel Aviv on what kind of bullet had killed Wissam. For months, with no independent report, the police were able to claim that he was the victim of an Arab gunman. No one challenged this account, neither government ministers nor the Israeli media. At the time of my meeting with Mahmoud Yazbak, the message being conveyed to the Israeli public on every Israeli television channel and in every newspaper article was that just as Barak had unmasked Arafat as an enemy of Israel at Camp David, so the intifada had unmasked the Palestinian minority as a dangerous – and armed – fifth column.

INCITEMENT BY THE HEBREW MEDIA BUILDS

A few Israelis observed that the anger that had driven the Arab population to the street derived not from nationalist militancy but from long years of severe and systematic discrimination and their political parties' exclusion from power. These long-standing grievances had been inflamed over the summer by several developments: first, there had been a wave of demolitions of Arab homes inside Israel heavily enforced by the police; second, the state was threatening to prosecute a leading Arab Member of Knesset, Muhammad Barakeh, for incitement over his trenchant attacks on the police role in the demolitions; and third, the failed negotiations at Camp David in June looked to Arab citizens more like cynical manoeuvring by Israel to cheat their Palestinian kin in the occupied territories of a state. The final blow was the barrage of images of the Palestinians being savaged by Israel's sophisticated military hardware.[50]

The veteran Israeli journalist Gideon Levy, who has reported from the occupied territories for many years for *Ha'aretz*, argued that the sudden outpouring of anger by the minority in October 2000 should be seen in the context of decades of quiescence. Ever since 1976, when six Arab demonstrators were killed by the security forces during protests against a wave of land confiscations, Arab citizens had demonstrated unswerving loyalty, he observed. "Twenty-five years of exemplary, almost exaggerated loyalty, almost groveling obedience to the state whose wars are not their wars, whose national anthem is not their anthem, whose language is not their language, whose holidays are not their holidays."[51]

But the few voices of calm were all but drowned out by a sea of accusations from Israeli politicians and commentators that the country's Palestinian minority was really a "second front" of the intifada, of the war being waged by Arafat against the Jewish state.[52] The claim was entirely baseless but it gripped the Israeli imagination with a vice-like power from the first moments of the clashes between the police and Palestinian citizens. One of the first people to articulate the theory was Ariel Sharon, who published a commentary in the *Jerusalem Post* two days after the bloodshed began inside Israel. Sharon suggested that the Arab Members of Knesset had connived with Palestinian leaders in a "carefully orchestrated operation to ignite riots in large-scale violence in Judea, Samaria [the Biblical names used by Israelis for the West Bank], Gaza, and Israel proper among its Arab Israeli citizens".[53]

The idea that Israel's Palestinian minority was really a second front of an intifada planned and orchestrated by Arafat resonated with most Israelis, and was instantly adopted by politicians of the right and left. It fitted the unsupported "intelligence" assessments of General Amos Gilad, who had claimed that Arafat had been plotting the overthrow of the Jewish state through a mix of demographic war and armed intifada. So if the Israeli Arabs staged a simultaneous intifada inside Israel there could only be one explanation: their activities were being directed by Arafat too. Barak himself would later suggest that the intifada had effectively crossed the Green Line into Israel.[54] It was also the kneejerk position of prominent liberals like Uri Dromi, head of the Israel Democracy Institute and spokesman for former prime minister Yitzhak Rabin. Days after the outbreak of the intifada, Dromi speculated: "Because the Arab Israelis consider themselves to be part of the Palestinian people, they are susceptible to the calls for struggle against Israel urged by both Palestinian leaders in the territories and their own leaders."[55] Dan Schueftan, a professor at Haifa University and lecturer at the Israeli army's National Security Academy, observed that the Palestinians' goal during Oslo had been "to secure an irredentist Arab base in the West Bank and the Gaza Strip, from which Palestinians could undermine the Jewish state". He added that the Palestinians in the occupied territories were "bent on waging a demographic war against this state with the enthusiastic cooperation of a national minority (Arab citizens of Israel) that challenges the very legitimacy ... of a Jewish homeland".[56]

To get a sense of the atmosphere of the time in Israel it is worth quoting at length one of the most influential columnists, Yoel Marcus of *Ha'aretz*, a man whose opinions are generally considered to reflect the thinking of the security and political establishments. Five days after the protests by Arab citizens began he wrote:

> When one in every six Israeli citizens challenges the very authority of the state in which he or she is represented in the national legislature, we find ourselves in a situation that is far more problematic than our relationship with the [Palestinian Authority]. Sooner or later, we will reach an agreement with the PA, permanent borders will be established and the State of Israel will be physically separated from the State of Palestine. However, Israeli Arabs live in our midst, they are part of us. This is a ticking time bomb whose explosion will trigger a civil war... The Green Line has been destroyed, the line between law-abiding citizens and citizens who violate the country's laws has become the difference between citizens who do not use firearms

> against police officers and innocent civilians, and those who do... The worst nightmare for any general in the midst of battle is the opening of a second front. That was precisely Barak's predicament when the rioting in the heart of Israel merged with rioting in the territories.[57]

Marcus and others adopted this view even though there was not a shred of evidence to support it. Despite six decades of suffering gross discrimination, the Palestinian minority had never engaged in organised violence against the state and only a minuscule number of individuals had ever been prosecuted for subversive activity. Clashes had remained localised, usually spontaneous outbursts of protest against specific instances of land confiscations or house demolitions. The previous lethal clash between the police and large numbers of Arab citizens had occurred a quarter of a century earlier, in 1976, during the minority's first ever general strike called in response to large-scale confiscations by the state of farming land in the Galilee. On that occasion, six unarmed Palestinian citizens had been shot dead by the security forces in circumstances not dissimilar from those in October 2000.[58]

Nonetheless, Marcus was not alone in his views. In a survey for Israel's biggest-circulation newspaper, *Yediot Aharonot*, taken shortly after the October 2000 events, three out of four Jews said they believed Israeli Arabs had behaved treasonously. A poll in the rival *Ma'ariv* newspaper showed that only 17 per cent of Jews thought the police had overreacted, and 60 per cent wanted Arab citizens expelled from the country.[59]

The second front theory gained universal currency because the police were quick to spread misinformation that chimed with the "intelligence" climate being created by Gilad. The police claimed that they had resorted to lethal force only after armed Arab protesters attacked them and tried to storm nearby Jewish communities. An attack on Jews by Israeli Arabs, as several senior policemen made clear, was a "red line" in which police had no choice but to use extreme violence, including live ammunition.[60] In a society primed rarely to question official arguments presented in terms of security, the police's account was dutifully accepted. An editorial in *Ha'aretz*, for example, reproduced without question statements from the chief of police, Yehuda Wilk, that Israeli Arabs had fired on the police in Acre, Nazareth and the village of Fureidis.[61] As late as February 2001, a prominent columnist and settler leader, Israel Harel, was still observing that the main thrust of an investigation into the 13 deaths should be an examination of the question of "where did the Israeli Arab rioters obtain firearms?"[62] Similar claims of live fire by Israeli Arabs were promoted by the Israeli historian Benny Morris in the updated edition of his book *Righteous Victims*.[63] Despite later investigations, which showed that the protesters had not been armed and that there was no evidence suggesting any Jewish community was threatened let alone invaded, the impression of a second front was permanently fixed in the Jewish public's imagination.

EVIDENCE OF POLICE BRUTALITY OVERLOOKED

When I visited Nazareth a few months after the October events, it was hard to find a family not smarting still from the deep wound left by their treatment at the hands of the police. In contrast to the popular account of what had happened, Nazareth's victims of police brutality had not left the city during the clashes, and some had not even been participating in the demonstrations.

A case in point was my neighbour, a jovial, overweight man in his late fifties by the name of Ibrahim Suleiman. One day he lifted his shirt to show me a raw, scarlet 20-inch scar from his rib cage to his belly button. Suleiman had been shot on 2 October from close range with a rubber bullet by a policeman standing a few metres from his home. He had not been throwing stones or demonstrating; he had been with his family on the high flat rooftop of their home watching the early stages of the police invasion unfold below. "At that stage I assumed the police were arresting the demonstrators, so I was not afraid to stand and watch," he told me. Unexpectedly, however, one policeman turned towards the family and shot a rubber-coated bullet at the face of his 22-year-old daughter Nur. The round punctured her forearm as she instinctively shielded her head. Suleiman rushed downstairs to fetch his car to take his daughter to hospital. As he emerged into the street, he saw the same policeman aim his gun again and fire a rubber-coated bullet into his chest. The operation to remove the projectile, which twisted and turned its way through his innards before lodging close to his heart, has left Suleiman without a spleen or pancreas.

Bassem Abu Ahmad, aged 50, had an injury almost as horrific. His back, pockmarked like Swiss cheese, showed the deep impressions left by 13 rubber bullets fired at him from point-blank range by a policeman. Photos from the time show his lower back an angry mess of purple, black and yellow bruises around the points where the bullets tried to penetrate his skin. Abu Ahmad had been shot on 2 October after he joined a march from the central Peace Mosque in Nazareth to protest against the killing of 26-year-old Iyad Lawabny in the city earlier that day. When police fired over the heads of the crowd to force them to disperse, Abu Ahmad took shelter behind a low concrete wall. He was spotted by a policeman who ordered him to leave. As he tried to flee, the officer opened fire.

Some of the police brutality in Nazareth, the effective capital of the country's Palestinian minority, was captured on amateur videos. On 3 October, one Nazareth resident filmed two police marksmen on a rooftop shooting intermittently at unseen protesters below. It is unclear whether the officers are shooting live rounds or rubber bullets. Neither appears to believe he is in any danger. At one point, the two policemen can be seen breaking off from their shooting; they grin at each other and give an excited "high-five" slap in the air, presumably after they hit a demonstrator below. Another video shows a woman psychologist, Nasreen Aseeli, being surrounded by a dozen policemen as she watches from afar the demonstrations in the centre of Nazareth. The officers start to punch and kick her before knocking her to the ground. As she gets up, one hits her shoulder with his rifle butt. Her shoulder was broken in the incident.[64]

None of this evidence emerged in the Israeli media. It was collected by the families of the dead and their lawyers. Instead, for months on end the media dutifully repeated the police account of the October events, especially the most outrageous lie of all: that at no time had the police used live ammunition against the demonstrators. In truth, the police had fired large quantities of live rounds, often as a first line of defence, and, as already noted, had brought in police sniper units that were supposed to be used only against terrorists.

The evidence to shatter the story was not hard to find if someone in authority or the Hebrew media had cared to look. On one street in Nazareth, for example, the steel lamppost close to where Iyad Lawabny died after being shot in the chest while throwing stones had been punctured at head height by a live round shot from the direction where a police unit had confronted the demonstrators. The hole's size matched the handfuls of bullet cases stamped with IMI (Israel Military Industries) that Nazareth schoolchildren were offering anyone showing an interest. And on the hill just above the centre of Nazareth close to the neighbouring Jewish town of Upper Nazareth where Wissam Yazbak was killed could be found a concrete wall slashed with a row of deep holes, all again at head height. The holes were from the direction of the dirt hill where a police unit had been stationed on the night Yazbak died. This evidence alone appeared to be incontrovertible proof that not only had the police used live ammunition as well as rubber bullets on that occasion but that, contrary to their claims, they had not been aiming at protesters' legs.

In fact, despite the subsequent denials by everyone in authority, from Barak downwards, and the willing acceptance of these statements by the media, it had been widely reported inside Israel at the time of the clashes that the police were using live fire. A report from Umm al-Fahm in *Ha'aretz* dated 3 October records that the police "used sniper rifles".[65] The next day in the same newspaper it was reported that, following a three-hour meeting between Barak and the Arab leadership, the government had agreed among other things to "order the security forces to withdraw from the Arab towns and villages and not to use live ammunition other than in the most extreme circumstances". The report added: "The decisions were made under pressure from the Arab delegates."[66] And on an Israeli TV news broadcast presented from Nazareth on 2 October, reporter Majdi Halabi noted that the police were using snipers and live ammunition against the demonstrators.[67] All of this was well known to the Arab population, even if Israeli Jews refused to listen. A lengthy email dated 10 October sent by one observer in Nazareth detailing events in the city a few days earlier stated: "Hundreds of police swarmed [over] the town. Police snipers positioned on the rooftops shot at demonstrators with live ammunition."[68]

One incident in Nazareth seemed to refute in particularly dramatic fashion the police story of restraint. Unlike the 13 dead who could no longer tell their stories, the victim on this occasion survived – if only just – her brush with the police. On the evening of 2 October, Marlene Ramadan and her husband, Dr Amr Ramadan, a paediatrician, had been driving home to Nazareth in the dark, unaware that they were close to the scene of earlier clashes in the city centre. As Dr Ramadan slowed his Mercedes car at an intersection blocked by a barrier, the couple reported hearing what sounded like loud banging on the exterior of the car. Seconds later, as they realised the car was being fired on, Dr Ramadan accelerated up a side street. Although he was unhurt, his wife was hit four times. When police forced the car to a stop, Dr Ramadan was made to lie on the ground and refused permission to treat his wife.[69] The police then left the scene without calling an ambulance.[70] Dr Ramadan later told me:

> My wife was hit once in the hand and arm, and twice in the chest. One of the bullets was only 1 cm from her heart, according to doctors at the hospital. The bullets were removed but there was severe nerve damage to her hand and she has lost the use of it. When I inspected the car, I found 22 bullet holes.[71]

Under questioning many months later, the police admitted snipers had been in hiding when they fired at the car without warning, aiming at the torsos of the driver and passenger. At the time, the police justified the use of live ammunition on the grounds that a Molotov cocktail was thrown from the car. That was what the entry on the incident in the Nazareth police log book shows. Later the police admitted that the commander at the scene, David Ankonina, invented the story to explain the shootings.[72] With the Molotov cocktail story discredited, the police snipers offered a different excuse: they opened fire because they felt their lives were in danger as the driver accelerated towards them. This contradicted the Ramadans' version, that the Mercedes had come under fire when it slowed down; it also conflicted with ballistic tests done on the car showing that the police continued firing at the car after it passed them.[73] Ankonina later confessed that he had told the men under his command to "shoot to kill" the people inside the car.[74]

The truth about those early days in October 2000 began to filter out belatedly because of the domestic political calculations of the prime minister, Ehud Barak – calculations that did not apply to the mounting Palestinian death toll in the occupied territories, where investigations were almost never held. Barak's governing coalition was coming apart in the wake of the failed negotiations with Arafat at Camp David and the outbreak of the intifada. Barak knew he desperately needed both the support of the ten Arab Members of Knesset to keep his minority coalition in power and the support of Arab citizens to win the impending election. He had won a direct election for the premiership in 1999 largely on the back of blanket support from the Palestinian minority, which had been impressed by his pledges to ease discrimination, seek peace with the Palestinians and withdraw troops from South Lebanon. Once elected, Barak had made good only on the last promise, pulling Israeli troops out of Lebanon in May 2000. Rather than fighting discrimination, Barak had avoided any dealings with the Arab minority's leaders. The only generous interpretation was that he feared contact with them might taint him in the eyes of the Jewish public and thereby undermine the negotiations he was carrying out with the Palestinians.

A less forgiving interpretation, however, was that, in a tradition of Israeli leaders of the right and left, Barak had a deep-seated distrust of "Arabs" fed by profoundly racist instincts, as was suggested by several later interviews. In one, with the historian Benny Morris in the summer of 2002, Barak observed: "Palestinians are products of a culture in which to tell a lie ... creates no dissonance. They don't suffer from the problem of telling lies that exists in Judeo-Christian culture. Truth is seen as an irrelevant category."

BARAK REFINES HIS 'SECOND FRONT' THEORY

In the same interview Barak reiterated the second front theory, on this occasion setting out clearly the logic of his position. The Palestinians were not just waging an armed struggle, the intifada, against Israel, Barak said, they were also using the Israeli Arab Knesset members as a "spearpoint" to weaken and possibly destroy Israel from within. Their method was the political campaign that had been launched in the late 1990s by the Israeli Arab leadership to turn Israel from a Jewish state into a state of all its citizens.

> Then they will push for a binational state and then, demography and attrition will lead to a state with a Muslim majority and a Jewish minority. This would not necessarily involve kicking out all the Jews. But it would mean the destruction of Israel as a Jewish state. This, I believe, is their vision. They may not talk about it often, openly, but this is their vision.[75]

Barak's view was widely shared. It explained why Israeli Jews – politicians, the police and the public – had found it so easy to ignore the evidence and accept instead that the country's Arab citizens were trying to overthrow the state in October 2000. It explained why the police and politicians had sanctioned and used lethal force so readily, and it explained why ordinary Israelis had condoned the security forces' brutality.

In Israel, Barak was well-known as a *bitkhonist* – the Hebrew word for a security obsessive – much like his military mentor, Ariel Sharon.[76] As the historian Avi Shlaim observed, as far as Barak was concerned:

> All developments in the region, including the peace process, are considered from the narrow perspective of Israel's security needs and these needs are absurdly inflated – not to say, insatiable. It is only a slight exaggeration to

say that Barak approaches diplomacy as if it were an extension of war by other means.[77]

Statements by Barak and Sharon suggest both were convinced that Arafat had been coordinating the activities of the Israeli Arab leadership since 1994 when he had been allowed under the Oslo Accords to return from exile in Tunis to establish the Palestinian Authority in the West Bank and Gaza. Arafat had been given his tiny state-in-the-making, but in the view of Barak and Sharon he still wanted to keep a strategic foot in Israel, where he hoped one day to realise the right of return of the Palestinian refugees and so bring about the demographic destruction of the Jewish state. Neither Barak nor Sharon was willing to believe that the Israeli Arabs were the true authors of the political demand for a state of all its citizens that emerged in the late 1990s. Instead they were convinced – presumably on the basis of intelligence reports similar to the ones offered by Amos Gilad at the outbreak of the intifada – that Arafat was using the Arab citizens to help destroy the Jewish state demographically.

When Arafat rejected Barak's offers at Camp David, it was proof to the *bitkhonists* that the Palestinian leader was not interested in a deal. He wanted it all. The assumption of both Barak and Sharon was that Arafat had devised a twin-track strategy, hoping either one or both approaches would bring about the Jewish state's downfall. First he had tried to undermine the legitimacy of a Jewish state by demanding a state of all its citizens via his partisans in the Knesset, and second he had begun an armed struggle (the intifada) to weaken Israel and the international community's resolve. In the worst case, he would achieve far bigger concessions from Israel than Barak had dared to offer at Camp David; in the best, he might force Israel to reform itself into a binational state under the threat of being labelled an apartheid state. Then he could wait for demographics to return Palestine to him.

When questioned later about the outbreak of the intifada, Barak explained his thinking. According to intelligence reports, he said, Arafat had been looking for a pretext to wage war on Israel and found it in Sharon's visit to the Noble Sanctuary. "The visit was legitimate. We know that for Arafat it was just an excuse [for launching a popular uprising], and if [the visit] had not taken place he would have found another excuse."[78] About the October 2000 events inside Israel, Barak set out Israel's difficulty as he saw it. "We are coping with a very problematic phenomenon, an effort to use the democratic process to undermine the foundations of the state. They call for a binational state, which will end up as a state with a Jewish minority." Asked who "they" were, Barak identified Azmi Bishara's National Democratic Assembly, the Islamic Movement and the Sons of the Village – the main Arab political streams. He accused them of "abusing" democracy. Bishara, the man who had developed the slogan of "a state of all its citizens", was "a very smart man who knows what to do and what not to do to achieve his ends", said Barak.[79]

Like the rising death toll in the occupied territories, the events that led to the killing of 13 Arab demonstrators inside Israel would probably have remained uninvestigated but for a short-lived experiment with the Israeli electoral system. For a brief period – in three national elections between 1996 and 2001 – the Israeli public had the chance to vote for the prime minister directly. It was a brief window when Palestinian citizens' vote had a marginal impact on the outcome of the election. Their influence was limited to tipping the balance in favour of one of the two Zionist candidates – from Labor or Likud. In 1999 they turned out in overwhelming numbers to support Barak against the incumbent, Binyamin Netanyahu of Likud. But by late 2000, they were disenchanted with Barak: he had refused to meet any of their leaders and had done almost nothing to end discrimination. Their impression was that, because Barak knew there was no "better" candidate on offer, he could rely on their support however he behaved. The direct election system was abolished for the 2003 contest, partly out of a shared recognition by Jewish politicians that it gave too much influence to the Arab minority.

But that brief experiment had one outcome no one could have foreseen when it was introduced. Faced with the simmering rage of the Arab population inside Israel in the wake of the 13 deaths, Barak needed to win back their loyalty if he was to stand a chance of being re-elected.

A DESPERATE ATTEMPT TO WIN BACK VOTERS

After the October events, Barak's political future looked bleak indeed. He was aware that, as far as Palestinian citizens were concerned, blame for the 13 deaths fell squarely at his door. The election would be against his chief political rival, Ariel Sharon, whose inflammatory visit to the Temple Mount a few months earlier had been widely interpreted as the first leg of his campaign trail. Sharon could win the election on a hawkish platform that appealed to rightwing

Jews; Barak, on the other hand, would need more support than he could muster from the ranks of Israel's dwindling left.[80] The prime minister, therefore, acted quickly to try to win back Arab voters to his side. He promised to reverse some of the decades of economic discrimination by investing $1 billion in the Arab community over the next four years – a pledge that neither he nor his successor, Sharon, ever honoured.[81] Also, according to Amnon Lipkin-Shahak, a former army chief of staff and Israeli negotiator at Camp David, Barak decided for the sake of appearances to attend the Taba talks in early January 2001: "Taba was bullshit! Taba was an elections exercise ... Taba was not aimed to reach an agreement. Taba was aimed to convince the Israeli Arabs to vote."[82]

In addition, Barak promised a low-level committee of examination into the October events under the chairmanship of a retired district court judge. With no powers to call witnesses or compel the production of documents, the committee failed to impress the bereaved families and their lawyers. They demanded a full and independent commission of inquiry. Their model was the Saville inquiry that was belatedly investigating the killings of 13 unarmed Catholic demonstrators in Derry in 1972 by the British army in what came to be known as "Bloody Sunday" – an event that had more than superficial similarities to what had happened in the Galilee.[83] The Arab families' lawyers met regularly with their Irish counterparts.

Barak soon caved in, appointing a three-man commission of inquiry on 8 November. Sitting alongside the chairman, Supreme Court judge Theodor Or, would be the distinguished academic Shimon Shamir, a former ambassador to Egypt and Jordan, and a little-known Arab district court judge, Sahel Jarah, who was replaced four months later by another Arab judge, Hashem Khatib.[84] The inquiry was not a criminal trial; it was empowered to investigate and report on the events of early October, subpoenaing witnesses and demanding documents it needed to complete its work. Its report would identify failings to the government, and the panel could recommend criminal prosecutions against any of those it warned.

Barak was keenly aware of the dangers of opening up the early days of October 2000 to forensic inspection. Depending on the evidence, the chain of command responsible for the killings at the start of the intifada – both inside Israel and in the Old City of Jerusalem – could stretch back to his public security minister, Ben Ami, and ultimately to himself. Possibly as a result, Barak insisted on sabotaging the inquiry's mandate in two ways. First, he set a very narrow window for the inquiry to inspect the circumstances surrounding the 13 deaths. The panel could only examine the events that began unfolding from 1 October. Sharon's visit to the Temple Mount three days earlier, Barak's reasons for approving it against advice, and Barak and Ben Ami's decision to use snipers against the Palestinian demonstrators were all outside Justice Or's remit. Second, as well as examining the behaviour of the police, Barak required the inquiry to investigate the "conduct of the inciters". It was clear from the wording that the incitement Barak was referring to was to be found in the Arab and not the Jewish community – and that was precisely how Justice Or proceeded to interpret his mandate. As the lawyers of the victims' families pointed out, however, Barak's phrasing presumed that incitement by the Arab leadership had actually taken place, and did so before the commission had even begun its work.[85]

There was another problem with Barak's mandate. If the Arab leadership's role needed investigating, why not also look at the incitement of the Jewish leadership? What about the politicians and columnists who had accused the Palestinian minority of being a fifth column? Had they not encouraged the Jewish mobs that had attacked Arab homes and cars? And what about Sharon's visit to the Temple Mount? That could be seen as a very direct form of incitement.

The suspicion was that Barak wanted to divert attention from his own and his government's role in the 13 deaths – and in the outbreak more generally of the intifada through the events at the Temple Mount – by scapegoating the Arab representatives in the Knesset. But it also served another useful purpose: by assuming that the Arab leaders had incited the demonstrators, Barak was forcing the Or Commission to adopt the same ideological framework as the one created by Amos Gilad's discredited intelligence reports. He was ensuring its conclusions would reinforce, rather than challenge, the "second front" theory: that Arab citizens had simply been pawns, willing or not, of a subversive strategy incited by the Arab MKs and born in the fevered imagination of Yasser Arafat himself.

Justice Or's ready acceptance of the terms of the remit imposed by Barak was not an auspicious start. In fact, there were strong grounds for believing that the mandate violated Israeli law as well as all established international precedents for a commission of inquiry. Adalah, a legal centre for the Arab minority that represented the families of the dead and the Arab leadership during the hearings, observed tellingly: "The aim of establishing a Commission of Inquiry is to investigate state authorities in cases in which their behaviour created a loss of trust by the public. This is different from investigating the conduct of citizens, who are subordinated to the state authorities."[86] In other words, the role of the inquiry was to hold accountable state officials and institutions, not to usurp the role of a criminal trial into the behaviour of ordinary citizens, including Arab Members of Knesset.

None of this did much to salvage Barak's reputation. For many weeks after the October events he refused to meet the bereaved families. When in late December he finally agreed to pay a visit, as the inevitable election drew nearer, they refused his offer.[87] By the time of the election in early February 2001, a full-blown campaign to boycott the vote was under way in Arab communities, under the slogan "We will vote when our sons can vote".[88] In a last-minute bid to win favour with the country's Arab minority, Barak gritted his teeth at a cabinet meeting on the eve of the poll and said: "On behalf of the government and myself, I express deep sorrow for the killing of Arab citizens. In demonstrations, even if they are illegal, civilians are not supposed to get killed."[89] It was too little, too late.

Sharon won with a handsome majority of 62 per cent of the vote, aided by the lowest Arab turnout in Israel's history, at about 18 per cent. (A significant proportion of those Arab votes were assumed to come from the mainly loyal Druze community.) According to figures supplied by the Israeli Arab lobby group Mossawa, only 10 of more than 13,000 eligible voters in the town of Sakhnin cast a ballot; in Umm al-Fahm it was 350 out of 18,000 voters; in Kafr Kana 100 out of 8,000 voters.[90] The boycott was a sign of how gravely the minority viewed its treatment by the police, especially since a boycott was deeply opposed by Arab world leaders, who preferred a second term of Barak as prime minister. In another sign of how implausible the "second front" theory was, Israeli Arab voters ignored appeals from Palestinian leader Yasser Arafat to turn out for Barak.

The general attitude of the Palestinian minority at the election was summed up by Hassan Asleh, whose 17-year-old son Aseel, a peace activist, was shot dead by police on 2 October in the town of Arrabe. "As we see it, the policies of all the Zionist parties are the same," he told the Hebrew media. "There might be some differences in terms of tactics or methods, but they all relate to us as though we are enemies."[91] He was not speaking idly. On the cover of the report into the cause of his son's death he received from the hospital were stamped the words "Enemy operation".[92]

Asleh had become an articulate spokesman for the grieving families. At a meeting in his home shortly after the election, he took me to the olive grove on the edge of the town where his son died. There, a fading black shroud of cloth hung from a tree where Aseel had been shot in the back from close range by a policeman. "I have no doubt this was an execution," he said. "Aseel's only crime was that he was an Arab in a Jewish state." The coming testimonies before the Or Commission would do nothing to dispel that impression.

2
A False Reckoning

In vain we are loyal patriots, our loyalty in some places running to extremes; in vain do we make the same sacrifices of life and property as our fellow-citizens ... The majority may decide which are the strangers; for this, as indeed every point which arises in the relations between nations, is a question of might.

Theodor Herzl (1896)[1]

Break their bones.

Yitzkak Rabin (1988)[2]

The rubber bullet introduced by the Israeli army during the [First] Intifada symbolised the recognition that Israel's commitment to democratic values and its investment in its internationally recognised status as a democracy set limits to the legitimate use of force in the cause of the Jewish state.

Yaron Ezrahi, professor of political science at Hebrew University, Jerusalem (1997)[3]

The Arab town of Shafa'amr, located halfway between Haifa and Nazareth, is known for two things: its ice cream and its human rights lawyers. In July 2000, however, when I first visited Shafa'amr, most Israeli Jews had no more heard of the law firm Adalah ("Justice" in Arabic) than they had tasted the town's ice cream. I had to search for the white villa that serves as the firm's office at the end of a dirt path on the edge of town.

Since its founding in 1996, Adalah and its charismatic director, Hassan Jabareen, had been working mostly unnoticed to chip away at the glass wall that separates the Arab minority from the Jewish majority. It was a thankless task. A glance at the annual report for the year 1999 that Jabareen thrust into my hands revealed a catalogue of relentless discrimination: the daily battles that Palestinian citizens face living in a Jewish state and Adalah tries to challenge in the courts. The chapter headings for the legal petitions the lawyers submitted that year seemed to include the violation of just about every right I could think of: language rights, education rights, religious rights, land and housing rights, women's rights, political rights, social rights, economic and employment rights. Almost as an afterthought the report included a final section on racism and hate speech, the informal indignities that pale in comparison to the real problem – state-sanctioned and state-organised discrimination.

Under those headings were to be found some of the stories that gave an impression of Arab life in a Jewish state in 1999, a year when a government of the left was in power. Adalah had petitioned against the refusal by the government and local authorities to include road signs in Arabic (despite it officially being a state language), as well as the refusal by the state-owned banks to use Arabic in their literature or on the screens of their cash machines, and by the labour courts to accept evidence in Arabic. It had petitioned against the government for classifying more than 500 exclusive Jewish communities as "national priority areas A", entitling them to extra municipal funding, access to mortgage grants and tax breaks for local industries, while denying such status to all but four tiny Arab communities, even though the bottom of every socio-economic index was crammed with Arab towns and villages. It had petitioned against the Ministry of Religious Affairs for setting aside for Arab communities less than 2 per cent of its budget, even though their inhabitants comprise nearly a fifth of the population, and against the ministry's refusal to provide any budget at all for non-Jewish cemeteries. It had petitioned against the Health Ministry's refusal to provide health care clinics in any of the Negev's "unrecognised" communities, home to some 70,000 Bedouin Arabs, Israel's poorest citizens, and against a much wider failure to provide social services to the Bedouin by the Labour Ministry. It had petitioned against a decision by the Airports Authority to stop construction of the country's new airport after it was discovered that Arab workers were employed on the building site. And so the list went on.

"We're dealing with just the tip of the iceberg," said Jabareen.

> There are an endless number of issues of discrimination we could pursue – some much worse than these cases – but at the moment we are a small organisation and can only fight the cases we think we are most likely to win. We find the weak points in the system, we confront the judges with cases where the discrimination clearly violates the country's legal codes, and try to tease out a remedy.

But given the depth of discrimination, even victory can be hollow. Although in March 1999, for example, the Supreme Court ordered the Health Ministry to build three clinics by the end of the year to provide health care for the "unrecognised" Bedouin population, the state did nothing. Several requests by Adalah for a progress report from the government went unanswered until the Health Ministry finally admitted a year later it had not yet hired a building contractor, let alone begun work. In the meantime, the ministry had drastically cut the public transport available to the Bedouin to reach clinics in neighbouring towns. Despite the court decision, things had actually got worse. Adalah's report noted that, with an outbreak of pneumonia among the Bedouin in the Negev, "the issue of the clinics had become a matter of life and death".[4]

Adalah was ploughing a lonely furrow when I first met Jabareen, but a few months later he and several of his lawyers would become faces recognisable to every television viewer in the country.

In February 2001 the Or Commission opened its inquiry into the killings by the security forces of 13 unarmed demonstrators inside Israel at the start of the intifada. The early sessions gripped the country as Jews and Arabs tuned in to hear the testimonies. The bereaved families recruited Adalah to represent them at the Commission, to sift the evidence and question state officials, and to act as a spokesperson in front of the television cameras. It would prove to be, as Jabareen later told me, not an entirely comfortable experience.

As well as rapidly earning a reputation for professionalism, Adalah also found itself widely maligned for its trenchant criticism of the Commission's methods and for the regularity with which it unearthed disturbing evidence about the October 2000 events, material that the official investigators never seemed to find. Soon the law firm was the subject of almost as much scrutiny as the inquiry's revelations. In a sign of how much Adalah was upsetting the system that was supposed to keep the Arab minority weak and on the other side of the glass wall, the government's charity commissioner began investigating Adalah midway through the Or hearings. He alleged that the firm had abused its mandate, was financially mismanaged and had forged an affiliation with a political party. These grave charges were made without anyone from Adalah being interviewed or any documents being requested.[5] After Jabareen publicly challenged the charity commissioner to produce evidence, the allegations were quietly dropped.

Adalah doubtless knew what it was letting itself in for: Israeli politicians had lost no time in discrediting the Or Commission and the Arab leaders who had demanded it, even before the inquiry started. Likud leaders, in particular, observed that it had been, in their words, "born in sin" – a reference to Barak's attempts to win back the votes of the Arab minority.[6] It was not a little paradoxical then that, by the time Justice Or began his hearings in the Supreme Court building in Jerusalem, Barak was already out of power and Ariel Sharon safely installed as prime minister. The Or Commission started its work in an atmosphere of open hostility from the new government. Two months into the hearings Uzi Landau, the new public security minister, took the unprecedented step of warning the inquiry that he would not feel bound to implement its recommendations.[7] He also approved the promotion of two senior police commanders, Moshe Waldman and Benzy Sau, who were both under suspicion of having acted with gross negligence during the October 2000 events.[8] Landau's deputy, Gideon Ezra, threatened to resign his post should the police be criticised in Justice Or's final report[9] and the justice minister, Meir Sheetrit, made what he described as a "solidarity visit" when the police commander who had been in charge in the north, Alik Ron, testified before the inquiry.[10]

BEREAVED FAMILIES SEEK A FAIR HEARING

In many ways, the establishment of the Or Commission should have been a triumphant moment for Israel's Palestinian citizens. When in 1976 the security forces suppressed a general strike in the Arab town of Sakhnin by killing six unarmed protesters, the prime minister of the day, Yitzhak Rabin, refused to countenance an inquiry. This time, hoped some Arab observers, the security forces would not be allowed to kill with impunity. A few had even higher expectations of the Commission. They trusted that once Justice Or began his work he would find it difficult not to be drawn into the wider context in which the October events occurred: the decades of discrimination in budgets and resources, the systematic exclusion of the minority's parties from power, the repressive policy of land confiscations and house demolitions, the still-prevalent philosophy of "Jewish labour" in the workplace. If he did so, it would be the first time an independent public body had ever critically examined the state of relations between the Jewish majority and the Arab minority. Maybe the very nature of a Jewish state would also come under scrutiny.

The Adalah lawyers, the bereaved families and most of the Arab public, however, remained sceptical about how far a state-appointed inquiry could relate to their wider concerns. Such fears were hardly allayed by Justice Or's decision in April 2001 to build a glass wall to separate the families in the public gallery from the main room where the panel and state officials sat, after attacks by two fathers on policemen in the witness stand. But in truth a glass wall existed from the outset. Neither Adalah nor the families were informed about the first hearing, on 19 February 2001; they heard via rumours from the commission's investigators. Even though the proceedings were being held in Jerusalem, a two or more hour drive for most of the families and their lawyers in the Galilee, the inquiry started each day at 8.30 am promptly. Initially, the families were refused permission to testify in Arabic, even though several of the older people knew little Hebrew.

But the biggest blows, remembers Marwan Dalal, one of Adalah's senior lawyers at the hearings, came from Justice Or's legal decisions. The Supreme Court judge refused Dalal and his team any official standing before the inquiry, thereby preventing them from issuing subpoenas and cross-examining witnesses, from seeing much of the evidence submitted by the state, and from being given advance warning of the issues to be raised at the hearings. At one point Hassan Jabareen complained bitterly that hundreds of injured Arab demonstrators were being denied the chance to testify and to clarify the events of October 2000.[11] To no avail: Adalah had no influence on whom the panel called as a witness. Justice Or's decisions, according to the opinion of a British legal expert, Lord Gifford, violated the internationally recognised principles of a commission of inquiry.[12] Israeli commentators, however, took Justice Or's side. In a typical *Ha'aretz* editorial, the newspaper criticised what it regarded as "interference" in the inquiry:

> Ever since the commission began its work [Arab citizens] have not hesitated to challenge the procedures of its deliberations, to demand that bereaved family members be allowed to cross-examine witnesses, to regard some of the witnesses as guilty, and to question the commission's credibility. This behavior is unfair and irresponsible.[13]

The families and their lawyers were on the point of boycotting the hearings when an unexpected early development occurred. The inquiry had agreed to let low-ranking policemen testify first, some of them anonymously. When these officers started to explain what had happened in October 2000, much of the façade carefully maintained for several months by the security forces, Justice Ministry investigators and the government crumbled. The policemen's admissions and revelations, it should be noted, were usually made inadvertently, often by officers who had no idea that what they were saying suggested a profound degree of racism. Some told of shooting rubber-coated bullets and live ammunition at unarmed protesters who posed no threat to their safety; few had any idea of the safe range for using rubber-coated bullets, or seemed to think it important that they knew; others agreed that they had received different orders when dealing with Jewish citizens; and yet more spoke of their suspicion or hatred of Arabs.

Avraham Bar, for example, told the inquiry that his unit had been ordered to fire a rubber-coated bullet at a demonstrator in the village of Jatt "as a deterrence". The bullet, fired from close range by a Druze patrolman, Murshad Rashad, penetrated the face of 21-year-old Rami Jarra through his eye, later killing him.[14] Rotem Buzaglo, a member of the Border Police, a paramilitary unit that operates inside both Israel and the occupied territories, was quoted by the inquiry as having told a newspaper at the time of the clashes: "There was an atmosphere in the unit of: 'We'll stick it to them [the Arab demonstrators] and get it over with.'"[15] Another police officer, Ophir Elbaz, who the inquiry heard had fired more than 30 rounds of rubber-coated bullets in Umm al-Fahm, hitting at least 15 demonstrators and disabling several, admitted that, while off-duty several days later, he had joined the mob from Upper Nazareth that attacked Arab homes in Nazareth, including that of Azmi Bishara, an Arab Member of Knesset.[16] A veteran Arab officer in the Border Police, Muhana Nijim, told the inquiry that he had overheard many of the policemen who were brought to Kafr Manda saying that it was their chance to kill an Arab. He recalled that more than 200 officers had fired a barrage of bullets into the town. "I saw bullets [being fired] in bursts, flying over the mosque of Kfar Manda," he said. "It was like war... there was a lot of shooting."[17]

These revelations, however, were overshadowed by the far greater reluctance on the part of police witnesses to cooperate with the inquiry. Repeatedly during testimony the Commission members made it clear they felt they were being misled or that important evidence was being withheld. During the questioning of Yaron Meir, the operations commander in the Galilee, for example, Justice Or observed bluntly that the senior officer was "giving untrue answers" about the use of live ammunition.[18] When pressed on inconsistencies in his testimony, Meir confessed that he had viewed an earlier Justice Ministry inquiry as "an investigation among friends".[19] He was not alone. Other senior officers also admitted failing to take earlier inquiries seriously. Moshe Waldman, who was in charge in Nazareth, told Justice Or that he had not checked any of the evidence, including bullet rounds, passed to him after a protester was killed in the city.[20]

As one regular observer of the proceedings, Ori Nir of the *Ha'aretz* newspaper, commented:

> Some of [the police] are coordinating their testimonies. In other cases, testimony given to the panel contradicts what the same person said earlier under oath to the commission's investigators. Some of the comments made by policemen in their testimony sound untrue to the commission. Many of the policemen are struck by an attack of unreasonable forgetfulness on the witness stand. Very often they reply to questions with "I didn't see," "I didn't hear" or "I don't know" – even in cases where they were only a few meters from the events in question.[21]

MURDER IN AN OLIVE GROVE REMAINS A MYSTERY

Nir was referring in particular to the circumstances surrounding the death of Hassan Asleh's 17-year-old son, Aseel, who died in Arrabe on 2 October 2000. What little international media interest there had been at the time of the 13 deaths inside Israel concentrated on the killing of Asleh, mainly because he appeared such an unlikely threat to the police or the Jewish state. Asleh had been a prominent and very committed member of Seeds of Peace, an American-sponsored group dedicated to encouraging bonds of understanding and coexistence between young Jews and Arabs in the Middle East. He had met President Clinton on the White House lawn as part of a Seeds of Peace delegation and had numerous Jewish friends in Israel and America. On the day he died, he was wearing a green T-shirt bearing the Seeds of Peace logo.

The police account of Asleh's killing was little different from the stories they were promoting relating to the other deaths. For many months the district police commander in the Galilee, Yehuda Solomon, had been telling the media that Asleh and another Arrabe youth, 18-year-old Ala Nassar, had been shot dead as the police defended a nearby Jewish kibbutz called Lotam. In Solomon's words, the police had their "backs to the wall" as they protected Lotam from "a civil rebellion with an intent to kill".[22] However, there was no evidence that any police officer had been injured in the attack, or even that the attack had taken place. The kibbutz's secretary, Nitzan Rosenbilt, said the community had received no warning from the police of an attack nor had they been given "any special alert".[23] The police version also conflicted with the testimonies of the Arab demonstrators, who insisted that they had remained close to the outskirts of Arrabe all day.

Solomon also denied vehemently to the media the demonstrators' claims that Asleh had been shot in the back by the police. No autopsy had been carried out on Asleh because the Justice Ministry, which was responsible for investigating the death, had released his body for burial without demanding a post-mortem examination – in violation of its legal obligations.[24] Solomon, when finally confronted with a surgeon's report from Nahariya hospital, where Asleh died, which showed a fatal gunshot wound to the teenager's upper back, told a reporter: "Which doctor is that? Some Muhammad or Mustafa?"[25]

Solomon's account began unravelling in June 2001, as soon as the Or inquiry investigated the death. The panel heard that on 2 October a large group of demonstrators from Arrabe had marched to the outskirts of the town, close by an olive grove, where they burned tyres on the road and held noisy protests over the killings of three Arab citizens close to Umm al-Fahm the day before. Several members of the Asleh family had been present, including Aseel's father and his uncle. Aseel, it seemed, had not been directly involved, but sat under a tree in the olive grove, a curious spectator watching the events from afar. All morning a police unit was stationed some distance further up the road to protect a junction that led to Kibbutz Lotam. But after arson was suspected in a fire that broke out in a nearby wood, reinforcements were called for, including three paramilitary units of the Border Police and a team from the Drug Squad. The police units moved down towards the demonstration, provoking stone-throwing from the youths. The Border Police responded at first with rubber bullets, they told the panel, and later with live ammunition when their supply of rubber bullets was exhausted. Superintendent Michael Shafshak, an intelligence officer from the Drug Squad, said his team had not been supplied with rubber bullets and so they had used live rounds. "If we had had rubber bullets, a lot of what happened later wouldn't have happened," he said.[26]

At about 2.30 pm the police units took the decision to storm the area by the olive grove to disperse the demonstrators. Police witnesses told the commission they broke up into three-man teams to chase after and arrest troublemakers. Hassan Asleh, who was some distance from his son, said he saw him surrounded in the olive grove and beaten by police officers with the butt of their rifles. He told the inquiry:

> [Aseel] was knocked forward by the force of the blow and ... fell down. I didn't see him after he fell because the olive trees blocked my view, but I heard shots and when the three [policemen] left without Aseel, I understood that they had shot him. I started to shout "My son has gone" and then I fainted.[27]

A physician confirmed to the commission that Aseel had received a blow to the back of the head as well as a fatal gunshot wound.[28]

Aseel, it was known, had died from a bullet wound high on the back of his shoulder, fired from point-blank range, that severed an artery. The accounts of Arab and police witnesses agreed on the fact that he had been chased and that he had stumbled and fallen. Either he had been shot from behind while running, or – as his father contended – he had fallen or been knocked down and then executed while he lay face down on the ground, possibly unconscious. But who pulled the trigger? Even though 17 police witnesses were called, none could say. Several admitted that Asleh had been targeted for arrest only because he was separate from the main body of the demonstrators and close to the police.[29] Avadia Hatan, an officer from the Drug Squad who admitted chasing the teenager, said he saw a bloody wound to his shoulder as they ran after him, which may have caused him to stumble. Another policeman, Avi Karso, said he was not sure when Asleh was shot, and heard no shots before, during or after the chase. Hatan called Asleh's death "a mystery".[30]

The one policeman whose name kept cropping up during testimony and who several witnesses said was the first to reach Asleh – Yitzhak Shimoni – was not called before the hearings into Asleh's death. He appeared only much later, when he was permitted to testify from behind a screen. Shimoni claimed that he had found the teenager on the ground badly wounded and had tried to get him medical help.[31] All three members of the inquiry did little to conceal their disbelief.[32]

'UNIFIED RESPONSE' TO EXPLAIN ARAB DEATHS

The Israeli public and media, which had been fed a constant diet of insinuations about the Israeli Arabs as a fifth column and that their "riots" had been orchestrated by Arafat himself, were troubled by the early revelations. Senior police commanders, caught off guard, hastily recruited extra media advisers to present a more sympathetic account. The least damaging version of events, it was apparently decided, was that police officers had been poorly prepared and equipped for such a hostile confrontation. They had resorted to lethal force largely because government underfunding meant they lacked the resources to tackle the clashes by other means. There was some speculation about whether police commanders were creating a "unified response" to the commission's questions – euphemism for a cover story – concentrating especially on the lack of riot control equipment. As one police source observed, the force had mistakenly expected the media's coverage of the inquiry to "start on page one, but eventually slide to the back, and then out of the newspapers".[33]

Despite their attempts at managing the news, the police failed to stop the inquiry unearthing a hugely damaging revelation. Allowed to speak from behind a screen to conceal their identities, several witnesses revealed that they belonged to an elite squad of police snipers used in anti-terror operations. Drawn from the same sniper unit deployed by Barak and Ben Ami on 29 September at the Temple Mount, where at least four Palestinians had been shot dead, they were called in to Umm al-Fahm and Nazareth on 2 October to disperse the demonstrations.[34] Although at Umm al-Fahm the snipers were initially told to shoot only if demonstrators endangered policemen's lives by using firearms, the order changed after an officer was injured by a stone. From then on, a legitimate target was redefined as anyone holding a slingshot.

It was never properly established who was in charge of giving orders to the anti-terror unit in Nazareth, or why they were brought there in the first place. Moshe Waldman, the city's commanding officer, initially told the inquiry that the use of sniper fire had been viewed in terms of "fear and deterrence". Under further questioning from a clearly troubled Justice Or, however, Waldman changed tack, suggesting that the sharpshooters were needed to guarantee the safety of police officers.[35] That hardly fitted with the accounts given by the dozen snipers who were stationed in the city for two days, on 2 and 3 October. The snipers had fired more than 20 bullets at Dr Amr Ramadan's Mercedes car, for example, severely injuring his wife, even though it was admitted that the couple posed no threat to the police at all. In another incident the unit was located on a roof in the city centre, while the rest of the Nazareth force kept out of sight in the main police station, to act as "spotters" during the funeral for

Iyad Lawabny. Members of the funeral procession who noticed the snipers surrounded the building and started throwing stones. Police witnesses told the inquiry that reinforcements had to be drafted into the city to "rescue" the unit, leading to yet more casualties among local inhabitants. Justice Or observed pointedly to one of the snipers that had he not been stationed on the roof in the first place there would have been no need to fire on the funeral crowds.[36]

As the officer in charge of the sniper unit testified to Justice Or, it was the first time to his knowledge that the unit had ever been ordered to open fire at Israeli citizens. The public security minister, Shlomo Ben Ami, who had been insisting for months that no live ammunition had been used, told Channel Two television that night "No one ever told me, upstairs, of this detail" – the "upstairs" presumably a reference to the prime minister, Ehud Barak.[37]

COMMANDER ALIK RON'S SECURITY OBSESSIONS

The man responsible for calling in the snipers was the police commander of the northern region, Alik Ron, who himself once headed the sniper unit and therefore knew better than anyone that its role was to target armed terrorists. At Umm al-Fahm he personally directed the sniper fire by radio, authorising the unit to shoot at individual demonstrators. When questioned by journalists stunned at the snipers' revelations, Ron replied: "So what's new? What's special in this?"[38] But as most of the reporters understood, the testimony suggested two extremely uncomfortable possibilities. The first was that Ron and his boss, police chief Yehuda Wilk, had engineered a complex cover-up lasting many months to conceal from the public and government their decision to use live fire and sharpshooters against unarmed civilians. The second, more disturbing scenario was that they had been ordered by the government to use full force, including live ammunition, to deter the protests and had then assisted in the cover-up. This was the conclusion that had been reached many months earlier by some in the Arab leadership, who had never been deceived by the campaign of police misinformation. Knesset member Azmi Bishara had observed six months earlier: "Either Barak and Ben-Ami ordered the army and the police to open fire with live ammunition in the territories and inside Israel, or they have lost control of the army and the police. Either way, they are responsible for what happened."[39]

During the first days of October, there had been protests and riots across the country, staged by Jews and Arabs, and yet two patterns were discernible. The first was that only Arabs had been killed by the security forces; the second was that all 13 deaths had occurred in the north, the most populous Arab region in the country and the one under Alik Ron's command. Similar protests by the Bedouin in the southern desert area of the Negev,[40] and by Arabs in the mixed cities of Jaffa, Lod, Acre and Haifa had been ended by the police without loss of life or major violence. There, local leaders and police commanders had kept up some kind of dialogue.[41] In Haifa the dovish mayor, Amram Mitzna, and an Arab Member of Knesset, Issam Makhoul, had calmed protests in the Arab neighbourhood of Wadi Nisnas with only minimal police involvement. Only where Ron was in charge, in the Arab heartlands of the Galilee and the Little Triangle, had citizens died at the hands of the police.

Ron, a former Israeli army commando officer and head of the northern police force since the late 1990s, was a very typical product of the Israeli security establishment. Later, under questioning from the Or Commission, Ehud Barak would heap lavish praise on Ron, describing him as "someone who has made an enormous contribution to Israel's security".[42] During his public career, however, Ron had made it clear that he was naturally suspicious of Arabs and keen to show who was boss. Facing imminent retirement, like many senior Israeli security men before him, he was known to have political ambitions. According to rumours in early 2000, he was in negotiations with Ariel Sharon about running on a future Likud electoral list in what some observers termed an "anti-Arab alliance" of the Jewish rightwing: settlers, Orthodox Jews, Russian immigrants and Mizrahim (Jews originally from Arab countries).[43]

During the months before the outbreak of the intifada, Ron had dangerously and publicly widened the rift with the Arab population in his region. He had inflamed tensions in three aspects of his role as regional police commander. First, he had adopted a policy of "zero-tolerance" against what he termed "law-breakers" – Arab citizens participating in political demonstrations and protests against house demolitions – which had led to a series of localised and nasty clashes between Arab communities and the police. One such instance had occurred on 30 March, when thousands of Arab citizens took part in the annual march in Sakhnin marking Land Day, the commemoration of the killing of six unarmed demonstrators by the security forces during a general strike in 1976. During Land Day of 2000, Ron chose a violent confrontation with the demonstrators that led to the death of one woman after inhaling tear gas and injuries to dozens more, including Muhammad Zeidan, the leader of the minority's supreme political body, the Higher Follow-Up Committee. He was photographed surrounded by policemen beating him with batons.[44]

Also over the summer, Ron arranged a series of dawn raids to enforce a controversial policy of house demolitions against Arab homeowners. Israeli governments have been confiscating private and municipal Arab land for decades and passing it on to Jewish communities for their exclusive use, as part of an official policy of "Judaising" Arab areas. Palestinian citizens, facing a chronic shortage of land and refused building permits, have had little choice but to build homes illegally. In the language of Ron, they too were "law-breakers" who had to be dealt with using the full force of the law. In the summer of 2000, the police had helped enforce the demolition of homes using high levels of violence.

The second confrontation engineered by Ron was a high-profile media campaign against the Arab leadership, who he repeatedly claimed were steering the local population towards extremism – a refrain that echoed the criticisms of government ministers and later the Or inquiry itself. Ron began his attacks as early as 1999, criticising the northern Islamic Movement, based in Umm al-Fahm, and especially its popular leader, Sheikh Raed Salah.[45] He accused Salah, the mayor of Umm al-Fahm, of incitement for staging large rallies in his city warning that the al-Aqsa mosque, the centrepiece of the Noble Sanctuary in Jerusalem, needed protection. At his "Al-Aqsa is in Danger" rallies Salah claimed that rightwing leaders such as Sharon were conspiring with extremist Jewish groups to end centuries of Muslim control of the Sanctuary.[46] At the same time as his attacks on Salah, Ron accused the Arab MKs of "inciting in a bloodthirsty way against the police".[47]

By May 2000, Ron was again censuring the Arab leadership, calling the MKs "inciters" and the Islamic Movement "the most despicable movement".[48] A delegation of MKs from the one, small Jewish–Arab party, Hadash, met with the public security minister, Shlomo Ben-Ami, to suggest Ron be removed from his job.[49] Tamar Gozansky, a Jewish MK in Hadash, pointed out to Ben Ami that a few days earlier the police had dealt with two demonstrations, one Jewish and one Arab, but had acted violently only against the protesters in the Arab town of Shafa'amr. "There was a confrontation in [the Jewish town of] Kiryat Shmona that same day. No bullet was fired and no one was beaten. Why are protesters in [Shafa'amr] different?" In a comment that would foreshadow the imminent events of October 2000, she added: "Democratic rights are the rights of all citizens. The right to protest is not just a right of Jewish citizens."

Ron was not to be diverted. He stepped up his criticisms over the summer, and by mid-September – days before the outbreak of the intifada – he was holding a press conference at the Nazareth police headquarters to recommend that an unnamed Arab MK be investigated for "inciting Israeli Arabs to attack police" during confrontations over house demolitions.[50] It later emerged that the MK in question was Muhammad Barakeh, of the joint Jewish and Arab Hadash party.[51] Ron's anger had been inflamed by a statement from Barakeh to the media defending Arab citizens who were trying to prevent that summer's wave of house demolitions. "The right to a roof over one's head takes precedence over the duty to obey the law," Barakeh said.[52] The attorney-general, Elyakim Rubinstein, immediately approved the investigation.

At the same press conference, Ron provoked a third confrontation. This accusation was even more serious. He announced the arrest of 41 Israeli Arabs from two independent "terror cells" based in the Umm al-Fahm area. They had, he claimed, been plotting against "collaborators" (Palestinians working for the Israeli police and intelligence services) and trafficking in arms. Ron described the cells as the biggest nationalist conspiracy against the state uncovered in nearly twenty years. He again implicated the leader of the Islamic Movement, Sheikh Raed Salah, saying his party was closely linked to the cells. The revelations prompted one normally moderate commentator, Roni Shaked of *Yediot Aharonot*, to observe: "The organising [into cells] of dozens of people planning to harm national security is no longer 'wild weeds' ... It is doubly worrisome because this was not a Hamas or Islamic Jihad initiative, but rather a home-grown initiative from among Israeli Arabs."[53]

In truth, Ron's information was entirely misleading. There were early indications that the terror plot foiled by the police was nothing of the sort. Of the 41 Israeli Arabs and three Palestinians from the West Bank accused by Ron, 18 of them had been released before the press conference was even staged.[54] A few days later the Haifa district attorney, Lili Borishansky, announced that only 12 had been charged, adding: "There was no evidence of nationalist motivation for any of the offences."[55] It soon became apparent that the "terror cells" really comprised a small number of petty criminals, and that the "gun-running" was not part of a conspiracy to overthrow the government but a trade in weapons by criminal gangs and a few local families who liked to celebrate weddings by shooting into the air. (It is worth noting that, paradoxically, Ron's claims of a brewing armed insurrection in Israel were not borne out by the subsequent protests inside Israel a few weeks later, in October 2000. Although no one disputed that some families in the Umm al-Fahm area owned illegal guns, the Or inquiry discovered that none used them during the several days of clashes, even when the police started opening fire at the demonstrators.)

There were two interpretations – neither of them mutually exclusive – of Ron's behaviour towards the Arab leadership and public, both of which suggested the northern police commander was playing a dangerous game of incitement himself. The first was that Ron's instinctive mistrust of the Arab population was feeding his political desire to discomfort Barak, whose government coalition had been put under immense strain through most of the year as the prime minister entered negotiations with Yasser Arafat. In the wake of the failed Camp David negotiations, Barak was desperately clinging on to what was left of his ragged Jewish coalition, and relying on the unofficial support of the ten Arab MKs to struggle through a series of no-confidence motions introduced by the rival Likud party.[56] Ron's repeated attacks on the Arab MKs as "inciters" made Barak's dependence on their parliamentary backing far more problematic. After Ron's press conference, Barak was forced to issue a call to the Arab leaders "to refrain from steps or statements which are liable to place in question the rule of law in the state".[57] Doubtless Ron's interventions endeared him to Likud – and its leader, Sharon – whose blessing he might need to launch a political career.

The other possibility was that Ron was conjuring up a phantom to frighten the Jewish public.[58] By suggesting that the Arab leadership was plotting against Israel, and that there was a network of "terror cells" operating in the north, he was crafting an early version of the "second front" theory that was about to wash over the country. To most Israeli Jews, Ron's allegations would have sounded plausible. As already noted, an assumption had been gaining ground since the late 1990s that the Arab population was really the "enemy within" – a subversive nationalist minority conspiring with the Palestinian leadership in the occupied territories against the Jewish state through a campaign for "a state of all its citizens". Ron was not devising his "second front" theory in a vacuum. It would fit neatly with the explanations of the outbreak of the intifada offered a few weeks later by Sharon and Barak. So neatly in fact that it is more than reasonable to assume both the police and the government were basing their interpretation of events on the same intelligence.

SHIN BET IDENTIFIES THE 'ENEMY WITHIN'

The notorious General Security Service, the domestic secret service better known as the Shin Bet, is Israel's main intelligence-gathering bureau along with Military Intelligence. On matters relating to Israel, rather than the occupied territories, the Shin Bet has almost exclusive jurisdiction. The great bulk of its work is directed at the Arab, rather than Jewish, population: it is responsible for collecting information from suspects, often through the use of torture;[59] recruiting collaborators among local populations; running undercover operations, sometimes using Jews disguised as Arabs; and vetting teachers in Arab education. Its intelligence reports, and its forecasts, are the main source of information available to the government and police on political developments and trends in Arab communities. The secret service's activities, developed over nearly six decades inside Israel and four decades inside the West Bank and Gaza, are extensive and require a huge investment of personnel and resources. A survey by the children's human rights group Defence for Children International, for example, found that in late 2003 there were at least 40 attempts a month by the Shin Bet to recruit children as informants and collaborators in Gaza alone.[60] Sixty per cent of the children interviewed reported being subjected either to torture or coercion, often in the form of threats against other family members.

For their interpretation of political developments inside the Arab minority, therefore, the government and police were entirely reliant on the Shin Bet. Its intelligence, and its analysis of it, created the framework within which the government and police decided to act. Shin Bet officials appeared before the Or Commission in January and February 2002 in sessions from which the public, lawyers and media were excluded to protect "national security". We cannot know, therefore, what approach they recommended to the police concerning the Arab population in the period before the events of October 2000, or what strategies they devised for dealing with the unrest when it erupted. Instead we can only infer from the evidence of how the police and government responded in practice: from the confrontational policies being pursued by Ron in the Galilee earlier in the summer and his all-too-quick accusations of terror plots; from the decision to put the police on their highest level of readiness, "Paam Gimel", following Sharon's visit to Temple Mount; from the decision to invade Arab communities in a "pre-emptive strike" and use live fire as a first line of defence; and from the decision to use for the first time inside Israel an anti-terror unit of snipers.

How the Shin Bet's assessments may have coloured the view of the police and government was suggested in an article in *Ha'aretz* about similar conclusions being reached by the army in the wake of the second intifada. Like the police, the army relies on the Shin Bet for analysis of developments inside Israel. Uzi Benziman, a veteran reporter with exceptional contacts inside the security establishment, revealed that the army and defence establishment were operating according to a new security paradigm in which they were

> convinced that there is no difference between the negation of the existence of Israel as a Jewish state by the Palestinians who live in Nablus [in the West Bank] and the Palestinians who live in Umm al-Fahm [inside Israel]. The segment of the Palestinian population that lives in Israel and is counted among its citizens reluctantly accepts its civil affiliation with the state but opposes the country's definition as a Jewish state.[61]

Benziman was comparing the ambitions of Israel's Arab citizens with those of the Palestinians in Nablus, the most militant city in the West Bank, well known for its armed groups and for dispatching suicide bombers into Israel. In the view of the defence establishment, both Israeli Arabs and the occupied Palestinians wanted the "negation" – destruction – of Israel. The armed factions in Nablus hoped to achieve this through armed struggle against occupation. But what was the struggle of the Israeli Arabs that posed an equal threat to Israel? The answer, said Benziman, was the "yearning" of Israeli Arabs for a state of all its citizens. In the view of the army, and therefore presumably of the Shin Bet, the Arab citizens' discourse about democratisation had become the ideological equivalent of the Palestinian suicide bomb.

This assessment of the Shin Bet's role in shaping the security discourse is supported by Dr Ilan Pappe, of Haifa University, one of a small group of academics known as Israel's "new historians" because of their willingness to break with the traditional founding myths of Israel's creation and examine its history through detailed research of archival material. He argues that the giant apparatus of the Shin

Bet was increasingly threatened by political developments following the signing of the Oslo Accords. As the major towns and cities of the West Bank and Gaza were handed over to the Palestinian Authority, a significant part of the Shin Bet workload was eroded.

> My fear even before the outbreak of the intifada was that the Shin Bet was under-employed in the occupied territories because of the withdrawals agreed under the Oslo Accords. The security apparatus [in Israel] is huge, and a lot of people work for it – 50 per cent of academics, for example, are employed in some capacity as advisers or counsellors – so there's a lot of interest in keeping it going.
>
> Because the service still had the same manpower and the same means at its disposal, it needed to change target – and to justify this change of target it had to come up with a new story: that there had been a fundamental change in the way the Palestinians inside Israel were behaving. The Shin Bet argument was that Israel needed to increase the involvement of the secret services *inside* Israel, that the police could not operate alone ... They had to prove that there was a sinister side to activity by the Palestinian minority that could only be deciphered by the secret service and could only be confronted by the secret service. The first sign of this trend was a few weeks before the outbreak of the intifada when Muhammad Barakeh was summoned by the police over comments he had made at a rally [espousing the right of Arab citizens to defend themselves against the demolition of their homes]. How did the police know what he said at the rally? They admitted they used *mistarvim*, special agents dressed like Arabs, a technique they often use in the occupied territories but never inside Israel itself. This was a really dangerous precedent. They were sending elite secret agents to the political rallies of democratically elected leaders of the Arab population of Israel.

Pappe believes that the Shin Bet's redefinition of its security role neatly fitted the new outlook of politicians of the right and left. At Camp David, Barak wanted to reach a final-status settlement by solving all the outstanding issues separating the two peoples. The price of an Israeli concession on limited statehood for the Palestinians in the West Bank and Gaza was a new mood of intolerance towards the political ambitions of the Arab minority inside Israel.

> Camp David meant: This is it, the Palestinians will have a state. If Palestinian citizens don't like things inside Israel, then they can move to Palestine. Barak was saying, "Inside Israel we won't tolerate any signs of Palestinian nationalism, ambitions of autonomy, talk of Israel as a state of all its citizens."

> At the pragmatic, ideological, rhetorical levels there emerged a very clear position not from the right but from the heart of the Israeli establishment: we will not tolerate "Palestinianism" among Arabs inside Israel if we're going to continue with the peace process ... From now on there would be no questioning of the legitimacy of the Jewish state by anyone within the state and especially not the Palestinians. Any signs of civil disobedience would be met with all force, and it was up to the police and the Shin Bet to decide what means they wanted to use to secure Israel's strategic superiority.[62]

According to Pappe, the Shin Bet painted the picture of the Arab minority that determined the police responses in October 2000 and before.

> Alik Ron was like a robot that had to be fed. It was not his interpretation of the situation, it was how the research and analysis section of the Shin Bet depicted the situation. They have a legal department which is involved in explaining how dangerous illegal building in the Arab sector is and how it is connected to the minority's irredentist, secessionist tendencies. The clash in October 2000 was prepared by the secret services.

So how did Ron justify his lethal show of force against demonstrators in October 2000 to the Or Commission, what intelligence did he say he had at the time? Given his high-profile confrontations with the Arab minority a few weeks before the outbreak of the intifada, in which he warned of incitement and terror cells, he might have been expected to claim that the October events had proved his warnings prescient. But he did not. Instead he argued to the Commission that the protests had hit him and the northern police force under his command "like thunder in a blue sky".[63] "I am not sure anybody knew what was to come – not even those who incited the violence. We never expected such rioting. It was like an apocalyptic dream," he said.[64] Neither the police nor the Shin Bet security services, he told Justice Or, had received any intelligence warning of an outburst of Arab protest on this scale.

Ron's new position of feigned surprise was driven by the new realities. Facing the Or Commission, he had every reason to fear that a full investigation of his earlier confrontations with the Arab population and its leaders might suggest to Justice Or that, far from predicting the clashes of October 2000, Ron had directly encouraged them. Ron's warnings, the inquiry might conclude, were less prophetic than self-fulfilling. But there was another, more important reason why Ron dramatically changed tack before the inquiry: he needed to maintain the police's by now well-developed "unified response". Everyone from the chief of police, Yehuda Wilk, to the lowest ranks were making the same argument to the panel: the police had been forced into their harsh responses to the October events because they had been deprived of resources and training. Ron toed the line: he called his budget "pitiful" and observed that his officers were still wearing flakjackets from the 1960s. "If we knew what was ahead of us, we would have needed 7,000 police reinforcements," he declared.[65] In Ron's version, the police were the real victims, victims of political misjudgments.

When Ron testified before the Commission in September 2001, Justice Or challenged the northern commander's claims of ignorance. He alluded to a classified intelligence document, presumably from the Shin Bet, that warned of the possibility of widespread disturbances among the Arab minority. Prime Minister Ehud Barak's military secretary, Gadi Eizenkot, also told the inquiry that Wilk and Ron had been warned to ready themselves for large-scale demonstrations inside Israel immediately after the violence on the Temple Mount on 29 September.[66] But in truth, the police had been making preparations long before that for just such an eventuality. Since 1998, the Commission learnt, the police had been refining a plan codenamed "Kessem Ha-Mangina" or "Magic Tune".[67]

OPERATION MAGIC TUNE SETS THE STAGE

"Magic Tune" was one thread in a much bigger strategy known as "Field of Thorns". The Israeli security services began developing "Field of Thorns" following a bloody confrontation between Palestinians and the Israeli security forces in the Old City of Jerusalem in September 1996, after the prime minister of the day, Binyamin Netanyahu, decided to open a 400 ft tunnel to the Western Wall close by the complex of mosques of the Noble Sanctuary. This and subsequent clashes led to 15 Israeli soldiers and at least 75 Palestinians being killed.[68] "Field of Thorns" was supposed to be put into effect should Arafat declare statehood and the army need to reoccupy areas of the West Bank and Gaza already in the hands of the Palestinian Authority. The operation's guiding principle, simply stated, was that the more force the army used against Palestinians the fewer casualties it would suffer in return.[69]

It was assumed that should "Field of Thorns" be implemented, there would be mass violent demonstrations by Israeli Arabs in support of the Palestinians. "Magic Tune" established protocols for the police, permitting the use of snipers and high levels of force to disperse protesters.[70] There were several reasons for believing that the plan was implemented by Alik Ron in October 2000. As much was admitted by a senior northern police officer, Yaron Meir, during his testimony to the Or Commission in June 2001.[71] And a report in the *Ma'ariv* newspaper on 2 October 2000, when the police markedly stepped up the use of force against the demonstrators, stated:

> The Israeli police are now working according to procedures that had been intended for a situation in which a Palestinian state was unilaterally declared. The police claim that the most radical scenarios predicted by these plans have come to pass, namely demonstrations by Israeli Arabs, almost at the heart of the state.[72]

During 1999 and 2000, according to documents unearthed by Adalah, the police had conducted training exercises as part of "Magic Tune", culminating in a war game called "Storm Wind", at the police headquarters in Shafa'amr – close by Adalah's offices – on 6 September 2000. Police commanders, the Israeli army and senior members of the Shin Bet took part.[73] During the training operation, it was agreed that the police should use extreme force to prevent demonstrators blocking key highways, specifically the Wadi Ara road that runs past Umm al-Fahm, where less than a month later the worst clashes would develop and three demonstrators would be killed. According to documents obtained by the Adalah team, the police concluded that roads had to be kept open "because the Jewish people must travel there" and to "prevent territorial contiguity between Nablus and Lebanon". Ron's deputy, Avi Tiller, was recorded as stating that the police response to Israeli Arab protests must be quick and harsh to stop demonstrators gaining confidence. Another document stated that completely different procedures should be used in the event of violent demonstrations by Jews, including the instruction: "The Jewish sector will be dealt with using extreme flexibility."[74]

Use of excessive lethal force against the Arab population was strictly in accordance with the pre-planned guidelines established by "Magic Tune". Within weeks of the "Storm Wind" war game, officers under Ron's command would be using just such tactics across the Galilee. This was confirmed by an independent expert on riot control practices, Dr Stephen Males, a former senior British policeman, who was sent to Israel in early October 2000 by Amnesty International. After studying the methods used by the police, he told me:

> My view was that the police failed in their policing role – they used weaponry and tactics more suitable for an armed conflict than for crowd control. Whereas the military try to identify the enemy and kill it, the police should be concerned with restraining disruptive elements in society within the rules of justice. In Israel, the distinction between military and police strategies appears to have been ignored.[75]

In the immediate aftermath of October 2000 – before the conduct of the police was subjected to critical scrutiny by the Or Commission – commanders not only appeared to be untroubled by their handling of the events in the Galilee but actually celebrated their record. Justice Or expressed astonishment that at a briefing at the national headquarters in November 2000, a few weeks after the 13 killings, the police congratulated themselves on the implementation of their harsh policy against Arab demonstrators. The national operations chief, Ezra Aharon, presented a report in which he praised the use of snipers in the Galilee as "helpful at deterring the demonstrators", even though the inquiry had heard endless accounts of how the presence of snipers had only served to inflame the situation.[76]

The self-congratulatory briefing at national headquarters suggests that the police commanders' later assessments to the Or Commission about the 13 deaths – essentially that they were the result of a lack of resources – were dishonest. But the briefing also began unravelling the story maintained by the two most senior political figures at the heart of the inquiry: the public security minister, Shlomo Ben Ami, and the prime minister, Ehud Barak. Both told the Or Commission that the Arab demonstrations were "an earthquake" for which they and the police were unprepared. But "Magic Tune" proved that the northern police force and the government had been expecting just such a confrontation. It suggested that the police had responded to the protests not according to the levels of violence they faced but according to a strategy that had been worked out well in advance. In parallel, the "Field of Thorns" plan indicated that the army's response in the occupied territories had been equally pre-planned.

Ben Ami was as deeply involved as Barak in the breakdown of peace talks with the Palestinians in the summer of 2000 and the subsequent lethal suppression of the intifada in the occupied territories and the demonstrations inside Israel. Under Barak, Ben Ami held two cabinet posts. His less prestigious title was public security minister, responsible for the police. But he was also foreign minister, and therefore one of the key players in the negotiations with the Palestinians at Camp David and later at Taba. A man with a distinguished record as a history professor, Ben Ami was known to enjoy striding the international stage and was reported to harbour ambitions to be prime minister. Ben Ami may well have seen the public security portfolio, by comparison, as beneath his standing and as a distraction from his real job as foreign minister. That certainly was the view taken by many Israeli observers, including the chief of police, Yehuda Wilk.[77]

Ben Ami's testimony suggested that he had many more pressing demands on his time than overseeing the national police force. The Commission heard that he issued a series of orders to Wilk during the October events, including that officers confronting Arab protesters be disarmed and that Alik Ron be removed from his post. Wilk, Ben Ami said, simply ignored him.[78] Despite his self-confessed inability to control the police force he was responsible for, Ben Ami's officials in the ministry painted a picture of their boss as a beacon of enlightenment. In the words of David Tzur, a police liaison officer in the ministry, the approach of Ben Ami and Barak had been "much more humanist and much less militant than the police command's".[79]

BARAK AND BEN AMI'S ROLES CLARIFIED

This characterisation of Ben Ami – and Barak for that matter – appears less than plausible given the evidence presented to the Or Commission. It was hard to believe that Ben Ami knew as little as he claimed. As one Israeli commentator observed, the Hebrew media had reported on the use of live ammunition and snipers at the time of the October events. Not only did Ben Ami appear to have no control over his police commanders, wrote Nehemia Strasler of *Ha'aretz*, but "he doesn't even read the papers".[80] As noted before, Ben Ami had approved bringing a unit of anti-terror snipers to Temple Mount on 29 September 2000, a decision that contributed to the violent atmosphere there and led to the killing of several Palestinian demonstrators. Even if Ben Ami had not been consulted by Ron and Wilk about using snipers in Umm al-Fahm and Nazareth, the minister had effectively sanctioned their use by deploying them himself a few days earlier in Jerusalem. But as the inquiry discovered, there were at least three separate written directives permitting the use of snipers against demonstrators inside Israel;[81] Ben Ami's enduring ignorance of these orders verged on the miraculous.

Ben Ami's proclaimed ignorance about the use of live fire and snipers failed to fit the evidence unearthed by Adalah and the commission of inquiry. It was Ben Ami after all who approved the staging of the war game "Storm Wind", where these scenarios were worked out. And he had been invited to the national police briefing in November 2000, where the use of snipers was praised.[82] Muhammad Zeidan, the head of the Arab Higher Follow-Up Committee, who was on the Nazareth hillside on the night of 8 October when Wissam Yazbak and Omar Akawi were shot dead, told the inquiry that he had been speaking to Ben Ami by mobile phone at the precise moment the police opened fire. As the sound of machine gun spray could be heard, Ben Ami cursed the police, according to Zeidan, saying: "I told those sons of bitches not to use live ammunition."[83]

Equally problematic was evidence – again unearthed by Adalah – that legal officials in the Public Security Ministry had drafted a report, known as the "Kistoho Document", shortly after the 13 deaths setting out the arguments Ben Ami could use to "cover up", as his officials put it, any suggestion that he was culpable over the use of lethal violence during the October 2000 events. When the Kistoho document was written, Ben Ami's officials believed he would be facing not a commission of inquiry but a low-level committee of examination that would lack the power to challenge his or the police evidence. In the document Ben Ami was therefore advised to divert criticism from himself by arguing that the police faced live fire from protesters and had no choice but to use lethal force in return. The document stated, entirely falsely, that those who had been killed by the police "shot, burned, injured and incited to murder and kill, all intentionally and in an organised manner, and actually acted as soldiers fighting an enemy".[84] In other words, Ben Ami too had been encouraged to present the second front theory: that the Israeli Arab demonstrators were pawns of a much bigger plan, presumably hatched by Arafat.

The most damning evidence refuting Ben Ami's claims of ignorance was an event that also deeply implicated the prime minister, Ehud Barak. On the evening of 1 October 2000, Barak invited Ben Ami and the national police commanders to a meeting at his home to discuss the day's dire developments inside Israel, including the vicious clashes at Umm al-Fahm where the police had tried to keep the Wadi Ara road open, leaving one protester dead, two more fatally wounded and dozens seriously injured.

The significance of the Wadi Ara road, a busy highway that passes by Umm al-Fahm and connects the Jewish city of Hadera in the centre of the country to the Jewish city of Afula in the Lower Galilee, cannot be overstated in the police and government's thinking. In the territory and security-obsessed frameworks within which the Israeli defence and security establishments operate, the Wadi Ara is seen as a vital strategic road linking the Jewish-dominated centre of the country to the Galilee region in the north, an Arab heartland lying next to Lebanon. The fear of the police and government was that, if the Wadi Ara road was blocked, Israeli forces defending the northern front might be cut off and vulnerable to a cross-border attack from the Lebanese militia Hizbullah. As Dov Lutzky, Alik Ron's number three, observed: "The decision-makers considered the highway a central and strategic artery which was supposed to serve anyone on his way to the battlefront."[85]

Barak, the police command and the Israeli public instinctively shared the logic of the "second front" theory being proposed publicly by people like Sharon: that Arab protests were being organised by Arafat, who was plotting to overthrow the Jewish state through two intifadas, one inside the occupied territories and another inside Israel. Barak and the police were frightened that if they allowed what they saw as a second front to build in Umm al-Fahm, they might expose themselves to an assault from a third front in Lebanon.

The security establishment's overarching obsession with the Wadi Ara road derived from the abject failure of Israeli governments over many decades to "Judaise" the Triangle area in which it is located: that is, to persuade Jews to settle there and bring it decisively under Jewish dominion. In Israel's two other Arab heartlands, the Galilee and the Negev, Jewish settlement drives had been far more successful: the famous rural Jewish collective communities of the kibbutzim and moshavim, and luxury hilltop settlements known as mitzpim, all heavily subsidised by the government, have attracted large Jewish populations. The purpose of Judaisation, as one Haifa University academic, Avraham Dor, enthusiastically put it, is to make possible "a maximum distribution of [Jewish] settlement sites and the 'conquest' of the territory by means of access roads to them and by means of the permanent Jewish presence in the area".[86] But this strategic goal had not been achieved in Wadi Ara, a valley lying close to the West Bank, where few Jews were prepared to move.

In hindsight the "second front" theory may have looked as indefensible to some of the decision-makers as it undoubtedly was at the time. Ben Ami, for example, admitted to the Or Commission that the information he had received from the police about a "rebellion" and "a war situation" was "exaggerated".[87] Rather than defending the decision to use lethal fire against protesters in Umm al-Fahm on 1 and 2 October to keep the road open – effectively triggering the violence that erupted across the Galilee and the increased death toll – Barak, Ben Ami and Yehuda Wilk all insisted to the Or Commission that at the time they had called for restraint. Ben Ami said he had ordered the police to close the Wadi Ara and that he had not been updated about the later police actions.[88] Barak claimed, despite ample police testimony that the road had been treated as a "red line" that must be defended at all costs, that he had issued no orders to keep the Wadi Ara open. Wilk backed that view, claiming that he had set down no red lines precisely to prevent his officers from using "extreme measures".[89] Ron had disobeyed him, he said, in deciding to keep the Wadi Ara road open when it was clear a violent confrontation would ensue.

But the testimonies of all three flew in the face of the only evidence that remains of the meeting that took place in Barak's home on the night of 1 October. Not much is known about what was discussed that evening because no meaningful record of it has survived. Barak's military secretary, Gadi Eizenkot, who was responsible for documenting the meeting, had some incomplete handwritten notes that were almost indecipherable. A tape that was also made of the meeting, Eizenkot told the inquiry, was discovered to be blank when it was taken for transcription.[90]

What can be deduced from the meeting is a verbal account provided by Barak himself the next morning when he was interviewed on Reshet Beit radio. This vital piece of evidence was only examined by the inquiry because of the work of Adalah in locating the transcript. Far from suggesting that he wanted to calm the situation and stop the deaths among Arab citizens, Barak told the radio interviewer:

> We cannot accept and will not accept either the blocking of roads or disruption of the ordinary lives by citizens inside the state. In a discussion which went into the night yesterday at my home, I instructed the minister of public security [Shlomo Ben Ami] and the police commanders, who by the

> way deserve great compliments for their self-restraint yesterday during the demonstrations, ... that you have a green light for any action necessary to bring about the rule of law, to preserve public order and to secure freedom of movement for the citizens of the state, anywhere in the state.[91]

Questioned about the interview by Justice Or, Barak said his statements were meant only to reassure the Jewish public and that in private he had adopted a different position. "The serious events of those days warranted a strong feeling for the need to back the police," Barak added.[92]

The implied "mood" of the meeting provided by Barak's radio interview neatly fitted Ron's account of events, in which he said he was ordered by Wilk to use force to clear the demonstrators away from the Wadi Ara after the chief of police's meeting with Barak the night before. Taking his cue from Barak and Ben Ami's decision to use snipers on the Temple Mount a few days earlier, and presumably after approval by the Shin Bet, Ron brought the same anti-terror unit to Umm al-Fahm and Nazareth. Although we can only surmise about his precise actions, it seems likely that Ron also conveyed Barak's "green light" to his senior officers, permitting them to take "any action necessary", including the use of live ammunition, against demonstrators, whether armed or not. Implementation of "Magic Tune", at least as far as Ron was concerned, had been approved by the prime minister himself at that meeting. The high casualty toll of eight dead and hundreds injured on 2 and 3 October was the outcome.

INQUIRY FAILS TO FIND THE CULPRITS

From the evidence heard by the inquiry, it might have been expected that Justice Or would draw similar conclusions. Much of the damning evidence presented to the panel – from the Barak radio interview to amateur videos and spent shell cases – had been unearthed through the labours not of the Commission's investigators but of Adalah's dedicated legal team and the bereaved families.[93] They hoped that with the evidence they had accumulated Ben Ami and Barak would receive the same treatment meted out two decades earlier to the then defence minister, Ariel Sharon, by the Kahan Commission of Inquiry. Justice Yitzhak Kahan had investigated the massacre of Palestinian civilians, including hundreds of women and children, in the refugee camps of Sabra and Shatilla in Lebanon in 1982. Sharon had engineered the invasion of Lebanon, pushing his forces into

Beirut and then sealing off the camps. Under the watch of Sharon's soldiers, Christian militias opposed to the Palestinian presence in Lebanon were allowed to inflict their own savage form of retribution on the refugees. The Kahan Commission found Sharon "indirectly responsible" for the massacres and recommended that he be barred from serving as defence minister again.

In comparison, the publication of Justice Or's 800-page report in September 2003 was a sore disappointment to the families and to Adalah. The Commission had called before it 350 witnesses and sat in session for two and a half years, but the report's conclusions were "tepid and lacking teeth" in the words of an editorial in the *Ha'aretz* newspaper.[94]

Having noted that relations between Jews and Arabs inside Israel were "the most important and sensitive domestic matter on the state's agenda",[95] Justice Or slipped the government off the hook. He observed that Barak had given the police a "green light" to keep the Wadi Ara road open but could not determine whether he had done so "at any cost", including the use of live fire. Although Barak's failings as prime minister were noted by the Commission, no recommendations were made against him. Barak was reported to have breathed a sigh of relief as he heard that the Commission had not raised any obstacles to his running for prime minister again.[96] Shlomo Ben Ami received a harsher rebuke, accused of being "insufficiently conscious" of the risks posed by the use of rubber bullets in crowd dispersal and failing to deploy police officers in sufficient numbers. Ben Ami was banned from being public security minister again – a punishment, as one analyst wryly commented, "that is good news for someone who never wanted to be anything but prime or foreign minister".[97] Meanwhile, Sharon's visit to the Temple Mount, which had ignited the intifada and the violent clashes between the police and Arab citizens, merited a passing mention in the report of five words.[98]

Marwan Dalal, who had represented the families on behalf of Adalah at the hearings, commented to me:

> Barak was really given an easy ride by the Commission. They appeared to take the view that he had far too many other things on his mind to be held accountable. They were only too willing to accept that the political echelon had no idea about the use of snipers, however improbable that seemed to those of us who heard the evidence. Israeli journalists were reporting on the use of live fire by the police at the time. So how did the media know and not the government? If you look back at the coverage, it reads like a form of

reassurance to the Jewish public: "Don't worry we are using snipers to keep the Arabs under control." But the real failure was the Commission's refusal to untangle the meeting held by Barak on the evening of 1 October to see what really happened there. That meeting held the key to explaining the 13 deaths. The Commission decided to leave the box unopened.

The police force's behaviour attracted the bulk of Justice Or's censure, though individual officers received minor punishments. Justice Or recommended banning the use of rubber-coated bullets against demonstrators inside Israel and concluded that the police "must instill in its people that the Arab public is not an enemy and should not be treated as an enemy". The two most senior officers, Yehuda Wilk and Alik Ron, were both severely criticised over their "substantial professional failures", with Ron's decision to deploy snipers singled out for particularly harsh admonishment. Justice Or recommended that neither fill a senior domestic security position again. Both had already retired from service. Another six senior officers were reprimanded, with the panel recommending that Moshe Waldman, the commander in Nazareth, be dismissed from service and that Benzy Sau not be promoted for a period of four years. The recommendations in both cases were ignored. Waldman and Sau had already been promoted during the Commission hearings. Police commanders continued to back Waldman, who was now a brigadier-general, saying he should be allowed to finish his term until his retirement in 2005.[99] And Sau, who had risen to become the Border Police's chief in Jerusalem in April 2001, was promoted again in 2004, this time to commander of the Border Police.[100]

The biggest blow to the Arab minority, and in particular the bereaved families, was Justice Or's failure to identify any of the policemen responsible for shooting dead the 13 protesters in October 2000 and so open the way to their prosecution. The report's conclusions suggested that there was only evidence to link two policemen to specific deaths: Murshad Rashad was believed to have shot 21-year-old Rami Jarra in the eye with a rubber bullet from close range in Jatt on 1 October; and Guy Reif was assumed to have been responsible for the deaths of two young men from Sakhnin on 2 October. But the inquiry could take no credit for the findings. In these cases, there was no dispute about who had pulled the trigger: Rashad alone had admitted firing into the crowd of demonstrators in Jatt, and Reif had confessed to confronting the stone-throwers in Sakhnin single-handedly with live ammunition. The other deaths, including those of Wissam Yazbak and Aseel Asleh, were no nearer to being solved. As Asleh's sister, Nardine, observed as the report was published: "The truth was there, they didn't reach for it. This commission gives a green light for someone to do this in the future."[101]

Equally baffling, according to Marwan Dalal of Adalah, was the fact that the Or report had not a word to say about the failure of the Justice Ministry to investigate the deaths in the days and weeks following the October events or about its conspiracy of silence regarding evidence that live ammunition had been used by the northern force. The report's indulgence was entirely consistent with Justice Or's treatment of the Justice Ministry and its investigations unit, Mahash, throughout the hearings. The unit had made tentative inquiries into two shooting incidents in October 2000 – those involving Guy Reif and two snipers who shot Marlene Ramadan while in her car – but froze them as soon as Barak announced the appointment of the Commission of Inquiry a month later.[102] The Justice Ministry justified the decision on the spurious grounds that Mahash's work might prejudice, rather than assist, the hearings. The Commission then recruited two of the Mahash investigators to its own team sifting the evidence.[103] Justice Or neither encouraged his own team to begin the forensic work of a proper investigation nor ordered Mahash to reopen its files. For nearly three years no one apart from the bereaved families and the Adalah legal centre made any effort to acquire new evidence. Aseel Asleh's father, Hassan, observed that they had submitted "bulging files", including photos of the dead, evidence found at the scene of the shootings and information on the type of weapons used. "The commission completely ignored these files," he said. "Had they wanted to, they could have used them. It was a complete disappointment."[104]

JUSTICE MINISTRY STALLS NEW INVESTIGATION

In his report Justice Or requested that Mahash restart the investigations it failed to carry out three years earlier and open new investigations into the other deaths. In a sign that government officials wanted to prepare the public for a low probability of success, the justice minister, Yosef Lapid, told reporters the next day: "It is extremely complicated to begin three years later to investigate events in which hundreds of people were involved. The bodies have long since been buried. There are no bullets, no scraps of evidence, and no witnesses."[105] This was a convenient excuse but hardly true: there were hundreds of witnesses yet to give evidence, particularly injured Arab demonstrators who had never been called by Justice Or to testify; there was evidence, much of it hidden away in forensic laboratories, including the round that killed Wissam Yazbak; and there were the bodies of those still alive but severely wounded, such as Marlene Ramadan and Ibrahim Suleiman. It was also known from the evidence provided to the Or Commission that senior commanders, including Alik Ron, had approved sniper fire at stone-throwers, almost certainly in violation of the law.

Lapid's comments seemed ample justification for the cynicism of one family at the Or Commission hearings who had daily held aloft a sign reading: "13 dead, 0 responsible".[106]

Finally, on 18 September 2005, less than a fortnight before the fifth anniversary of the 13 deaths, Mahash issued the conclusions of its belated investigation of the killings. Its director, Herzl Shviro, said the unit would not be bringing charges against any police officers for the deaths. Even in the two cases where the Or Commission had suggested criminal responsibility – in the killings of three Arab citizens by policemen Guy Reif and Murshad Rashad – Mahash rejected the inquiry's findings, claiming that the officers' actions were "justifiable" because their lives had been in danger.[107] Mahash also concluded that, though it had identified the two snipers who shot Marlene Ramadan, the officers would not be indicted. Again contrary to the evidence unearthed by the Or Commission, Mahash believed the officers had grounds for being suspicious of the behaviour of the car in which the Ramadans were travelling.

Professor Shimon Shamir, one of the Or Commission's three panel members, called the decision disgraceful. "If two important and respected judges [on the Or Commission] are of this opinion, is there not a way to bring at least these two cases [Reif's and Rashad's] to trial?" he asked. Shamir also criticised Mahash's handling of the investigations:

> I believe that [Mahash's] conclusions regarding some of the incidents stretched our patience to the very limits, and sometimes beyond those limits, regarding the claim that the police faced an immediate and substantial threat to their lives as justification for firing live bullets and using snipers ... A situation in which 13 people were killed and no one is accused is a situation that is hard to accept.

Shamir pointed out that since the October 2000 events another 18 Israeli Arabs had been killed by the police in unexplained circumstances. In almost all of these incidents, Mahash had not submitted an indictment. "There are too many fatalities and not enough [Mahash]," said Shamir. The attorney-general, Menachem Mazuz, was scornful of Shamir's criticisms. "None of us wants to live in a country in which indictments are filed just to mollify one sector of the public or another," he said. "There shall be none of this in the state of Israel."[108]

Mahash's main justification for closing all the investigations was the refusal by four of the bereaved families to have their son's bodies disinterred for an autopsy five years after their deaths. Against its own regulations, Mahash had agreed to the burial of the bodies back in October 2000 without first carrying out post-mortem examinations. Shviro claimed that the families were now obstructing Mahash's investigations. But as Adalah observed, there could be no justification for putting the families through the distress of exhuming the bodies when Mahash had not yet shown any serious intention of pursuing the investigations. "After all this time, the exhumation of the bodies must be the last stage in the inquiry, not the first," said Marwan Dalal. Adalah noted pointedly that, while Mahash was demanding autopsies on the four bodies, it had not begun investigating the other nine deaths where it did not need to exhume the bodies, including the four bodies that already had autopsy reports. Also, Mahash had access to the bullet that killed Wissam Yazbak, which was removed from his body by a surgeon in Haifa. Why had it not begun a proper investigation into his death? Mahash needed to "indicate that the exhumation of the body is the only remaining means of uncovering the truth", wrote Adalah.[109] There was no evidence that Mahash had even begun a serious investigation.

THE 'FIFTH COLUMN' LIBEL STANDS

There was a final reason for the Arab minority's profound disenchantment with the Commission's report. Describing the October protests as "unprecedented riots", Justice Or accused three leading Arab public figures of incitement – thereby echoing his mandate from Barak. He recommended no punishments against the secular nationalist Azmi Bishara, and two Islamic Movement leaders, Abdul Malik Dehamshe and Sheikh Raed Salah, but all three were accused of extremism. These admonishments effectively "balanced" the criticisms of the police.

As has already been noted, there was a legal problem with Justice Or's condemnation of the Arab leadership: a commission of inquiry is supposed to investigate only public officials, those representing the executive branch of the state. The Arab leaders, as the Adalah lawyers had pointed out, should have been outside the inquiry's frame of reference. But there was another problem with Justice Or's approach. Sensing precisely the line the Commission was about to adopt, Aseel Asleh's father Hassan observed a few days before the report was published. "I found that the commission's only aim was to achieve a 'balance'. [Panel member] Shimon Shamir said at one point, 'There was an illegal protest and an illegal response by the police'. I reject that equation."[110]

The equation, however, was deeply satisfying to the "second front" theorists, including Sharon and Barak. On several occasions during his testimony to the inquiry, Barak had described the Arab protests as "echoing" the events in the occupied territories. He blamed what he called "a small extremist group that does not accept the vision of Israel as a Zionist Jewish democratic state", pointing the finger in particular at Azmi Bishara's National Democratic Assembly party.[111] In Barak's thinking, the Israeli Arab leadership had conspired with Arafat and incited its public by denying Israel's legitimacy as a Jewish and democratic state. Barak singled out Bishara – more so even than Islamic fundamentalists like Sheikh Raed Salah – because he was vociferously demanding that Israel be transformed from a Jewish state into a state of all its citizens.

If Sharon and Barak saw the state of all its citizens ideology as sedition, and Bishara's espousal of it as incitement, then Justice Or appeared to be giving them succour. The evidence that had been presented to the Commission during the hearings suggested that the police had hugely overreacted to angry demonstrations by the Arab community, wrongly treating the protests as an organised insurrection and responding with a pre-arranged plan, "Magic Tune", to crush the protests quickly and ruthlessly. The Shin Bet, police and government's mistaken assessments had been possible because of a deeply rooted culture of anti-Arab racism at all levels of the security and political establishments. Justice Or should have challenged the legitimacy of this approach; instead he accepted that the Arab leadership had incited the demonstrators. This left open the question of what form the incitement took and to what purpose the Arab leadership thought the angry protests could be put. It left a disturbing cloud of suspicion hanging over not only the Israeli Arab leadership but also the whole Arab population. Justice Or, whether intentionally or not, had allowed the fifth column libel to stand – and by extension the unsupported claims of Military Intelligence that Arafat had been plotting the intifada with the Arab leaders in an attempt to overthrow the Jewish state.

As a result, much of the debate in the Israeli media that followed the Or Commission report was framed in terms that compared it to another Commission report published 30 years before.[112] The Agranat Commission had investigated the failures of the army to deal effectively with a sudden military strike launched against Israel by its Arab neighbours during the Yom Kippur holy day in 1973. The defence establishment's failure to foresee the carefully planned military aggression of Egypt and Syria was equated with the security establishment's failure in 2000 to foresee the "civil rebellion" by Arab citizens. Both were viewed as intelligence failures. The Israeli media seemed to be agreed that the police command, like the army command before it, had not been alert to the imminent threat it faced. The media's reading of both the 1973 and 2000 commissions of inquiry was the same: the Israeli security forces had failed when faced with a hostile and organised enemy.

Nonetheless, Justice Or's report did pose problems for the government of Ariel Sharon. The judge identified wide-ranging and systematic discrimination against the Arab minority and recommended comprehensive government measures to reverse it. He found that "poverty, unemployment, a shortage of land, serious problems in the education system and a substantially defective infrastructure" blighted Arab communities. The state, said Or, must "speedily and vigorously and clearly [set in motion] a program to narrow the gaps".

Sharon's response was subdued. A fortnight after the report's publication, on 14 September 2003, the prime minister established a cabinet committee under the justice minister, Yosef Lapid, to investigate ways of implementing the Commission's recommendations. Not a single Arab was included on the committee; instead it was stuffed with extreme rightwingers, including ministers such as Effi Eitam and Gideon Ezra, both of whom opposed the establishment of the Or Commission. In a move designed to outrage the Arab population, Sharon also included on the committee Benny Elon, leader of the Moledet party, which advocates the emigration, forced or otherwise, of Arab citizens from the country. Many observers assumed the creation of the committee was a delaying tactic, with Sharon hoping that pressure to implement Justice Or's recommendations would dissipate over time. Sharon responded by promising that the committee would report back within two months; nothing was heard for the next nine.

By the time the Lapid committee published its report in June 2004, it had severely watered down Justice Or's proposals. The committee recommended a governmental authority for promoting the Arab sector, and the creation of a compulsory non-military national service programme for Arab youths.[113] The measures, both of which were later forgotten, were greeted with howls of scepticism even from the Hebrew media. Uzi Benziman of *Ha'aretz* observed: "There is a strong stink of lack of seriousness from the recommendations of the Lapid Committee."[114] The Or inquiry had recommended that two other key reforms be instituted. First, the judge suggested that Arab symbols be added to the state's national symbols, such as the flag and anthem, to encourage Arab citizens to identify with the state. The Lapid committee translated this into a recommendation that there be a new "Solidarity Day" shared by Jews and Arabs – another proposal that quietly vanished. Second, Justice Or urged that the state provide Arab communities with desperately needed land on which to build homes legally. He recommended that the Israel Lands Authority, a state body that manages 93 per cent of land in Israel, be required to allocate additional lands to the Arab minority. That recommendation, designed to repair some of the damage done by more than 50 years of state-organised land theft from the Palestinian minority, was simply ignored.

On the anniversary of his report's publication, in September 2004, Justice Or took the highly unusual step of castigating the public bodies responsible for implementing his recommendations. He said virtually nothing had been done by the government to carry out his proposed reforms, with discrimination still rife in budgets, land, housing and employment, including in the civil service. He reiterated his criticisms in June 2005.[115] His public rebukes changed nothing. It appeared that the government of Ariel Sharon was happy to wait out its critics, hoping that eventually the events of October 2000 and what they revealed about the democratic pretensions of a Jewish state would be forgotten.

3
The Battle of Numbers

We shall try to spirit the penniless [Palestinian] population across the border by procuring employment for it in the transit countries whilst denying it any employment in our own country ... Both the process of expropriation and the removal of the poor must be carried out discreetly and circumspectly.

Theodor Herzl (1895)[1]

It must be clear that there is no room in the country for both peoples ... There is no way but to transfer the Arabs from here to the neighboring countries, to transfer all of them, save perhaps for Bethlehem, Nazareth, and the old Jerusalem. Not one village must be left, not one tribe. The transfer must be directed at Iraq, Syria, and even Transjordan. For this goal funds will be found.

Joseph Weitz, director of the Jewish National Fund's Land Department (1940)[2]

[Israel must] implement a stringent policy of family planning in relation to its Muslim population. The delivery rooms in Soroka Hospital in Be'er Sheva [serving the Negev's Bedouin population] have turned into a factory for the production of a backward population.

Yitzhak Ravid, head of the Rafael Arms Development Authority (2003)[3]

The vast empty spaces of the Negev, Israel's southern desert, are a playground for the Israeli army and the smugglers who cross its long open border with Egypt to trade in anything for which there is a demand: from cars and cigarettes to guns and women. The desert forms 60 per cent of Israel's land mass but is home to fewer than 7 per cent of its citizens. Many are to be found in Be'ersheva, a grim oasis of concrete that is the capital of the Negev and Israel's fourth largest city. In early August 2003 I travelled there to meet Morad as-Sana, a Bedouin lawyer who had just returned from a honeymoon in Istanbul. He and his wife Abir, a lecturer in social work, had come back to a new law that made it illegal for them to live together. As they crossed over the border from Jordan, they were forced to part: Morad to his apartment in Be'ersheva, and Abir to her parents' home in the West Bank city of Bethlehem.

While they were away, the Knesset had passed a temporary amendment to one of Israel's founding pieces of legislation, the Nationality Law of 1952, making it impossible for an Israeli citizen to obtain a residency permit for a Palestinian spouse from the occupied territories.[4] In effect, Israel had banned marriages between Israelis and Palestinians. Under the new law, 27-year-old Abir was barred from joining her husband in Be'ersheva, and Morad, aged 30, was banned by military regulations from entering a Palestinian-controlled area like Bethlehem.[5] Israel had revoked a fundamental human right of its Arab citizens: the right to love and to raise a family.

The pair were far from alone in their enforced separation. The amendment, known as the Nationality and Entry into Israel Law, discriminated against hundreds of Arab citizens recently married or preparing to marry a Palestinian from the occupied territories. It also promised an uncertain future for thousands more long-established couples: Palestinian spouses who had been stuck for years in Israel's interminable naturalisation process would now find their applications for a residency permit or citizenship frozen or refused. Without a permit, the families would either be forced into hiding or torn apart.

Morad and Abir were determined to live together. "We will live like fugitives," said Morad, who had few illusions about what that would entail. "We won't be able to give out our address, Abir will not be able to leave the house or work in Israel, or go to the doctor if she gets sick. We will learn to fear every knock at the door."

The terrible plight of couples like Morad and Abir briefly caught the world's attention. The amendment to the Nationality Law provoked outrage from international and Israeli human rights groups, which had no hesitation in calling the measure racist.[6] Technically the law also applied to Israeli Jews who married Palestinians, but in practice only the rights of Arab citizens were being harmed. (The law, of course, did not apply to the other inhabitants of the occupied territories – the Jewish settlers.) B'Tselem pointed out that the legislation violated Israel's Basic Law on Human Dignity and Liberty as well as a pledge in the Declaration of Independence that the state would "ensure complete equality of social and political rights to all its inhabitants irrespective of religion, race or ethnicity".[7] Amnesty International and Human Rights Watch submitted a joint letter of protest to the Knesset shortly before the vote on the amendment, urging parliamentarians to reject it because it contravened international law.[8] Even the dovish interior minister, Avraham Poraz, who had been required to legislate the amendment by the prime minister, Ariel Sharon, was apologetic. He admitted: "It would be best if the bill never made it to the law books, because an enlightened and humane society should allow reunification of families."[9]

Such regrets were of little consolation to Morad. He had met Abir three years earlier on a peace-building programme in Canada designed to encourage Israelis and Palestinians to trust each other and partly sponsored by the local Israeli embassy. "I am an Israeli citizen and this is supposed to be my state. What other country treats its citizens in this way?" he asked. "And what message does this [law] send us apart from that our government not only doesn't trust the Palestinians but it doesn't trust us either." He paused briefly as he contemplated his future, and then added: "Where does it stop? What will they do next?"

As the bill passed the Knesset vote, Israeli officials strenuously denied that it had any racist intent. The law, argued the head of the Shin Bet, Avi Dichter, was "vital for Israel's security".[10] He claimed that the government had been forced to block the entry of Palestinian spouses into Israel after a small number had abused their naturalised status to participate in terror attacks. Despite a petition to the courts, it was never clarified how many naturalised Palestinians had been involved in such attacks or in what ways. Several commentators suspected that the measure had been drafted not with security in mind but out of a fear that Palestinian applications for Israeli citizenship through marriage would eventually erode the country's Jewish majority. Naturalisation through marriage offered Palestinians from the occupied territories the one and only legal route to acquiring Israeli citizenship. A *Ha'aretz* editorial sounded less than convinced by Israel's official arguments: "On the assumption that the bill is indeed for security purposes, as the government claims, [it] appears to be both an unnecessarily vehement and unbalanced reaction to the security situation."[11]

The story of "the separation wall through the heart", as one international human rights lawyer called the legislation,[12] slowly dropped off the media's radar. Over the next two years large Knesset majorities renewed the temporary amendment. Only in May 2005 did the issue briefly flare up again, when the government made further modifications to the law, ostensibly designed to suggest a slight easing of the restrictions but which in practice made almost no difference.

THE NEED FOR 'A MASSIVE JEWISH MAJORITY'

Shortly after the cabinet vote on the new legislation, the prime minister, Ariel Sharon, held an impromptu press conference to explain the decision. At the time he was on his way to Washington, on a trip designed to soften up the Bush Administration over the terms of Israel's imminent evacuation of 8,000 settlers from the Gaza Strip. Tens of thousands of feet above the green–blue waters of the Atlantic Ocean, Sharon publicly addressed the issue of demographics for the first time as prime minister. His comments marked a dramatic turning-point in the government's official policy. He told the press corps:

> The Jews have one small country, Israel, and must do everything so that this state remains a Jewish state in the future as well. There is no intention of hurting anyone here; there's merely a correct and important intention of Israel being a Jewish state with a massive Jewish majority. That's what needs to be done, and that's exactly what we're doing. This is considered normal everywhere.[13]

Before his flight to Washington, Sharon had made a similar observation to senior ministers and security officials. "There's no need to hide behind security arguments," he reportedly told them. "There is a need for the existence of a Jewish state."[14] His officials took him at his word. The website of the *Yediot Aharonot* newspaper reported that the National Security Council, the body that advises the prime minister on the country's security needs, was preparing to recommend other restrictions on citizenship as a way of "improving the demographic situation in Israel".[15] Later it emerged that further changes to the Nationality Law would exclude not just Palestinians but any non-Jew marrying an Israeli.[16] According to a report in the *Ha'aretz* newspaper: "There is broad agreement in the government and academia that the policy must be strict and make it difficult for non-Jews to obtain citizenship in Israel."[17]

The Jewish state already had some of the toughest naturalisation laws in the world, requiring of non-Jews who married Israelis that they remain in the country on temporary residency permits for at least five years and renounce their existing citizenship. Even then, their application could be rejected if they failed to meet undisclosed criteria set by the Population Registry in a government procedure over which, uniquely, there was no judicial appeal. Now Israel was intending to tighten the rules to the point where non-Jews would be ineligible for citizenship or possibly even residency, and the children of an Israeli and a non-Jew would lose their citizenship rights too.

The new uncompromising mood was almost certainly a reflection of much wider demographic concerns that were preoccupying Sharon's government during the second intifada. They were most notable in Sharon's sudden conversion to the cause of "unilateral separation" in general and disengagement in particular.

There had been much speculation about the reasons for the "Gaza Disengagement Plan", as it was named, since Sharon announced it in February 2004.[18] He advanced it in the face of bitter and relentless criticism from the right wing, especially from senior members of his own Likud party, including his chief rival for the party's leadership, Binyamin Netanyahu, and militant settler groups who called the move "a transfer of Jews" and staged violent protests, including blocking public roads and attacking public buildings, to prevent its implementation. Why had the man widely seen as the chief architect of the settlement project in the occupied territories – the politician-general who infamously told his followers in 1998 to "grab hilltops" to prevent occupied land being handed back to the Palestinians under the Oslo Accords[19] – turned on the settlers now? Why the sudden change of heart, even if only in Gaza?

There was more than a suspicion among commentators in the Hebrew media that, faced with pressure from President George W. Bush to help create a "viable Palestinian state" as part of a US-sponsored diplomatic peace plan known as the Road Map, Sharon needed a concession to get the Americans off his back.[20] He needed to give the Palestinians something that could be presented as the first step on the path towards Palestinian statehood.[21] Gaza was a small limb of the Zionist project and could be sacrificed without too much pain: it had no religious or historic significance to the Jewish people, and only a few thousand settlers were living there. More importantly, though, in severing its connection to the tiny but hugely overcrowded Gaza Strip, Israel was also disposing of an unwanted Palestinian population estimated at about 1.3 million, more than a quarter of all the Palestinians who fell under its rule.[22] The rapidly growing Gazan population had been a demographic thorn in Israel's side for some time. An earlier prime minister, Yitzhak Rabin, had once publicly wished Gaza "would fall into the sea". He had added: "Since that won't happen, a solution must be found for the problem."[23] In disengaging, Sharon seemed to have found the best solution available.

During the course of the second intifada it had become increasingly apparent to Israeli politicians, diplomats, academics and generals that the country's continuing military rule in the occupied territories was losing legitimacy – even in American eyes. The Oslo years, when Israel had been able to mask its control through Yasser Arafat's corrupt and largely dependent regime of the Palestinian Authority, were effectively over. Israel was clearly back in charge, running the show directly from Jerusalem, even if it made great play of the occasional handover of a West Bank city to the Palestinian security forces. In response, campaigns by the global Churches to withdraw their investments from Israel were being stepped up,[24] and the biggest British union of university lecturers passed a motion in April 2005 to boycott two Israeli universities.[25] Even though lobbying by Israeli and Jewish academics in Britain managed to overturn the motion a short time later, the psychological and emotional barriers that once prevented groups in the West from punishing Israel were starting to fall.

GAZA AND FEAR OF THE APARTHEID COMPARISON

The new harsher climate of opinion had been partly created by bolder voices in Europe prepared to compare Israel's rule in the occupied territories to that of white South Africa during the apartheid years.[26] Paradoxically, security-minded Israeli academics were making much the same calculation, warning their leaders of the pressing need to withdraw from Palestinian territory.[27] Their thinking was driven by political and ethnic arithmetic:[28] between the Mediterranean sea and the River Jordan – in the land once known as Palestine and today longed for by many Israelis as the enlarged state of "Greater Israel" – the populations of Jews and Palestinians had reached virtual parity. According to Israeli demographers, there were 5.2 million Jews compared to a little over 4.9 million Palestinians, the combined Palestinian populations living in Israel, the West Bank and Gaza.[29] Given the far higher Palestinian birth rate and Israel's continuing hold on the occupied territories, Jews would soon be a minority in Greater Israel.[30] Once the region contained a majority of non-Jews, so the argument went, the Palestinians needed only to demand one person–one vote for the artifice of the "Jewish and democratic state" to crumble. Greater Israel would have to adopt the discredited apartheid model to enforce its rule or find itself transformed by demographics into Greater Palestine.

In November 2003 Ehud Olmert, a member of Sharon's inner circle in the cabinet, set out the new predicament facing Israel in an interview with the *Ha'aretz* newspaper. In doing so, he was also undoubtedly reflecting the prime minister's new thinking.

> There is no doubt in my mind that very soon the government of Israel is going to have to address the demographic issue with the utmost seriousness and resolve. This issue above all others will dictate the solution that we must adopt ... We don't have unlimited time. More and more Palestinians are uninterested in a negotiated, two-state solution, because they want to change the essence of the conflict from an Algerian paradigm [of armed resistance to occupation] to a South African one. From a struggle against "occupation", in their parlance, to a struggle for one-man-one-vote. That is, of course, a much cleaner struggle, a much more popular struggle – and ultimately a much more powerful one. For us, it would mean the end of the Jewish state.

Olmert concluded with what sounded much like a justification for the Gaza disengagement Sharon would shortly announce: "[The] formula for the parameters of a unilateral solution are: To maximize the number of Jews; to minimize the number of Palestinians."[31]

Professor Arnon Sofer, the head of geopolitics at Haifa University and the most prominent of the demographic prophets of doom, summarised Israel's plight in even starker terms in July 2004, shortly after Sharon unveiled the disengagement plan. Placing himself in the Palestinians' position, Sofer described how they might see the future of the conflict from what he called their "prisons" of Gaza and the West Bank:

> The Jews won't permit us to have an army, while their own powerful army will surround us. They won't permit us to have an air force, while their own air force will fly over us. They won't allow us the Right of Return [of refugees]. Why should we make a deal with them? Why should we accept a state from them? Let's wait patiently for another 10 years, when the Jews will comprise a mere 40 percent of the country, while we will be 60 percent. The world won't allow a minority to rule over a majority, so Palestine will be ours.[32]

Like Olmert and Sofer, Sharon doubtless regarded cutting Gaza adrift as the minimum price to be paid to maintain Israel's international standing and its control over most of the West Bank. Losing some 1.3 million Gazans would buy the Jewish state a little time as it sought a way to deal with its urgent demographic problems.[33] Throughout 2004, however, as the debate about disengagement raged, Sharon personally avoided referring to questions of demography, preferring the country's usual justifications based on "security". Yossi Alpher, a former adviser to Ehud Barak, noted the most likely reason: "Sharon apparently downplays demography because to highlight it would put the spotlight on his own central role of settling the West Bank and Gaza in the course of the past three decades, thereby creating the demographic problem in the first place."[34] Only as Israel began evacuating the settlements in August 2005 did Sharon allude to the fact that a demographic imperative lay behind the disengagement. In a short televised national address, he offered a single substantive reason for leaving Gaza: "We cannot hold on to Gaza forever. More than a million Palestinians live there and double their number with each generation."[35] Vice-Premier Shimon Peres was more plain-speaking. "We are disengaging from Gaza because of demography," he told the BBC's *Newsnight* programme.[36]

A JEWISH CONSENSUS EMERGES

Although no one was making the connection, the disengagement, the effective ban on Israeli Arabs marrying Palestinians, and the proposal to prevent Israelis marrying non-Jews were all products of a new tide of Jewish chauvinism sweeping Israel, winning converts across the political spectrum and at the highest levels.[37] In the vision being formulated by Israeli officials during the second intifada, the Jewish state was a place where only Jews were welcome and only Jews counted. The obsessive number-crunching of demographers, and their media elevation to guru status, suggested the shallowness and profoundly anti-democratic trend of the approach. Some Israeli leaders still used "security" as the defence of policies that violated the rights of non-Jews, but with far less conviction. The distinction between security and demographic issues had always been blurred in Zionist thinking but now it was vanishing. As Ilan Saban, a professor of public law at Haifa University, observed disconsolately: "We have, unfortunately, become a Jewish and demographic state."[38]

Such obsessions were far from novel. Surveys since the 1970s had shown a remarkable consistency in the replies of Jewish respondents when asked about the ideal traits of their country. For example, a poll undertaken by Haifa University in 1995, near the height of optimism about the Oslo peace process, showed that 95 per cent of Israeli Jews rejected the idea of Israel as a liberal democracy. In a series of surveys taken between 1980 and 1995, the team found that on average about 60 per cent of Israeli Jews believed the Jewish character of their state was more important than its democratic character.[39]

These results were confirmed again in 2003 in a major opinion poll, the Democracy Index, organised by the Israel Democracy Institute, which reported "alarming findings". It concluded: "The picture emerging from the various indicators shows that Israel is mainly a formal democracy that has not yet acquired the characteristics of a substantive democracy." According to the survey, only 77 per cent of Israeli Jews believed democracy of any sort was a desirable form of government, giving Israelis the lowest ranking in a comparative survey of public attitudes in 35 democratic states. More than half of Israeli Jews said they opposed equality for Arab citizens; more than two-thirds objected to Arab political parties joining the government; and 57 per cent thought Arab citizens should be encouraged to emigrate, either through inducements or force.[40]

Although a strain of anti-democratic and anti-Arab thinking had been prominent among the Jewish public for decades – a legacy of its Zionist training from the cradle – there was something discernibly new about the political climate in Israel after the eruption of the second intifada. It was evinced in a willingness by the country's leaders, including its leftwing elites, to speak out in public using the same chauvinistic language more usually heard on the street or from the far right. In the new consensus, rabbis, politicians, generals and intellectuals of all political stripes agreed that the country needed to return to what was seen as its founding vision: a Jewish state that was for and of Jews only.

Increasingly shrill reports on the demographic growth of the Palestinian minority served only to fuel the alarm. Prof. Sofer of Haifa University, for example, warned that the population growth of Israeli Arabs, at about 3.5 per cent a year, was comparable to sub-Saharan Africa but that their mortality rate was close to Europe's. He also noted that the Bedouin in the Negev had an even higher rate of increase: at 4.5 per cent, one of the biggest in the world. According to Sofer's forecasts, there would be 2.1 million Arab citizens by 2020. Given a Jewish birth rate of only 1 per cent, he predicted demographic calamity as the "non-Jewish" minority grew to 32 per cent of the population within a few years. This would give Israeli Arabs an electoral influence that could, he warned, undermine Israel's democratic features and pass effective control of the Knesset to the Palestinian leadership in the occupied territories.

> The leaders of the Palestinian Authority have been using the electoral power of the Arabs of Israel for their own needs ... [Israeli Arabs] can tip the balance on decisions about the future of Golan or the future of Jerusalem if these decisions are put to a referendum or incorporated into a party's platform. In their hands lies the power to determine the right of return or to decide who is a Jew ... In another few years, they will be able to decide whether the State of Israel should continue to be a Jewish-Zionist State or whether it should "turn into a State of all its citizens".[41]

Given this kind of logic, the Palestinians of the West Bank and Gaza were far less of a problem than Israel's own substantial Arab minority. A mixture of building walls and disengaging could keep the Palestinians of the West Bank and Gaza out of the Jewish state. But once that task was complete, Israelis would still face the difficult question of what to do with the rapidly growing Palestinian population who lived in the heart of Israel, supposedly as equal citizens. How was the threat that their demographic growth posed to the Jewishness of the state to be countered? How could they be prevented by democratic means from bringing Palestinians back into the state through marriage? And how could a fifth of the population continue to be excluded from the centres of power when all they were demanding was democratic reform, the creation of a "state of all its citizens"? As Sharon's government began formulating responses to these questions, politicians and academics of the left fell into step.

THE BIRTH OF A NEW BENNY MORRIS

Benny Morris, a distinguished historian who had done much to explode the myths of the traditional Zionist account of Israel's founding, came to personify the terrible intellectual contortions needed by the left in the new political era. He began over the course of the second intifada to argue that Zionism's pre-state leaders had failed in their historic mission to create a fully Jewish state when they allowed a rump Palestinian population to remain inside the borders of Israel during the 1948 war. The 150,000 Palestinians of 1948 had become the more than one million Israeli Arabs of today, a population group he referred to as a "time bomb".

Morris's thinking was first articulated in Britain's *Guardian* newspaper in 2002, when he quoted extensively and approvingly from the writings of early Jewish leaders in Palestine. He showed convincingly that they had known there was only one way to create a Jewish state: through the mass expulsion of the native Palestinian population.[42] Later Morris fleshed out these ideas in a lengthy interview with the *Ha'aretz* newspaper. After observing that Israel's first prime minister, David Ben Gurion, had made sure before the 1948 war that "there is an atmosphere of transfer" – the word most Israelis prefer over the more explicit phrase "ethnic cleansing" – he continued:

> I think [Ben Gurion] made a serious historical mistake in 1948. Even though he understood the demographic issue and the need to establish a Jewish state without a large Arab minority, he got cold feet during the war. In the end, he faltered ... I know that this stuns the Arabs and the liberals and the politically correct types. But my feeling is that this place would be quieter and know less suffering if the matter had been resolved once and for all ... If the end of the story turns out to be a gloomy one for the Jews, it will be because Ben Gurion did not complete the transfer in 1948. Because he left a large and volatile demographic reserve in the West Bank and Gaza and within Israel itself.[43]

Morris's concerns about this "volatile demographic reserve", he made clear, stemmed from his view of the Palestinian mind as essentially irrational and diseased, a position he appeared to have developed during his well-publicised interviews with former Prime Minister Ehud Barak. "When one has to deal with a serial killer, it's not so important to discover why he became a serial killer. What's important is to imprison the murderer or execute him." Asked how he proposed dealing with the murderous mentality of the Palestinians, Morris replied: "Something like a cage has to be built for them. I know that sounds terrible. It is really cruel. But there is no choice. There is a wild animal there that has to be locked away one way or another."

Morris, however, continued by suggesting that the cage policy might ultimately fail to contain the Palestinians, and then Israel would face the same moment of crisis as in 1948, when expulsion of the Palestinians was needed to save the Jewish state. This time Israel could not afford to hesitate.

> If you are asking me whether I support the transfer and expulsion of the Arabs from the West Bank, Gaza and perhaps even from Galilee and the Triangle

> [inside Israel], I say not at this moment ... But I am ready to tell you that in other circumstances, apocalyptic ones, which are liable to be realized in five or ten years, I can see expulsions.

Did he include expulsion of the country's Arab minority, the interviewer asked.

> The Israeli Arabs are a time bomb. Their slide into complete Palestinization has made them an emissary of the enemy that is among us. They are a potential fifth column. In both demographic and security terms they are liable to undermine the state. So that if Israel again finds itself in a situation of existential threat, as in 1948, it may be forced to act as it did then.

Morris was simply following to its logical conclusion Israel's founding ideology. As a "Jewish and democratic" state, Israel needed a convincing Jewish majority so that its decisions – even discriminatory and racist ones – could be justified as the will of the people. Morris believed that, as the ethnic arithmetic again turned against a Jewish majority, the country's leaders must confront the same questions faced by the generation of 1948. In Morris's mind, the most worrying demographic phenomenon was the relentless growth of the Israeli Arab population and what Morris characterised as its "radicalization" or "Palestinization". These terms, regularly used by Israelis when talking about the Palestinian minority, were rarely explained. They were a kind of shorthand understood by all Israelis, from Morris to Sharon. But what did they mean?

As we have seen, Sharon and Barak believed that the country's Arab citizens had been unmasked during the second intifada as a second front of the Palestinians in the occupied territories. They reached this conclusion from their premise that the Israeli Arabs could not have been the sole authors of the call for a "state of all its citizens", the main political programme of the minority's parties since the late 1990s. Someone else was behind the campaign. The culprit could be inferred from the goal of a state of all its citizens: the destruction of Israel as a Jewish state. As far as Barak, Sharon and apparently Morris were concerned, this was proof enough that Yasser Arafat and the Palestinian Authority were the true authors. The Palestinians, they believed, hoped to use Israeli Arabs as advance troops, subverting Israel from within through a political campaign for democratisation.

The Israeli leadership's demographic fears did not end there, however. The amendment to the Nationality Law showed that Sharon also believed the citizenship enjoyed by the country's Arabs could be further exploited by the Palestinian leadership. As Israel tried to separate itself from the Palestinians through wall-building and disengagements, Arafat could retake the initiative by converting marriage into a demographic weapon. If he encouraged Palestinians to wed Israeli Arabs, they would have the right to leave their prisons in the West Bank and Gaza and return to Israel as the spouse of an Israeli citizen. In the imagination of Sharon and Morris, the Israeli Arabs were a Trojan horse, carrying inside them the seeds of the Jewish state's destruction.

THE ISRAELI ARAB TIME BOMB

Senior political and military leaders expressed similar misgivings about the "time bomb" represented by the country's Palestinian minority. In October 2004, well after the Gaza disengagement had been announced, the public security minister, Gideon Ezra, told *Yediot Aharonot* that the presence of Palestinian citizens in the Jewish state was the most troubling aspect of the conflict. "There are Arab citizens in the State of Israel. This is our greatest sorrow. Finish things in Gaza, finish things in Judea and Samaria [the West Bank]. We'll be left with the greatest sorrow."[44]

Israel's military chief of staff through most of the second intifada, Moshe Ya'alon, described the crushing of the Palestinian uprising as "the conclusion of the War of Independence", implying that he regarded the military assault on the Palestinians as the completion of a job unfinished in 1948. He also compared the threat of the Palestinians to cancer.

> When you are attacked externally, you can see the attack, you are wounded. Cancer, on the other hand, is something internal. Therefore, I find it more disturbing, because here the diagnosis is critical ... My professional diagnosis is that there is a phenomenon here that constitutes an existential threat.[45]

As the sociologist Baruch Kimmerling noted, the Palestinians in the occupied territories were regarded by Israelis as an external problem, so in talking of an "internal" threat Ya'alon appeared to be referring to the country's Palestinian citizens.[46] Such an interpretation was confirmed by a later interview, in 2005, as Ya'alon prepared to step down from his post. He alluded to the coming apocalypse hinted at by Morris. As well as the "external existential threat" posed to the survival of the Jewish state by the Palestinians in the occupied territories, he said: "There is one internal existential threat which concerns me very much, but I will not discuss it as long as I am in uniform."[47] It was difficult to imagine what the threat could be apart from the "cancer" of the Israeli Arabs.

Morris's observation that Israel's Arab minority was a "demographic and security" threat reflected the blurring of these terms in Israeli discourse. The demographic threat of high Arab birth rates, which for Israelis like Morris meant the Jewish state was being swamped by a tide of Arab babies, was inescapably also a threat to the long-term survival – and therefore security – of a Jewish state. In the opinion of many Israelis, it was the biggest security threat facing Israel. This was the view endorsed by the former prime minister Binyamin Netanyahu. Shortly before Morris's interview, Netanyahu, then the finance minister in Sharon's government, addressed the Herzliya conference, the largest annual gathering of Israel's political and security establishment, telling them:

> If there is a demographic problem, and there is, it is with the Israeli Arabs who will remain Israeli citizens ... We therefore need a policy that will first of all guarantee a Jewish majority. I say this with no hesitation, as a liberal, a democrat, and a Jewish patriot.[48]

ZIONISM'S LONG DEMOGRAPHIC NIGHTMARE

The ideological path being pursued by Israel with increasing determination following the outbreak of the second intifada was laid out long before, in the events that forged a Jewish state on the Palestinian homeland. In the pre-state philosophy of Zionists like Vladimir Jabotinsky, an "iron wall" policy of force was needed to make the native Palestinian population submit. In practice, however, faced with enduring hostility from Palestinians over their national dispossession in 1948, Israel had built its walls to exclude as well. The Israeli historian Ilan Pappe characterised Zionism, the ideological foundations of the Jewish state, in the following terms: "The gates are kept closed, and the walls high, to ward off an 'Arab' invasion of the Jewish fortress."[49]

The "demographic problem", as Morris correctly noted, had been an enduring Zionist obsession since well before the creation of Israel.

At the turn of the twentieth century, as the movement sought to focus Jewish attention and resources on Palestine, many of its leaders claimed the country was a deserted wasteland waiting for the arrival of pioneer Jews – or in the slogan popularised by the British Jewish writer Israel Zangwill "a land without a people for a people without a land".[50] Elsewhere, Zangwill referred to the hundreds of thousands of indigenous Palestinians dismissively as "an Arab encampment".[51] A few Zionists tried to counter the movement's wishful thinking, including the Jewish thinker Asher Ginzburg, known by the Hebrew name Ahad Ha'am, who observed in 1891 after a trip to Palestine: "We abroad are used to believing that the Land of Israel is now almost totally desolate, a desert that is not sowed ... But in truth this is not the case. Throughout the country it is difficult to find fields that are not sowed."[52]

According to the report of an Anglo-American commission in 1946, on the eve of Israel's establishment, the population of Palestine stood at nearly 1.3 million Palestinians and, after waves of recent immigration, 600,000 Jews. The burning question facing the Zionists was how to establish a Jewish state on a land that was considered the Palestinian homeland by two-thirds of its inhabitants. Even the partition of the country proposed by the United Nations in November 1947 would have only postponed the problem for the Zionists, creating an Arab state populated almost exclusively with Palestinians, and a Jewish state populated with a small majority of Jews. Within a generation or two there would have been two Arab states.[53] Despite the Zionist movement's official support for the UN plan, its leaders were not disappointed by the Palestinians' rejection of partition and the pretext it offered them, according to Ilan Pappe, "for implementing a systematic expulsion of the local population within the areas allocated for a Jewish state".[54]

Undoubtedly, as the Mandate drew to a close, political arithmetic was the overriding concern of the Zionists preparing for the British exit. At the unilateral declaration of statehood in May 1948, the Jewish leadership began rewriting the demography of Palestine through three separate strands of policy: first, the mass expulsion of Palestinians under cover of war; second, the encouragement of massive Jewish immigration (and, conversely, the blocking of a right of return for expelled Palestinians); and third, financial and other support for improving Jewish birth rates at the expense of Arab birth rates. As early as October 1948, some months before the end of the war, Ben Gurion set an upper limit for the Arab population of the new Jewish state of 15 per cent, a figure that over more than half a century was never significantly deviated from.[55]

The biggest expulsion of Palestinians occurred during the year-long war of 1948, known by Israelis as the War of Independence. Some 750,000 Palestinians were driven from the newly established state, or 80 per cent of the 900,000 Palestinians who lived inside the new borders. The mythic account promoted by Zionists was that the Palestinians fled on their leaders' orders.[56] Only in the 1980s, when the historical records were opened for inspection, was this version finally laid to rest. Benny Morris, who spent many years trawling Israel's state and military archives, offers a far more plausible reason for the Palestinian flight: a systematic Israeli policy of massacres in Palestinian towns and villages, at least 24 according to his most recent, conservative estimates; the rape of women and girls by Israeli soldiers; and arbitrary killings.

Morris states:

> In Operation Hiram [in October 1948, in the country's northern Palestinian heartland] there was an unusually high concentration of executions of people against a wall or next to a well in an orderly fashion. That can't be chance. It's a pattern. Apparently, various officers who took part in the operation understood that the expulsion order they received permitted them to do these deeds in order to encourage the population to take to the roads ... Ben-Gurion silenced the matter. He covered up for the officers who did the massacres.[57]

Regular small-scale expulsions of Palestinians continued through the early years of the state.[58] In 1950, for example, the remaining population of 2,700 Palestinians in the town of al-Majdal were transported over the border to the Gaza Strip; in their place Jewish immigrants were settled in the town, which was given the Hebrew name Ashkelon. As many as 7,000 Bedouin were expelled from the Negev, either to Jordanian or Egyptian territory, over the period of a year from November 1949. And more than 5,000 Palestinians were forced out of their villages in the Wadi Ara region and made to cross over into the West Bank in the summer of 1949.[59]

Evidence exists that far larger expulsions were planned, though Israel's leaders appear to have balked at implementing their schemes, presumably because they feared the diplomatic repercussions. An investigation by an Israeli newspaper in 1991, for example, revealed that, under the cover of the 1956 Suez war, Israel hoped to expel

40,000 citizens – or about a fifth of the Israeli Arab population of the time – to Jordan. Operation Hafarferet was aborted after a unit of soldiers supposed to enforce a curfew on the Israeli Arab village of Kafr Qassem as part of the expulsion plan massacred many of the local inhabitants instead.[60] In the same period, according to a book published in Hebrew in 2005 based on documents from the country's state archives, Yitzhak Rabin, then a major-general in the army and later to become prime minister, proposed provoking a war against Jordan as a pretext for deporting West Bank Palestinians. "Most of them can be driven out," Rabin told a meeting attended by Ben Gurion. "If the numbers were smaller it would be easier, but the problem can be solved in principle. It would not be a humane move, but war in general is not a humane matter."[61] Although neither plan was implemented, Rabin, then in charge of the northern command, did manage during the 1956 attack to expel to Syria the 2,000 inhabitants of two Galilean villages near Lake Hulah.[62]

During the Six-Day War of 1967 and the subsequent occupation of the West Bank and Gaza, more than 300,000 Palestinians were expelled to Jordan and Egypt. Israeli government policy permanently blocked the return of the overwhelming majority of refugees from both the 1948 and 1967 wars. After the 1948 war, for example, Ben Gurion wrote: "I don't accept the formulation that we should not encourage [the refugees'] return: Their return must be prevented ... at all costs."[63] Any physical threat of a secret return over the border was averted through the wholesale destruction of Palestinian property, including the razing of more than 400 villages, and the transfer of Arab lands to Jewish farming communities like the kibbutzim and moshavim.

The second major "demographic fix" – the skewing of the Holy Land's ethnic arithmetic to ensure it permanently favoured Jews – was achieved shortly after the establishment of Israel through a piece of discriminatory legislation masquerading as immigration policy. The Knesset passed the Law of Return in 1950, giving anyone with Jewish ancestry the right to claim automatic Israeli citizenship.[64] Nearly three million Jews have so far taken advantage of the law and migrated to Israel, including at least one million immigrants following the collapse of the Soviet Union in 1990.[65] The extent to which these three million have been vital in ensuring Israel maintains a convincing Jewish majority is demonstrated by the population figures over five decades. Despite an Arab birth rate more than twice that of the Jewish one, the ratio of Jews to Arabs has stayed virtually unchanged. In 1949, Israel's 160,000 Palestinian citizens comprised 13.6 per cent of the total population. By 1970 the number of Arab citizens had more than doubled to 365,000, but their proportion in the population had shrunk slightly to 12.5 per cent.[66] Today, the Arab minority has grown to nearly 1.1 million, and about 16 per cent of the population. (If the figures include the 250,000 Palestinians annexed to Israel along with the lands of East Jerusalem in 1967, the proportion rises to 19 per cent, the figure cited by Israel's Central Bureau of Statistics.)

HEROINE MOTHERS OF THE JEWISH STATE

Given the Arab population's success in maintaining its demographic position despite large waves of Jewish immigration, Israel has also engaged in what has been called "a battle of wombs", encouraging higher birth rates among Jewish women. Historically, the main attempts to achieve this have concentrated on the manipulation of child-related benefits. The importance of such measures was evident to Ben Gurion as early as 1949 when he announced a monetary prize for every "heroine mother" on the birth of her tenth child.[67] Elsewhere, he stated: "Any Jewish woman, who, as far as it depends on her, does not bring into the world at least four healthy children is shirking her duty to the nation."[68] In the vision of the prime minister, pioneering parents would raise their Jewish children to go out and settle the new frontiers of the state, endlessly multiplying as they "redeemed the land" of its tainted Palestinian past. The Promised Land, which had been emptied of the vast majority of its Palestinian population during war the previous year, had to be filled with "Sabras", the assertive, independent new Jew that the creation of Israel was supposed to spawn.

Ten years later Ben Gurion abolished this clumsy welfare benefit as it became clear that the majority of claimants were Arab rather than Jewish mothers. The prime minister observed that in future such schemes "must be administered by the Jewish Agency and not the state since the aim is to increase the number of Jews and not the population of the state".[69] Unlike the government, the Jewish Agency, an international Zionist organisation with quasi-governmental powers in Israel, has a free hand to discriminate against Arab citizens.

Nonetheless, the state continued pursuing its own discriminatory policies. In 1967, the year Israel acquired a substantial new Palestinian population by occupying the West Bank and Gaza, a Demography

Council was established in the Prime Minister's Office with the goal of increasing Jewish women's reproduction. Demographic policy, the prime minister of the day, Levi Eshkol, declared, "is intended to create an atmosphere that will encourage childbearing, in light of the fact that it is crucial for the future of the Jewish people".[70] A year later a Fund for Encouraging Birth was established to provide child allowances to Jewish families with more than three children. Larger Jewish families were also entitled to extra welfare payments, about three times those granted to Arabs. Other benefits were offered courtesy of the 1983 Law on Families Blessed with Children.[71]

Conversely, the state hoped to lower Arab reproduction, although according to the anthropologist Rhoda Kanaaneh the state's selective pro-natalist policies remained "largely symbolic" given "the difficulty of encouraging the Jewish birth rate without encouraging the Arabs to multiply too".[72] A report in *Ha'aretz* in 1998 revealed that the government had secretly asked the country's health insurers in the 1960s to reduce the Arab birth rate by encouraging the use of contraceptives among the population.[73] Little appears to have been done in practice, however, until the 1980s when the Health Ministry began investing in family planning projects targeted disproportionately at the Arab population. "It was widely known among [health] ministry employees that approval for a general clinic in an Arab area was difficult to get, but approval was all but guaranteed if the proposed clinic included a family planning clinic," writes Kanaaneh.[74]

Only in the 1990s did Israelis start to believe that the long-standing "demographic pressures" on their country were easing through an unexpected windfall of huge Jewish immigration following the collapse of the Soviet Union and through a peace process instigated by the Oslo Accords that appeared to promise at its finish a Palestinian state, even if a very circumscribed one. It was during this period, in the mid-1990s, that the Demography Council was disbanded and for the first time in its history Israel equalised child allowances for Jews and Arabs.

The respite from the demography debate, however, was short-lived. As the flood of immigrants from the Soviet Union dried to a trickle through the latter half of the 1990s, the government was soon bewailing the failure to locate future reserves of Jewish immigrants. When Ariel Sharon proposed repeatedly from 2001 onwards that he would bring another one million Jews to Israel over the coming years, the country's demographers could barely hide their incredulity.[75]

Questions of ethnic arithmetic were also pushed centre stage by the collapse of the Oslo process in late 2000 and the outbreak of the intifada in the occupied territories, combined with the supposed threat of a "second front" of Arab citizens inside Israel. Politicians, diplomats, academics, businessmen, journalists and generals began reformulating the "demographic problem" with renewed urgency and in far more aggressive form.

RETHINKING THE IDEA OF CITIZENSHIP

A sign of this shift was the first conference of its kind held by the Institute of Policy and Strategy at the Interdisciplinary Centre in Herzliya in December 2000, shortly after the outbreak of the intifada. The conference, which attracted 300 of the most important figures in the Israeli establishment, became an annual event at which major policy decisions were unveiled, including three years later Sharon's unilateral solution to the conflict with the Palestinians, his "Disengagement Plan".[76]

The first Herzliya Conference effectively foreshadowed and helped shape Sharon's ideas of disengagement. The speakers, who included Sharon himself, Shimon Peres and Binyamin Netanyahu, examined the "demographic threat" facing Israel, concentrating less on the problem of the Palestinians in the occupied territories and more on the country's Arab citizens. A few months later, the conference issued a report recommending a range of solutions including population transfer. As one *Ha'aretz* writer observed: "The core of Israel's political and defense establishment has come out with a document that corresponds, in some of its recommendations and in general tone, with the views of the far right."[77]

Two possible responses to the "demographic threat" posed by the country's Arab minority were contrasted in the report: "adaptation" and "containment".

> The adaptation policy is the one propounded by those who view Israel as a country of all its citizens – adapting its national character, its symbols, and institutions to the changing demo[graphic]-political balance. Conversely, those who support the preservation of Israel's character as it was when it was founded – a Jewish State for the Jewish nation – and they still constitute a majority among the Jewish population in Israel, are forced to proffer a counter-strategy that will provide an effective response to the aforementioned trends [towards "a state of all its citizens"], while recognizing that, in a democratic

> country, the Jewish character of Israel can only be preserved if the Jewish majority does not dip below approximately three-quarters of the total population.[78]

The report was clear which view it took. "The increase in the demographic share of the Arab minority in Israel tests directly Israel's future as a Jewish-Zionist-democratic state," the report asserted.[79] We must not overlook the general context of the ethnic, ideological and political links between the Arabs inside Israel and the Palestinian people and the Arab world at large.[80] The authors suggested a range of solutions to consolidate the country's Jewish majority, including policies to encourage birth rates among the Jewish population and increasing Jewish immigration. Underlining the significance of the Law of Return, the report noted: "Diaspora Jewry has always constituted a traditional human reserve in preventing the creation of a Palestinian majority in Israel".[81]

The report's authors argued that, as well as consolidating the Jewish majority, the number of Arab citizens could be significantly reduced through government policies. One suggestion was that Israeli Arabs be "encouraged" to transfer their citizenship to a future Palestinian state while continuing to have residency rights in Israel. Emphasis was also placed on a further recommendation: that a densely populated Arab heartland in Israel – the "Little Triangle" region lying close to the West Bank – be moved, along with its population, to the control of the Palestinian Authority in a land swap in which the large Jewish settlement blocs inside the West Bank would pass to Israel.[82] (A similar suggestion was made in relation to East Jerusalem.) The organiser of the conference, Uzi Arad, a former adviser to Netanyahu, argued that transfer might be imposed on the 250,000 citizens of the Little Triangle against their will. "In a democratic state, it is the majority that determines where the national borders lie," he said.[83]

The idea of land swaps and a "transfer of citizenship", as some called it, found support among Israeli leaders of the left and right. In an interview in 2002, Ehud Barak suggested that it was "not inconceivable" that Israeli Arabs have their citizenship transferred, though he added: "I don't recommend that government spokesmen speak of it."[84] In fact, two years earlier he had privately pondered the same scheme – a "land swap" in which the Triangle and its residents would pass to the new Palestinian state – at Camp David, as the Israeli media later reported.[85] His enduring passion for transfer was not dimmed by surveys showing that 83 per cent of the inhabitants of Umm al-Fahm, the largest town in the Triangle, were vehemently opposed.[86]

Barak's successor, Ariel Sharon, was reported to be equally enamoured of the proposal. In February 2004 he floated the idea of transferring the Triangle in an interview with the *Ma'ariv* newspaper, adding that the issue was being examined by his legal advisers.[87] When Israeli Arab leaders denounced the proposal, Sharon's spokesman, Ra'anan Gissin, questioned their motives: "Palestinians hoping to conquer Israel with the demographic bomb [higher birth rates] are obviously opposed."[88]

A few weeks later, after Sharon's comments had been widely reported, he backtracked, publicly reassuring the inhabitants of the Triangle that they were "an integral part of Israel's population".[89] But investigations by the Hebrew media revealed that Sharon had been secretly studying the "transfer of citizenship" idea with officials since he was first elected prime minister in early 2001. According to reporter Ben Caspit, Sharon had discussed the plan with Shimon Peres, then his foreign minister, suggesting it was the best way to protect Israel's Jewish majority. Sharon reportedly told his confidants: "If we are already exchanging territory [with the Palestinians], why give empty land when we can transfer land with Arabs living on it?" Sharon's main problem, Caspit reported, was that such a transfer could be considered a war crime under international law. Government officials were therefore trying to "formulate a package 'to sell' to the world".[90]

POLITICAL TIDE TURNS TOWARDS TRANSFER

At the popular level, the word "transfer" – the Israeli euphemism for ethnic cleansing – quickly gained a new currency in the Knesset, on university campuses, in the media and on the street. Across the country posters littered walls, buildings, traffic signs and bus stops proclaiming "Expel the Arabs!" or "Transfer = Security and Peace". But it was the degree to which such language began to slip with ease from the lips of government ministers, advisers and spokesmen that suggested that the first Herzliya Conference, in December 2000, had marked a turning point. A year later, at the 2001 conference, Shlomo Gazit, a former head of Military Intelligence and an analyst with the influential Jaffee Centre for Strategic Studies at Tel Aviv University, stated without a trace of embarrassment: "Democracy has to be subordinated to demography."[91]

Until the second intifada few Israeli leaders except those drawn from the fanatical settlers talked openly of transfer of Arab citizens as a national goal. A closely related policy was emphasised instead: "Judaisation" highlighted not the expulsion of the country's existing Arab inhabitants but the process whereby their traditional heartlands, particularly the Galilee and the Negev, could be brought under Jewish dominion through state-sponsored settlement. This is not to suggest that since the state's birth the spectre of transfer had not haunted much Israeli policymaking; as we have seen, it undoubtedly had. But outside the inner sanctums of the political, military and security establishments the debate was rarely allowed to take on corporeal form. It was left to maverick extremists such as Meir Kahane, an American rabbi who immigrated to Israel in the early 1970s, to promote ethnic cleansing in public. His far-right Kach party was finally disqualified from contesting elections in 1988, four years after Kahane had been elected to the Knesset on an anti-Arab platform.

There were, however, plenty of Israeli politicians ready to inherit his mantle, though until the second intifada most made sure to temper their language and restrict their transfer talk to the Palestinians of the occupied territories. In polite Israeli debate only the inhabitants of the West Bank and Gaza were eligible for expulsion to Jordan or Egypt. This view was hardly controversial: it echoed the "Palestine is Jordan" option – creating a Palestinian state in neighbouring Jordan – which had once been a well-known ambition of several Labor and Likud leaders, including Ariel Sharon.[92]

But following the Herzliya conference it became acceptable, even customary, for Israeli officials to link publicly the fate of the country's Arab minority with that of the occupied Palestinians. A series of speeches and interviews by senior politicians, many of them members of Sharon's cabinet, made it clear that little or no distinction was now being made between Palestinians under Israeli rule, whether citizens or not, and that transfer could and possibly should apply to all of them. When in early 2002 the extreme rightwing MK Michael Kleiner presented a private member's bill to establish an "emigration package" to encourage Israeli Arabs to move abroad he found widespread support in the Knesset, even among ministers. Despite a warning from the parliamentary legal adviser that the bill was "problematic", the legislation oversight committee passed the bill for reading in the Knesset.[93] Only the calling of a general election later that year scuppered the bill's chances.

At times it seemed as though there was hardly a minister who did not feel free to express his contempt for the country's Arab population. In August 2003, Tzachi Hanegbi, the public security minister and a member of Sharon's Likud party, told the *Ma'ariv* newspaper that tens of thousands of Bedouin in the Negev were "criminals" who should be driven from their lands.[94] Six months later the deputy defence minister, Ze'ev Boim, claimed that Arabs suffered from a "genetic defect" that made them all naturally "murderous".[95] Infrastructure minister Avigdor Lieberman, a Russian immigrant, a former director-general of Likud and the current leader of the Yisrael Beiteinu party, described Bedouin citizens as "invaders".[96] He repeatedly suggested that Israeli Arab homes be transferred, along with their inhabitants, to the Palestinian Authority. Later, in May 2004, he developed his ideas into a political programme. During a visit to Russia he presented President Vladimir Putin with an alternative plan to Sharon's disengagement in which all Israeli Arabs would be expelled unless they could demonstrate their loyalty to the Jewish state, as part of what he called a "Separation of Nations".[97]

Another prominent cabinet exponent of transfer was Effi Eitam, a much-decorated army general who had become a religious Zionist following the 1973 Yom Kippur War. In 2002, as he took over the leadership of the National Religious Party and prepared to enter Sharon's cabinet as housing minister, Eitam gave an interview to *Ha'aretz*, in which, like Chief of Staff Moshe Ya'alon, he compared the growing Arab population in Israel to the spread of cancer. "Cancer is a type of illness in which most of the people who die from it die because they were diagnosed too late. By the time you grasp the size of the threat, it is already too late to deal with it." Asked whether he was suggesting transfer, Eitam replied: "The Israeli Arabs will remain citizens of the state if they do not cross the red lines."[98]

Another party in Sharon's cabinet had a long history of espousing what it called "voluntary" transfer. Moledet was created in the late 1980s – after the banning of Kahane's Kach party – by Rehava'am Ze'evi, an army general who went by the nickname of "Gandhi". Despite being an outspoken racist, he was much loved by the military establishment: Labor Prime Minister Yitzhak Rabin appointed him as a personal adviser in the 1970s, and his friend Ariel Sharon gave him the tourism portfolio in his first cabinet in 2001. Ze'evi was careful never publicly to include Israeli Arabs in his transfer plans but argued vociferously that the Palestinians of the occupied territories should be encouraged "voluntarily" to leave Greater Israel, by imposing on them economic hardship, unemployment and shortages of land and water – "in a legitimate way, and in accordance with the Geneva Conventions", he hastened to add.[99] Ze'evi campaigned in general elections under the symbol of the Hebrew character "tet", for transfer.

Ze'evi's ministerial term was cut short when he was assassinated by Palestinian gunmen in a Jerusalem hotel in October 2001. In a show of public mourning led by Sharon himself, the country eulogised Ze'evi's memory. The main Israeli-controlled road through the Jordan Valley, one fittingly that runs nearly the length of the occupied West Bank, was named "Gandhi's Road", and schools were required each year on the anniversary of his death to teach "the values in [Ze'evi's] personality – knowledge and love of the Land and loyalty to it".[100] In July 2005 the Knesset passed by an overwhelming majority a bill to establish a state-funded Ze'evi Heritage Centre, which would approve a national day of mourning and draw up a school curriculum to celebrate Ze'evi's legacy.[101] Yossi Sarid, a former education minister from the dovish Meretz party, who opposed the law, commented: "Israel will become the first country in the world that will include the theory of transfer within its education system."[102]

Ze'evi's successor as head of Moledet, Benny Elon, a settler leader and rabbi, found the new atmosphere in Israel conducive to developing a bolder platform of transfer.[103] He soon announced a campaign to encourage Arab citizens to emigrate from the country, proudly revealing that he had personally helped three Israeli Arab families to leave. The Moledet party boasted that it had located "overseas places of work, study and new residences for interested Arab applicants in order to encourage their emigration".[104] In an interview with the settlers' journal *Nekuda*, Elon explained how his "voluntary" transfer scheme might work in practice: "I will close the universities to you, I will make your lives difficult, until you want to leave."[105] Elon continued as the tourism minister in Sharon's cabinet while his party hung posters across the country reading: "Only population transfer can bring peace".[106] He was also a much-honoured guest in Washington where several Congressmen were reported to have been converted to the cause of transfer by his "Elon Peace Initiative".[107]

None of these statements by ministers were deemed illegitimate or examples of incitement in the opinion of the attorney-general, Elyakim Rubinstein. Instead he regarded them as part of healthy "public debate". "For now," he declared, "the issue belongs on trial by the public."[108] And, it seemed, the public was largely convinced by the arguments advanced by its leaders. In a poll of Israeli Jews published in April 2005, 59 per cent agreed that Arab citizens should be "encouraged" to emigrate.[109]

POLICIES SEEK TO CUT NUMBER OF NON-JEWS

Public expressions of support for transfer during the second intifada legitimised the development by the government of uncompromising policies to tackle the "demographic threat". One of the first acts was to reinstitute gross discrimination in child allowances. In June 2002, as part of general austerity measures, child benefit was cut by 4 per cent for all Israeli families but slashed by an extra 20 per cent for parents who had not served in the army.[110] It was a measure targeting Arab families specifically as Arab citizens alone are excluded by law from the national draft.[111] As well as the clear immorality of penalising children based on the perceived faults of their parents – and of penalising parents for behaviour over which they had no say – the cut harmed the country's economically weakest sector. Israeli Arabs were already losing a vast array of state benefits, from tax credits and employment opportunities to mortgage relief and housing grants, because they did not serve in the military, a withholding of welfare assistance the Israeli jurist David Kretzmer has termed "covert discrimination".[112] The loss of child allowance was yet another financial blow to Arab families, who were already five times more likely to be poor than Jewish families. It also flew in the face of statistics showing that 60 per cent of Arab children in Israel were living below the poverty line.[113]

Although it was not admitted at the time, the extra 20 per cent cut was implemented solely to reduce the Arab birth rate, as *Ha'aretz*'s social affairs correspondent Ruth Sinai reported three years later.[114] Senior Finance Ministry officials admitted as much as they tried to persuade the leaders of the main Jewish ultra-Orthodox party, Shas, to support the cut. The ultra-Orthodox were leading a campaign of opposition to the child allowance cut based on fears that it would harm their own community too. The ultra-Orthodox, whose members generally have large families, mostly refuse to serve in the army and are exempted by the state. Eventually in 2003, in the face of concerted opposition from the ultra-Orthodox, the government scrapped the extra cuts. But, as Sinai reported, the ultra-Orthodox had misunderstood the government's plan. They were not going to lose benefits, because Sharon had ensured that ultra-Orthodox couples would receive other benefits to compensate them for the loss of child allowance. The government's decision, wrote Sinai, "is aimed at transferring money to the ultra-Orthodox as an alternative to the child allowances that were trimmed". She called the government's policy "cynical, unethical and racist".[115]

In early 2005 government officials again admitted their true intentions in cutting child allowance, when they claimed credit for figures showing a reduction, even if a tiny one, in Arab women's birth rates in the two years since the universal, 4 per cent cut in child allowance had been imposed. A Finance Ministry spokesman observed triumphantly: "We are reversing the graph, to defend the Jewish majority in the country."[116] Appalled at the media tide of anti-Arab sentiment unleashed by the data, Yitzhak Kadman, the executive director of National Council for the Child, was a lone voice of dissent: "The declaration that Israel's Arab citizens are deliberately multiplying to harm the state is racist. The declaration that reducing the birthrate among the Arabs of Israel is a national goal is racism."[117]

Shortly after the announcement of the child allowance cuts, in September 2002, the government reconvened the defunct Demography Council. Whereas in its previous incarnation the council had kept a relatively low-profile, its re-establishment was greeted with much fanfare. In a speech marking its reopening, social welfare minister Shlomo Benizri referred to "the beauty of the Jewish family that is blessed with many children".[118] The Demography Council's 37 members, including three gynaecologists, were charged with devising ways to increase the birth rate of Jewish women and dissuade them from seeking abortions. Benizri told the council members: "We are the majority in this country and we have the right to preserve our image and the image of the Jewish state, and also to preserve the Jewish people. Every state has the full right to preserve its character."

In addition to its work on raising birth rates, the Demography Council was instructed to examine a new phenomenon: the problem of mixed marriages between Jews and non-Jews.[119] Intermarriage between Arabs and Jews inside Israel was rare, but ministers, including Ariel Sharon, were reported to be alarmed by the demographic implications of another large group of "non-Jews" inside Israel who were showing clear signs of assimilating. Waves of foreign workers, mainly from South-East Asia, Africa and Eastern Europe, had been pouring into the country since the early 1990s to replace Palestinian workers from the occupied territories who were barred from entering Israel by a "closure" policy enforced through checkpoints and roadblocks (severe restrictions on movement that were, in effect, Israel's perverse interpretation of the Oslo process). With more than 150,000 Palestinian workers unable to leave the West Bank and Gaza, Israeli firms desperately needed another cheap labour force. By 2002 the number of foreign workers had reached a high of more than 300,000. The fear of the government and the Demography Council was that if these figures remained unchecked a tide of marriages between Jews and foreign workers might be unleashed. Many of the children of such marriages would not be Jewish according to *halacha* (rabbinical law) and would therefore endanger the Jewishness of the state. The demographic threat from the foreign workers was comparable, in many Israeli Jews' eyes, with the menace posed by high Arab birth rates.

The seriousness with which the government judged the threat of the foreign workers was evident in a rash of policies rushed through in late 2002. In October of that year Sharon announced that no new foreign workers would be allowed into the country. At the same time large numbers of police were recruited to a special force under the direction of a newly created body called the "Immigration Authority".[120] It was set the goal of deporting 50,000 illegal workers in 2003, a target it easily exceeded as the media reported police teams violently arresting and assaulting foreigners found on the streets of Tel Aviv and elsewhere. An overtly racist publicity campaign funded by the government was launched under the name *Avodah Zara* – a Hebrew phrase meaning ambiguously both "Foreign Labour" and "Idol Worship" – warning ordinary Israelis that if foreigners were allowed to remain in Israel they would "marry our women".[121] Good citizens were encouraged to inform on foreigners through a freephone "migrant hotline".[122]

Foreign workers could be deported by the police on a technicality: many, perhaps two-thirds, were illegally in Israel because of a system of "tied labour" that several international and Israeli human rights groups had denounced as a "modern form of slavery".[123] Work permits issued to foreigners were in the name of a single employer, giving him a free hand in dealing with his foreign workforce. When an employer forced down wages, refused to honour holidays or time-off, exploited and physically abused staff, or reneged on promises, foreign workers had little recourse to law. Those who refused to endure their conditions of slavery had only two options: they could leave the country – if their passport had not been confiscated by the employer – and forgo the thousands of dollars they had paid for a permit; or they could disappear into the black market of illegal work, where they would be free to pick and choose their job and their employer but also risk deportation if caught by the Immigration Police.

Within 18 months of the creation of the Immigration Authority, 100,000 foreign workers had been banished from the country. On hearing the news, the government immediately set the police the task of removing another 100,000.[124]

Although Israel named the body responsible for deporting the foreign workers an "Immigration Authority", the name could hardly have been less appropriate. There is no immigration policy in Israel apart from the privileges afforded solely to Jews under the Law of Return.[125] Certainly there is no immigration track open to foreign workers. But in the political climate created in Israel by the second intifada even the limited residency and naturalisation rights afforded to non-Jews were being radically reassessed. The first sign of this was the sudden freezing in May 2002 of family unification procedures allowing married Palestinians and Israeli Arabs to live together in Israel.

ISRAEL CHANGES ITS NATIONALITY LAW

Since the creation of the Jewish state in 1948, the hundreds of thousands of Palestinians expelled from their homes, and millions of their descendants, had been refused the right to return to Israel. Whereas Israeli citizenship was automatically available to any Jew anywhere in the world, it was denied to every Palestinian apart from the small number who remained inside Israel in 1948. There was one exception to this rule, however. A Palestinian from the West Bank or Gaza who married an Arab citizen of Israel could apply for Israeli citizenship using a lengthy and uncertain naturalisation procedure under the Nationality Law. Marriage across the Green Line, between Palestinians living under occupation and Palestinian citizens of Israel, was not an uncommon phenomenon, particularly as several Arab towns and villages in the Little Triangle region in the centre of the country effectively straddled the line that separated Israel from the West Bank.[126]

Until the early 1990s few Palestinians who married an Israeli Arab applied for naturalisation. As couples could move freely between Israel, the West Bank and Gaza, few considered it a priority. But after

Israel began sealing off the occupied territories with regular "closures" in the early 1990s, many couples realised their future together was in jeopardy unless the Palestinian partner applied for Israeli citizenship under the family unification rules. Israel refused most applications from non-Jews for citizenship under the Nationality Law until the practice was challenged in the courts in 1999. In its ruling the Supreme Court stipulated that any Israeli, whether Jew or Arab, should receive equal treatment when applying for the naturalisation of a foreign spouse using the Nationality Law. Jews were mostly unaffected by the ruling because their non-Jewish spouses (at least if they immigrated with them) were entitled to citizenship through the Law of Return.[127] But the court's decision did force the government into a corner: it no longer had grounds for denying applications for naturalisation from Palestinians.

The complex procedure set down in the Nationality Law is that an eligible non-Jewish applicant for citizenship must wait six months before applying for a series of temporary residency permits. At the end of nearly five years, assuming the applicant has passed security and other checks, he or she is entitled to permanent residency, which may be possible to convert into citizenship if the applicant renounces his existing citizenship. The Supreme Court ruling meant that by late 2003 the state would have to begin approving the first cases of Palestinians receiving Israeli citizenship. Profoundly disturbed by this prospect, the government started compiling figures for the number of couples who had been claiming unification during the Oslo period. The Interior Ministry reported 22,400 applications from Palestinian spouses,[128] adding that if the applicants' dependants were included in the statistics, it was possible that more than 100,000 Palestinians were trying to gain citizenship "through the back door".[129] These improbable statistics – an investigation in 2005 by *Ha'aretz* suggested that the true figure was only 5,400 applications, and that the Population Registry had counted repeat applications[130] – had enormous value in shocking the Jewish public and preparing it for a draconian response.

The government's logic was no different from the reasoning of supposed leftwingers like Benny Morris. Cabinet ministers regarded the acquisition of citizenship by Palestinians through marriage to an Israeli Arab as the second of a two-prong demographic assault on the Jewishness of the Israeli state devised by Arafat and the Palestinian Authority. The first prong was the ideology of a "state of all its citizens", which was designed to fatally undermine Israel as a

"Jewish and democratic state" by offering Palestinians on both sides of the Green Line the chance to enter into a battle of wombs with the Jewish population. Given higher Arab birth rates, the Jews were bound to lose such a struggle. Once there were more Palestinians than Jews in the land between the Mediterranean and the River Jordan, then the Jewish state would fall through attrition of numbers.

The second supposed prong of the Palestinians' assault was their response to the evasive action Israel had taken in relation to a "state of all its citizens". Israel had disengaged from Gaza and started building walls across the West Bank, scaling back its greater territorial ambitions, precisely in order to protect its shrinking Jewish majority. The Israeli Arabs, however, could negate the demographic benefits for Israel by recruiting extra foot-soldiers to the battle, by marrying Palestinians in the occupied territories. In the words of the *Jerusalem Post*, family unification was allowing "tens of thousands of Palestinians to quietly exercise what has become a stealth implementation of the 'right of return'".[131]

The interior minister, Eli Yishai, was reported in January 2002 to have asked his officials to examine ways "to reduce the number of Arabs who receive Israeli citizenship by marrying Israeli citizens".[132] One method he was said to favour was imposing yearly quotas on unifications.

But despite the clear demographic fears that lay behind the government's desire to restrict Palestinian naturalisation, no official was allowed to make the connection explicit until Sharon did so himself during his flight to Washington three years later. Instead the government sought a security rationale, and found just such a pretext a short time later – in March 2002 – when a suicide bomber, Shadi Tubasi, detonated his explosive belt in a Haifa restaurant killing 16 people. The bomber, the Israeli media reported, had a blue Israeli ID because of family unification. (In fact, this was not true. Tubasi had been born an Israeli because of his mother's Israeli citizenship, though his father was Palestinian. Unification was not an issue in his case.[133]) The government immediately halted all naturalisation requests from Palestinians, arguing that the freeze was needed to protect the country's security. Exploiting the official line, the justice minister, Gideon Ezra, said: "Since September 2000 we have seen a significant connection, in terror attacks, between Arabs from the West Bank and Gaza and Israeli Arabs."[134]

The Interior Ministry's administrative freeze of May 2002 became a temporary law a year later, in July 2003, when the Knesset passed an amendment to the Nationality Law, effectively banning newly married couples from living together and forcing established couples into a legal limbo where the Palestinian spouse could not upgrade his or her temporary residency. The timing of the legislation was important too: by the end of 2003 the first applications from Palestinians for citizenship would have begun dropping on the interior minister's desk for approval. Orna Kohn, a lawyer representing several affected couples, pointed out that the legislation was designed to make life unbearable even for those thousands of families who were already in the system: without permanent residency or citizenship, Palestinian spouses would have great difficulty getting work inside Israel, opening a bank account, or obtaining National Insurance cover. "What are couples in this position supposed to do?" she asked me. "Maybe the state should prepare special prisons so that they can live together. Or maybe it really wants them to leave the country and live abroad."[135]

The situation remained unchanged for a year and half, until the Supreme Court, which was struggling to contain a flood of petitions from human rights groups, warned the government to legislate the matter properly, hinting that it might intervene if no weight was given to humanitarian concerns about the rights of married couples. In spring 2005, shortly before Sharon made his way to meet President Bush, the cabinet approved another amendment to the Nationality Law. The new law, which passed a vote of the Knesset two months later, prohibited Israeli citizens from bringing into Israel a Palestinian spouse, except under special circumstances. Technically, the interior minister could approve a dispensation in the case of a Palestinian husband aged over 35 or a wife aged over 25.[136] In practice, however, the modification made little real difference: the minister had a free hand to invoke security considerations in rejecting these applications, and, even if a permit was issued, it would be temporary and not entitle the holder to work in Israel or receive welfare benefits or medical care.[137]

To fully appreciate the direction Israeli society was taking, the change to the Nationality Law needed to be seen in its wider context, as part of a trend of "ethnic consolidation" in Israel that showed absolute intolerance towards the non-Jew, whether "Arab" or "foreigner". A report by the influential Association for Civil Rights in Israel (ACRI) in December 2004 accused the Interior Ministry, which oversees the naturalisation process, of "an endemic, systematic and pervasive bias against non-Jews", adding that it was "constantly trampling on their legal rights".[138] According to the report, the ministry was using "organized and methodical bureaucratic harassment" to "wear down" Israelis who wanted to marry non-Jews. Where such marriages could not be prevented, the ministry used coercion, particularly against Jews, to persuade them to divorce a non-Jewish spouse, who then lost all residency rights.

These dubious naturalisation practices were enforced by the Population Registry, a section of the Interior Ministry whose criteria for judging naturalisation cases had never been published and were "shrouded in mist", according to ACRI. Its officials did not provide written explanations of the Registry's decisions, and its decisions – uniquely for a government department – could not be challenged in the courts. The Registry was run for much of the period of the second intifada by a hawkish former brigadier-general, Herzl Gedj, a Likud activist and intimate friend of Sharon. He had earned the contempt of human rights groups after commenting on the death of an arrested foreign worker who hanged himself that the problem of the illegal foreign workers could be solved overnight if the state distributed ropes to them all.[139] He was also vehemently and publicly opposed to allowing Palestinians to marry Israelis, calling it "exercising the right of return through the back door". Gedj was reported to have produced unreliable and inflated figures suggesting the threat posed by both foreign workers and family unification.

AMNON RUBINSTEIN COMES TO THE RESCUE

But as the Population Registry came under the critical eye of ACRI, as well as a series of investigative articles run by the *Ha'aretz* newspaper in early 2005,[140] Israel began to rethink its untidy immigration policy for non-Jews. The government hoped to subsume the discrimination against Palestinians embodied in the Nationality Law and the improvised harassment of foreigners enforced by the Population Registry in a general law to curtail non-Jews' rights in a Jewish state. Israel wanted to put a legal gloss on existing racist practices. In April 2005, as the changes to the Nationality Law were being finalised, the government established an advisory committee of Jewish jurists – no Arab was appointed to the body – to devise the country's first definitive immigration policy. Its task was to impose strict conditions for the naturalisation of non-Jews to ensure "a solid Jewish majority in Israel".[141] Its chairman was the distinguished law professor and Israel's foremost constitutional law expert, Amnon Rubinstein, once considered of the left but like Benny Morris now almost indistinguishable from the cheerleaders of the hawkish right.

For some time Rubinstein had been working on behalf of the National Security Council, helping fight, in the words of the Council's director, Giora Eiland, "the demographic demon".[142] Rubinstein was a high-profile advocate of the amendment to the Nationality Law, and a behind-the-scenes adviser on it, as well as a vigorous supporter of Sharon's disengagement from Gaza. In one of his typical columns in the Israeli media, he justified the draconian amendment to the Nationality Law by claiming that a decision to allow Palestinians any right to acquire citizenship, to immigrate, would set a legal precedent and open the floodgates to the return of Palestinian refugees to Israel: "Not only does Israel not need to, but it must not, acknowledge a right of immigration to Israel. The very fact of raising such a demand means accepting the right of return." In similar vein, Rubinstein argued that even residency rights must be denied Palestinians to protect the Jewish majority: "Even if a distinction is made between 'residency' and 'citizenship' it is clear that descendants of [Palestinian] 'residents' will have the right to naturalisation. Losing the Jewish majority will be postponed at most by one generation."[143]

Rubinstein had spent much time studying foreign immigration laws, cherry-picking the severest restrictions he could find on each country's statute books and then suggesting that Israel would be justified in imposing similar measures. Rubinstein's guiding principle, he wrote, was that inside Israel there should be equality between Jews and Arabs but that "the key for entering the Israeli home is held by the Jews".[144] He and others working for the Security Council had discovered starkly discriminatory components to new immigration rules introduced by Denmark and the Netherlands. Both countries had recently adopted legislation requiring that potential immigrants demonstrate a deep connection to their new homeland before acquiring citizenship rights. It was widely assumed that Denmark and the Netherlands were intending to use these laws as a way to restrict Muslim applicants' rights to citizenship through marriage to a Danish or Dutch spouse.

Rubinstein promoted these laws on the basis that what was good enough for Europe was good enough for Israel. But a leading Israeli Arab lawyer, Hassan Jabareen of Adalah, pointed out that the harsher of the two laws, Denmark's, was still far less discriminatory than Israel's immigration laws – a combination of the new Nationality Law and the Law of Return. The Danish law did not include immigration tracks that discriminated on the basis of ethnicity – the criteria applied equally to all immigrants – and it included a right of judicial appeal. In any case, Jabareen added, the Danish law had not been subjected to review by the country's courts and was almost certain to be ruled unconstitutional. "The relevant question," wrote Jabareen, "is whether [Israeli] supporters of the law are willing to adopt the entire citizenship and immigration policy of Denmark. Their reply will certainly be negative, since they oppose turning Israel into a civil state with modern democratic policies."[145] Unlike Denmark, argued Jabareen, Israel already had at the core of its legislative framework the discriminatory Law of Return, a pseudo-immigration policy that offered privileges solely to Jews. The change to the Nationality Law and other reforms being considered by Rubinstein were designed to add yet another racist layer of legislation to a legal foundation that was already grossly discriminatory.

In Jabareen's opinion, Israel's amended Nationality Law – the application of which Rubinstein and the government wanted to extend to all non-Jews seeking to live in Israel – had no existing parallels since the abolition of apartheid in South Africa and the overturning of miscegenation laws in the southern states of America in the 1950s. Israel's law, according to Jabareen, was the beginning of a slide from discriminatory legislation into overtly racist legislation: whereas the Law of Return gave privileges to one group, Jews, based on their ethnicity, the new law denied basic freedoms to another group, Arabs, based on their ethnicity. "The amendment to the law reflects a transition from a situation of invalid discrimination to a situation of racist oppression," he wrote.

Jabareen's assessment was shared by Yoav Peled, a professor of political science at Tel Aviv University, who claimed Israel was reaching "a very dangerous turning point" where it could no longer be characterised as a democracy, even in the most formal sense.[146]

In pursuing disengagement and the changes to the Nationality Law, argued Peled, Sharon's cabinet had committed itself to the one surviving legacy of the failed Oslo process: the principle of the separation of Jews and Palestinians into two nations, if very unequal ones. "The logic of the Oslo process was a demographic logic. Israeli proponents of Oslo justified it to themselves with a demographic argument: 'You are over there; we are here'." The future Palestinian state promised by Oslo was meant to end not only the conflict with the Palestinians living in the occupied territories but *all* Palestinians, even those whose rights would be entirely ignored by the establishment of such a state and who would not benefit from it. Neither the Palestinian refugees living in squalid refugee camps across the Middle East nor Israel's Palestinian citizens had been included in the Oslo negotiations, and their status would continue to be unresolved by a Palestinian state created under the terms of the Oslo agreement. Israel's Palestinian citizens in particular would find themselves in an invidious new position: they would remain as second-class Israeli citizens without any room or possibility for improvement. If they complained, if they dissented, if they demanded their rights, Israel could simply wash its hands of them, telling them to seek their rights in the Palestinian state. "Their case was closed by Oslo, a decision to which the PLO was a party," said Peled.

As we have seen, Palestinian citizens responded to their new Oslo predicament by developing the ideology of "a state of all its citizens", an argument for full inclusion in the Israeli polity, which they believed was to separate imminently from the Palestinians in the occupied territories. But rather than winning approval from Israeli Jews, the campaign for a "state of all its citizens" simply antagonised the Jewish public and leadership yet further, inflaming the demographic fears that led to the changes in the Nationality Law. According to Peled, this new law marked a watershed. Whereas Israel had previously sought to disguise the discriminatory content of its laws, it was now making the discrimination explicit.

> Once a state says, "I admit I am discriminating because of ethnic difference", it changes. It is not the same state as it was before. It passes a threshold ... Now the road is open to all kinds of things, including 'silent transfer' – the manipulation of borders to deny citizens their rights.

Peled pointed out that the humanitarian language used by proponents of the "transfer of citizenship" policy, the moving of entire Israeli Arab communities such as Umm al-Fahm into the orbit of the Palestinian Authority, was dishonest and misleading. "Palestinian citizens who are transferred will not be transferred to another state – a Palestinian state where they can realise their rights – because there will be no other state. Their citizenship will not be transferred; it will be revoked."

In other words, the transfer debate is not about relocating Palestinian citizens' rights to another state but about irrevocably downgrading their status from citizens to non-citizens. Their rights will be moved to a pseudo-state, a stunted phantom state, which the world may call Palestine but which in reality will be under Israeli rule and tailor-made to suit Israeli needs. The Jewish state will continue to determine the fate of its former Palestinian citizens but without having to accommodate their demands for civil rights and political recognition. Like the disengagement, a transfer of citizenship will achieve the removal of the Palestinian presence from Israel, not so that Palestinians can exercise their rights in their own sovereign space but so that they are stripped of their voice entirely.

"Eventually we will have two separate and exclusive groups: Jewish citizens and Palestinian residents," says Peled. "Palestinian citizens will move from being Israelis with rights to residents of the occupied territories – and residents of the occupied territories have no rights at all."

4
Redrawing the Green Line

Let us approach [the Palestinian refugees in the occupied territories] and say that we have no solution, that you shall continue to live like dogs, and whoever wants to can leave – and we will see where this process leads. In five years we may have 200,000 less people – and that is a matter of enormous importance.

Moshe Dayan (1967)[1]

The real question that I have asked myself every day for the past ten years is what will happen when an Arab majority exists west of the Jordan River; what will happen when the number of Arabs who are citizens of Israel and the number of Arabs who are under Israeli rule exceeds the number of Jews, because that moment is not far off ... Because if that day comes and we don't have a border, if on that day there is no Palestinian state on the other side of a border, all hell will break loose here. I don't even want to think about what will happen in that case. It will be the end of the Zionist idea. So what I am saying is that a Palestinian state is the life-belt of the Jewish state.

Yossi Beilin (2001)[2]

[Israeli Arabs] have identification cards like us, the same license plates, and they can't be stopped on the roadsides. The answer to these problems is to bring more Jews to Israel.

Ariel Sharon (2005)[3]

In Hebrew, his name – Sofer – means "he who counts". And that is precisely what Professor Arnon Sofer does for a living: he counts Jews and Arabs. "My laboratory is the Galilee," he tells me, referring to Israel's Arab heartland, home to nearly 600,000 Palestinian citizens, which Israel has been struggling to "Judaise" – literally to make Jewish – for five decades. As head of geopolitics at Haifa University, Sofer charts the pattern of Arab life inside Israel and the occupied territories, recording where Palestinians live, how fast their families grow, and when and why they die; then he compares the statistics with those for Jews. He studies the data in minute detail, producing analyses and surveys on which Israeli governments base their short-term policies and long-term strategies. "I advise on demography and sociology and defence," he says. "We have to understand who are the Bedouin, and who are the Gazans compared with the people of the West Bank. Did you know they are two different populations? The Gazans came from Egypt – really they are Egyptians – while in the West Bank they are Jews who converted to Islam centuries ago. Arabs in the West Bank and Gaza have different stories, different noses, different blood."

Sofer demonstrates a discomforting habit of pouring forth fact and opinion in equal measure, in a cascade of verbiage that offers few chances to interrupt. Only after I had left his office did I have time to ponder how recent developments in the science of genetics appeared to have passed him by. Or, for that matter, how he could believe Palestinians from Gaza and the West Bank have "different blood" when hundreds of thousands of Gazans, like many West Bank Palestinians, are refugees from what is now Israel. They were forced to flee during the 1948 war from the same clusters of towns and villages that the new state of Israel razed after its military victory.

The professor may sound eccentric, but he is no maverick. One of the two founders of the National Security Studies Center, a leading research body at Haifa University, Sofer is hardwired into the country's security and defence establishments. He is an influential adviser on demographics to Israel's key decision-making bodies, from the Prime Minister's Office and the National Security Council to the Knesset Foreign Affairs Committee and the Jewish Agency. As an expert on urban warfare he has been responsible for educating a generation of senior security officials at the National Defence College and the Police Training College. "I have been teaching the army for 32 years. I can say nearly 100 per cent of army commanders were once my students." Likewise, said Sofer, he had the ear of the country's political leaders, including Ehud Barak, Binyamin Netanyahu and Ariel Sharon.

Our meeting took place in November 2001, before the building of the West Bank wall, at the height both of Israeli fears about Palestinian suicide attacks and of the public's demand for physical separation from the Palestinians. Sofer was in apocalyptic mood. "In my opinion in the next 15 years either we will see Israel surviving or we will see the end of the Zionist dream. We have 15 years and no more. We are counting down towards the end of Israel." There was only one option if the Jewish state was to be saved, said Sofer, and that was partitioning the land. "We can no longer think about Greater Israel; we have to think about divisions." The reason, he said, was that the Palestinians, particularly in Gaza, were breeding faster than Jews.

> It is impossible to talk about peace when in a few years there will be some 6.5 million Jews living among more than 10 million Arabs. Or when very soon we will have 2.5 million very poor people living in Gaza, in a prison. It is going to be terrible. Soon everyone will hear about Gaza ... The West talks endlessly about peace but I say no – peace, it's impossible.

He pointed to a series of large maps displayed on one wall. "The first is the Oslo map," he said dismissively.

> The other two are more interesting. One is an Arab map that has no borders; it shows an Arab state from the desert to the sea. The other is from the late 1950s and is the only official Israeli map showing the Green Line. Later, after the Six-Day War, Golda Meir banned the Green Line from being marked on all maps. But for me the Green Line is the most important thing. If I can separate from the Arabs completely, that would be wonderful.

Sofer wanted to reverse the all-or-nothing thinking he attributed to both Israelis and Palestinians. His large hands, moving back and forth across the map nearest to him, carved imaginary lines on paper he wished could be made concrete. As he severed the Negev from both Gaza and the West Bank, he made a succession of rapid demographic calculations:

> My philosophy is to settle more Jews to defend Israel, to separate the Bedouin in the northern Negev from the West Bank, and to separate Jerusalem. We need more Jews in the Galilee to separate it from the West Bank, and Jews along the length of the Jordan Valley [on the eastern flank of the West Bank].

Uncharacteristically, he faltered briefly before admitting it was not entirely clear to him what should be done with the Jordan Valley.

> On the one hand, it is better to keep Jews [settlers] there to stop the emergence of a big Palestinian state, but on the other hand I am in favour of seeing whether we can encourage the Palestinians to move eastwards beyond the Jordan River [into Jordan]. Maybe Jordan can be a magnet like it was in the 1950s and 1960s. But at the same time I have to isolate the West Bank from the rest of the Arab world to prevent attacks by rockets and missiles.

Inside Israel swift action was needed too, he said. "We have the Israeli Arabs in the Triangle and the Galilee. What to do about them? The identification between the Palestinians in the West Bank and the

Israeli Arabs only complicates the picture, makes it harder to find a solution." Pressed on what options were available, Sofer continued: "I'm ready to get rid of Wadi Ara and Taibe – no problem," referring to the Triangle area, home to nearly a quarter of a million Palestinian citizens.

> We can change our borders to lose the Triangle but we cannot give up the Galilee. We cannot make compromises there on territory. The important thing is that the Muslims must be isolated. Then we can make the problem manageable. We will be left with half a million Muslims. With the Muslims, we must use a carrot and stick.

But what if Arab citizens refused to accept the terms on offer? Would he consider expelling them from the state? "That depends on the Israeli Arabs. I'm prepared to live with you, give you equal rights, but if you don't like it and want to bring things to a confrontation then please be ready to face any possibility."

Like his problem choosing a fate for the Jordan Valley, Sofer was troubled by the Galilee, Israel's hilly northern expanse dominated by its indigenous Arab population. "We cannot make compromises there", he insisted, dismissing any suggestion of a land swap with the Palestinians. But a little later he observed: "Demography is much more important than territory." Israel had been struggling, and failing, for more than five decades to establish a Jewish majority in the Galilee. On his logic, why not give up the Galilee as well as the Triangle? Because, although Sofer did not want the Arab citizens of the Galilee included in his state, he also knew that Israel desperately needed the territorial advantages conferred by the Galilee: the sheer size of its area, its expansive, fertile valleys, and the large buffer it offered against neighbouring Lebanon. For the time being Sofer and Israeli Jews would have to live, even if grudgingly, with the Arabs of the Galilee.

I asked Sofer where he saw himself on the political spectrum. "There is no right and left at the moment. It is Jews versus Arabs. The wide centre is behind the idea of separation. When it comes to separation, I think only of the Jewish side. I don't care about the Palestinians any more." And by Palestinians, he appeared to be including Arab citizens.

The problem with creating an ethnic partition of the clarity demanded by Sofer was that Israel had been making every effort imaginable to forestall a territorial division since its victory in the

Six-Day War of 1967. In violation of international law, Israel had encouraged ever larger numbers of Jews to settle in the West Bank and Gaza to the point where by the 1990s the two groups – Palestinians and Israeli Jews – were entwined in a network of neighbouring, if separate, communities. It was difficult to see how these two populations could be separated without the evacuation of the settlers, the expulsion of Palestinians, or a dramatic redrawing of the Green Line.

THE GOAL OF GREATER ISRAEL

Jewish settlement of the Palestinian territories of East Jerusalem, the West Bank and Gaza – the last remaining areas of what had once been Mandatory Palestine – began in the immediate aftermath of the 1967 war. Religious Jews in particular coveted the West Bank, which they referred to by the Biblical names of Judea and Samaria, and East Jerusalem as the fulfilment of Greater Israel.[4] They did not see the occupation of the Palestinian territories as the final stage of the Palestinian people's dispossession; it was the completion of "Eretz Israel", the realisation of a Biblical birthright to the whole of the Promised Land. For a significant minority of Israelis, the victory on the battlefield in 1967 was nothing less than a miracle from God, a divine signal that Israeli settlement of the land was bringing the Redemption closer.

The wave of Messianism unleashed by the territorial triumphs of 1967 (which also included the capture of the Sinai from Egypt and the Golan Heights from Syria) rode a more general mood of religious nationalism that swept up even secular Israelis. The defence minister of the time, Moshe Dayan, was probably not being entirely cynical when he visited the Western Wall in the Old City of Jerusalem on the day of its conquest to declare: "We have united Jerusalem, the divided capital of Israel. We have returned to the holiest of our Holy Places, never to part from it."[5]

The settler movement quickly came to regard all Palestinian land occupied in 1967 as a holy place for Jews and parting from even one inch of it as inconceivable. As Rabbi Zvi Yehuda Kook, the spiritual leader of the religious settlers, observed shortly before the 1967 war: "Where is our Hebron? Do we forget this? And where is our Shechem [Nablus]? Do we forget this? And where is our Jericho? Do we forget this too? And where is the other side of the Jordan? ... Is it in our hands to relinquish any millimetre of this?"[6]

If few in the government shared the settlers' zeal, the politicians and generals mostly approved of the facts on the ground they were creating. The settlement enterprise neatly circumvented international law forbidding the transfer of civilians into occupied territory; it looked spontaneous and unplanned. The success of Jewish settlement of East Jerusalem emboldened Israel officially to annex the Palestinian half of the city in 1980, and to extend its land grab by expanding Jerusalem's municipal boundaries much deeper into the West Bank. In Gaza and the rest of the West Bank, meanwhile, the growing network of settlements offered Israel a pretext to rezone extensive swaths of Palestinian land on the grounds that it was needed to protect the settlers from attack. Wherever Jewish settlements sprung up, the land on which they stood and the surrounding area were declared "closed military zones" or "state land", using nineteenth-century laws dating from Ottoman rule. Bypass roads to connect the settlements to Israel and each other ate up yet more scarce land in the occupied territories.

The complicity of the state in the settlement drive was clear from the outset. In 1971 Prime Minister Golda Meir told a group of new immigrants to Israel: "The borders are determined by where Jews live, not where there is a line on a map."[7] At the same time, as Prof. Sofer had observed, she underscored the point by ordering Israel's cartographers to erase the Green Line from all maps they produced. In Israeli officialese, the Green Line was renamed the "seam zone" to avoid any reference to borders.[8] Few Israeli Jews regarded the captured Palestinian territories of the West Bank and Gaza as occupied, nor did they see them as bargaining chips that one day would have to be traded for peace. As Golda Meir pointed out in another of her famous maxims, there was no such thing as a Palestinian people. "How is it possible to return the territories? After all, there's no one to return them to," she declared.[9]

In other words, the still-dominant image of the settlers as rogue fanatics squatting in caravans on West Bank hilltops was never true. The settlers were encouraged and directed from their earliest days by Israel's political and military establishment. Governments of both the right and left offered ideological, territorial, financial and military help to the settlements. While many of the settlers believed they were on a mission from God, as far as the state was concerned they were useful pawns in a battle to convert occupied Palestinian land into a future Greater Israel. Although some sites were developed to satisfy religious claims, such as at Hebron, Shilo and Beit El, most of the settlement locations were determined by the leadership's understanding of the country's security needs: fortified towns such as Ariel and Ma'ale Adumim, which became home to tens of thousands of Jews, were built to separate Palestinian cities in the West Bank one from the next, carving up the territory into a series of ghettos.

DECEPTIONS OF THE OSLO PEACE PROCESS

The truth about the Israeli government's covert role in the settlement enterprise was most starkly illustrated during the Oslo period, when Israel was supposedly immersed in a peace process whose motor was the principle of land for peace and whose intended outcome was territorial separation. But while the Israeli left was talking about ending the occupation and Palestinian statehood, the facts on the ground told a very different story. In 1993 there were some 100,000 Jewish settlers in the West Bank; by the demise of Oslo in 2000 there were more than 191,000 – a near-doubling of the population in just seven years. A similar pattern was observable in East Jerusalem. While Israel's general population grew during that period by about 2 per cent a year – including the enormous boost provided by the arrival of hundreds of thousands of immigrants from the former Soviet Union – the population in the settlements was expanding six times faster, by 12 per cent a year.[10] The reason was not difficult to identify. As well as the religious zealots who wanted to live close by Jewish holy places were a larger number of economic migrants encouraged into the settlements by huge discounts on land and housing, tax credits, mortgage breaks, and massively subsidised municipal services. Even though most of the funding of the settlements was hidden deep in ministry budgets, surveys by Israeli human rights groups suggested the settlers cost the government an additional $500 million to $1 billion a year.[11] If military expenditure was included, the figure was even higher.

The dramatic growth of the settlements during the Oslo period offers an insight into what Israel really hoped the "peace process" would achieve. Initiated by dovish elements in the country's Labor party, including Shimon Peres, who himself had been deeply implicated in the operation of the settlements, Oslo was designed to begin a process of separating the two populations, Israelis and Palestinians. It created autonomous Palestinian areas, initially most of the Gaza Strip and the small West Bank city of Jericho, under the control of the newly established Palestinian Authority, the Palestinians' first-ever government. In return for Palestinian recognition of the Jewish state, Israel was supposed to make further unspecified troop withdrawals over a five-year period. At the end, Israel and the Palestinians would negotiate a final-status agreement on the most contentious issues: security, Jerusalem, borders, refugees and the settlements. The popular perception was that at the end of the process there would be an Israeli state with a smaller Palestinian state alongside it.

However, given its behaviour during the Oslo period, it is difficult to believe Israel really intended to create a Palestinian state in anything but name. Certainly this was Rabin's view of Oslo. He told the Knesset in his last address in 1995 before his assassination: "We would like this to be an entity which is less than a state, and which will independently run the lives of the Palestinians under its authority."[12]

Although it was rarely mentioned, the logic of Oslo – a gradual separation between the two peoples so that Israel could end its responsibility for most of the Palestinian population in the occupied territories – was largely driven by Israel's age-old demographic fears. Those considerations had grown more pressing with the relentless surge in the number of Palestinians in the occupied territories. In signing up to Oslo, Israel was pursuing a policy inspired by the familiar Zionist axiom: "The maximum amount of land with the minimum number of Arabs". Israel's leaders were not interested in justice for the Palestinians or in Palestinian statehood; they wanted only to absolve their Jewish state of demographic responsibility for the Palestinians. If that required creating an entity that others would call a state, then that was a sacrifice Israel's leaders were prepared to make.

Dennis Ross, President Bill Clinton's Middle East envoy during the Oslo period, understood this very well, it appears. In 2004 Ross told the *New York Times* columnist Thomas Friedman that in signing up to Oslo in 1993 the Israeli Prime Minister of the day, Yitzhak Rabin, had been trying to pre-empt the Palestinian demographic threat to the Jewish state.[13] So grave was his perception of this threat, said Ross, that two years later Rabin began contemplating building a wall to keep Palestinians out of Israel should the Oslo process fail to maintain Israel's demographic strength.

> [Rabin] said, 'We're going to have to partition – there's going to have to be a partition here, because we won't be Jewish and democratic if we don't have a partition.' Now, his preference was to negotiate the partition peacefully

> to produce two states. But if that didn't work he wanted, as you put it, a separation fence or barrier to create what would be two states, or at least to preserve Israel as a state.[14]

The same demographic principle was espoused by Yossi Beilin, one of the architects of Oslo and a chief negotiator at the Camp David talks, in his later assessment of the period:

> I definitely did not agree, and will not agree, to a permanent settlement that will ultimately worsen the demographic balance inside sovereign Israel. That is my sharpest red line. On that issue I am absolutely tough. I am generous geographically but tough demographically. A Jewish majority within the sovereign [borders of the] state of Israel is the main thing as far as I am concerned. For me it is the most important thing.[15]

How Israel interpreted the principle of separation embodied in Oslo has been carefully documented by the Israeli journalist Amira Hass. She notes that even before the signing of the Declaration of Principles, the legal foundation of the Oslo process, Israel had begun enforcing policies to restrict the movement of more than 150,000 Palestinian labourers into Israel. A "general exit permit" that had given Palestinians relatively unrestricted access to Israel for nearly two decades was cancelled in 1991 – on the eve of the Gulf War, and well before the first suicide bombings – and replaced with a system of individual passes granted only to those favoured by Israel. In his 1992 election campaign, Rabin exploited the Jewish public's antipathy towards the Palestinian labourers who were still a common sight, coining the slogan: "Get Gaza out of Tel Aviv".[16] By 1994, when Yasser Arafat and his Tunis exiles returned to the occupied territories, Israel had transformed the pass system into a key method of controlling the movement of the Palestinian population. "The pass system turned a universal basic right into a coveted privilege ... Some passes permitted an overnight stay in Israel, others required return by dusk, a few were for an entire month," wrote Hass.[17] Faced with an ever-expanding network of checkpoints, roadblocks and bypass roads supposedly built to protect Israel and the settlements – a physical infrastructure that could be used to enforce what Israelis called "closures" of the occupied territories – Palestinians found movement into Israel and inside the occupied territories ever more difficult. Those who managed to enter Israel without a pass were classified as "infiltrators".

The separation, of course, did not work in reverse. Jewish settlers, along with the Israeli army, continued entering the occupied territories freely and in ever bigger numbers. As we have seen, Israeli contractors laboured relentlessly on expanding the settlements during the Oslo years. Separation worked in one direction only: to exclude the Palestinians. When Ehud Barak stood for election as prime minister in 1999, as international pressure for progress on pushing ahead with the Oslo agreements built, he pledged to continue Rabin's legacy and campaigned under the slogan "We are here and they are there".[18] A more honest platform would have declared: "They are there, and we are here and there". In his first full year as prime minister, as he prepared for negotiations over Palestinian statehood at Camp David, Barak approved the construction of 4,800 new settler homes.[19]

Earlier, in 1993, following the signing of the Declaration of Principles at the White House, both Barak, then the military's chief of staff, and Sharon, a leading figure in the opposition Likud party, had expressed their opposition to the Oslo process – a fact that in Barak's case was largely forgotten once he was elected as prime minister.[20] Both believed that installing Yasser Arafat next to Israel was a strategic error of the gravest magnitude. They worried that the prestige conferred on him by leading the Palestinian Authority, and the platform it gave him to walk the world stage, posed a threat to the Jewish state's "security" in the long term: one day the international community might press for real, as opposed to illusory, separation. As we have seen, they also feared that Arafat's presence so close to Israel would encourage him to try to turn Israel's Palestinian citizens into an enemy within. Sharon, who famously called on the settlers to "grab hilltops" to prevent the return of land to the Palestinians, denounced Rabin as an "Oslo criminal" shortly before the prime minister was shot dead by a religious extremist in November 1995. But the Oslo process moved inexorably on, even during the hostile premiership of Binyamin Netanyahu.

BARAK'S TWO-STATE MAP AT CAMP DAVID

There are reasonable grounds for suspecting that Barak was as keen as Sharon to unravel the advances made by the Palestinian Authority during the Oslo period by insisting on unpalatable terms for a final-status agreement. Either Arafat would be compelled to reject the deal and thus be unmasked, or accept it and consign his state to terminal dependency on Israel. Dan Schueftan, a government adviser and an early proponent of separation, observed that Barak's terms at Camp David were designed to "call the Palestinians' bluff", as he phrased it.[21] Off the record, an Israeli negotiator at Camp David told one of the main documenters of the talks, Clayton E Swisher: "In Barak's view, Arafat was a wolf dressed as a sheep: only if you challenge him to end the conflict will you expose [the fact that] he is not willing to end the conflict."[22]

Certainly, as we have seen in Chapter 1, Barak made control of the holy places in Jerusalem a sticking point that persuaded one of his key advisers, Dr Moshe Amirav, he was using it to "blow up" the negotiations. Oded Eran, Israel's former ambassador to Jordan and one of the negotiators in the build-up to Camp David, says Barak's early maps offered the Palestinians the West Bank divided into three sectors. The Palestinians would receive 66 per cent of the land, with 20 per cent annexed to Israel and another 14 per cent under Israeli control for the foreseeable future.[23] Such a map is confirmed by Shlomo Ben Ami, Barak's foreign minister and a chief negotiator at Camp David. He observed:

> [Barak] was proud of the fact that his map would leave Israel with about a third of the territory ... Ehud was convinced that the map was extremely logical. He had a kind of patronizing, wishful-thinking, naive approach, telling me enthusiastically, "Look, this is a state; to all intents and purposes it looks like a state."[24]

At his most "generous" at Camp David, Barak may have offered the Palestinians as much as 88 per cent of the West Bank, though nothing was set down in writing. But whatever Barak's intentions, the result of the Camp David failure was the destruction of the peace process and a new round of blood-letting. The demise of Oslo did not, however, mark the end of the problems it had been designed to solve. Quite the opposite. Demographic concerns, as we have seen in the previous chapter, grew substantially after the eruption of the second intifada. In the Israeli peace camp such fears were compounded both by concerns that the Palestinians had spurned the "generous offers" of a Labor prime minister, thereby proving that there was "no partner for peace", and by the assumption that the country's Arab citizens were a second front of the intifada. The Israeli left's response was to search for a different route to separation.

"Why do I believe that Israel, in spite of the risks involved and prices to be paid, should nevertheless evacuate settlements and withdraw?"

asked Uri Dromi, Yitzhak Rabin's former spokesman and one of the heads of the Israel Democracy Institute, in May 2002. "Because of sheer numbers. We simply don't have enough Jews in the Land of Israel to keep all of it to ourselves."[25] The disenchantment of Dromi and others on the left was reflected in the urge to separate: not, as in Oslo, through negotiations and staged withdrawals but decisively and without consideration of Palestinian wishes. Thus emerged the idea of unilateralism.

It is important to note that unilateral separation was a policy born of the traditional Israeli left, particularly of the Labor party, not of the right.[26] The political father of the new unilateralism – the desire to separate and build walls around the occupied territories – was probably, as we have noted, Yitzhak Rabin. But if not Rabin, then it was certainly Ehud Barak. Disengagement from the Palestinians was something he was considering even before he began the final-status negotiations with Yasser Arafat at Camp David in the summer of 2000. Uzi Dayan, the army's deputy chief of staff, says he persuaded Barak of the need for unilateral disengagement as "a safety net to Camp David". "I said, 'OK, if we can't achieve such an agreement, let's go and do what is good for Israel and the whole region, and let's disengage from the Palestinians even if we don't have a partner.'"[27] This account is confirmed by Barak's deputy defence minister, Ephraim Sneh, who was asked to prepare with Dayan a plan for unilateral separation in case the talks failed. "I drew the map. I can speak about it authoritatively," Sneh later said. "The plan means the de facto annexation of 30 percent of the West Bank, half in the Jordan Valley, which you have to keep if there is no agreement, and half in the settlement blocs."[28]

It seems Barak was intending either to negotiate with the Palestinians over the map he had shown Ben Ami just before Camp David or impose it by force if it was rejected.

Barak had already proven his practical commitment to unilateralism. A few weeks before the talks, in May 2000, he had pulled soldiers out of Israel's "security zone" in occupied South Lebanon without negotiating an agreement with the Lebanese government or Hizbullah, the Shi'ite militia that is Israel's main military foe in South Lebanon. It was not therefore surprising that Barak was talking about "unilateral disengagement" long before the phrase first fell from Sharon's lips. "What Israel ought to do now is take steps to ensure the long-term viability of its Jewish majority," wrote Barak in May 2001, shortly after he was ousted from power.

"That requires a strategy of disengagement from the Palestinians – even unilaterally if necessary – and a gradual process of establishing secure, defensible borders."[29]

A UNILATERAL BORDER FOR THE JEWISH STATE

In the summer of 2002, A B Yehoshua, an Israeli novelist and high-profile member of the peace camp, wrote that Jewish identity in the Diaspora inherently lacked borders: "It wanders around the world, a traveller between hotels. A Jew can change countries and languages without losing his Jewishness." By contrast, he argued, the Jewish state needed territorial limits, it had to define the extent of the sanctuary it provided to Jews. "Borders are like doors in a house which claim everything inside as the responsibility of the master. That is what Zionism means: realising Jewish sovereignty within defined borders."[30] For more than 30 years, however, Zionism had meant exactly the opposite: it had flourished in a space without borders. The "master of the house", to continue Yehoshua's metaphor, had built ever larger extensions of his home on the land of his neighbours. Now, after decades of building without planning permission, Yehoshua appeared to be arguing, the homeowner demanded the right permanently to lock the doors of the house and evict his neighbours as trespassers. That, in short, was the new sensibility of the left.

If negotiations with the Palestinians had failed at Camp David, the conclusion of the "peace camp" was that Israel must find a border fast, fortify it and disengage from all responsibility for the Palestinians. "The absence of a partner should not paralyze Israel from taking defensive steps in order to protect its own vital interests, which will determine its identity and future," argued Barak. "We should say yes to two states for two nations, where Israel is recognized as a Jewish, Zionist democratic state."[31] Such an idea was far easier for the left to contemplate than the right, not least because the establishment of clear borders would necessitate the dismantling of at least some of the settlements. Most in the ruling Likud party, as well as in the small religious parties Sharon had brought into his coalition to keep it in power, drew a thick red line at the loss of settlements. But the left took a more pragmatic view: remoter settlements should be sacrificed to protect the Jewish state, both from Palestinian attacks and from the demographic time bomb of Palestinian birth rates.

Few on the left, however, were talking about a withdrawal to the 1967 Green Line. Shortly before his assassination, Rabin himself had warned that the Oslo accords were not intended to return Israel to the "1967 lines". Recalling Rabin's last address to the Knesset in 1995, Dore Gold, a former Israeli ambassador to the United Nations and an adviser to Sharon, wrote: "[Rabin] insisted on a map including a united Jerusalem, the settlement blocs and the Jordan Valley."[32] Barak echoed the sentiment: "We should say yes to secure and recognized borders for Israel but no to the 1967 lines."[33] Shlomo Avineri, a professor of political science at Hebrew University and a former director-general of the Foreign Ministry, expressed the consensual view of the centre-left: "Not a return to 1967 lines – this is impossible in Jerusalem; nor should most of the settlements be dismantled – but some of the isolated ones have no justification whatsoever, and a coherent line should be drawn."[34]

So what border was the left thinking of disengaging to? In June 2002 Barak gave an approximate idea, one that echoed Sneh's comments about his intentions shortly before Camp David:

> The disengagement would be implemented gradually over several years. The fence should include the seven big settlement blocs that spread over 12 or 13 percent of the area and contain 80 percent of the settlers. Israel will also need a security zone along the Jordan River and some early warning sites, which combined will cover another 12 percent, adding up to 25 percent of the West Bank.

In addition, there was the problem of East Jerusalem, where Jewish settlements had been implanted tightly in and around the Palestinian population. Barak continued:

> In Jerusalem, there would have to be two physical fences. The first would delineate the political boundary and be placed around the Greater City, including the settlement blocs adjacent to Jerusalem. The second would be a security-dictated barrier, with controlled gates and passes, to separate most of the Palestinian neighborhoods from the Jewish neighborhoods and the Holy Basin, including the Old City.[35]

In other words, Barak was talking about leaving the Palestinians with control over some 70 per cent of the West Bank and Gaza, territories that were only 22 per cent of their original homeland.

The problem in this new thinking was obvious to many, including on the right. The left was no longer talking about peace, or even about ending the occupation, but about pure containment of the

Palestinians, without regard to their wishes or to the consequences of such actions. Shlomo Gazit, a former head of Military Intelligence, observed that the left had "no doubt the Palestinian side will object to the separation line; they have no doubt the Israeli withdrawal will fail to put an end to the Palestinian violence; and they have no doubt that sooner or later renewed talks and negotiations will be needed as well as an additional Israeli withdrawal to a line agreed upon by both sides".[36]

The first sign that Barak's idea of unilateral separation was gaining ground came in the summer of 2002, when Sharon's government announced it was building a series of walls and fences around the West Bank. At the time, it was assumed that the plan had been foisted on Sharon as the price to be paid to keep the Labor party, then led by Binyamin Ben Eliezer, inside the national unity government.[37] Ben Eliezer had been persuaded by other leading members of his party who supported the idea of unilateral separation that it could be a useful way to revive his party's flagging fortunes. Sharon, it was thought, did not have the political courage to oppose the construction of a wall when polls showed that as much as 80 per cent of the Israeli public supported a physical barrier to stop Palestinian attacks.[38]

The prime minister was notably absent from a photo-call staged by Ben Eliezer in Salem, a village close by Jenin in the northern West Bank, where the first sods were cut in the construction of the barrier. Sharon's distaste for the fence-cum-wall was also inferred from his comments at the cabinet meeting immediately following Ben Eliezer's visit to Salem. Countering suggestions that the barrier would create the future borders of a Palestinian state, he declared: "The conditions are not ripe for the establishment of any kind of Palestinian state."[39] In response Ben Eliezer repeatedly tried to calm his fellow ministers, claiming that "under absolutely no circumstances" would the fence demarcate a border. "This is a wall, the aim of which is to stop entry. It is quite simply ... a barrier wall. There's nothing else. It is not a border."[40]

It is unclear what Sharon's real view of the barrier was at that stage. He may have been feigning opposition – a tactic he had used often before in his military and political careers to confuse his enemies – or he may have genuinely opposed the idea. Certainly, progress on the early sections of the barrier was slow, prompting claims that Sharon was trying to sabotage the plan. Uzi Dayan, one of the architects of the wall, claimed Sharon and his defence minister, Shaul Mofaz, were "not working on the fence ... They are trying not to do it."[41] But by early summer 2003 it was looking as though the prime minister had become a committed supporter. His conversion to the building of a wall – and later to the other outcome of unilateral separation, disengagement – was underlined in May 2003 when he addressed his parliamentary Likud faction. In comments that mystified observers at the time, Sharon announced that the Palestinians were living under an occupation that must end:

> The idea that it is possible to continue keeping 3.5 million Palestinians under occupation – yes, it is occupation, you might not like the word, but what is happening is occupation – is bad for Israel, and bad for the Palestinians, and bad for the Israeli economy. Controlling 3.5 million Palestinians cannot go on forever. You want to remain in Jenin, Nablus, Ramallah and Bethlehem?[42]

The only reasonable interpretation of Sharon's words was that for the first time he was advocating a Palestinian state.

So what had happened between June 2002 and May 2003 to explain his ideological transformation? In short: a sudden and unwelcome decision by the American Administration to engage in the Middle East peace process for the first time since President George W. Bush's election.

PANIC AS THE US UNVEILS THE ROAD MAP

In late 2002, shortly after work had begun on the first stages of the West Bank barrier, President Bush's envoy to the Middle East, William Burns, unveiled a new diplomatic initiative called the "Road Map".[43] The peace plan – overseen by an international quartet of the US, United Nations, European Union and Russia – deeply troubled Sharon for three reasons: first, it envisioned the rapid establishment of a Palestinian state "in provisional borders";[44] second, it assumed the creation within a tight, three-year timetable of a "viable" and "sovereign" Palestinian state; and third, it shared oversight of the plan's implementation with the United Nations and Europeans, both of whom were seen as hostile to Israel. Israel hurriedly submitted 14 "reservations" to the Road Map, but behind the scenes Sharon's officials were scrambling to find a way to kill it in its tracks.

The fear invoked by the Road Map was that Israel would no longer determine the pace and outcome of the peace process. The Road Map risked reviving the cold cadaver of Oslo: negotiations with the Palestinians over a just solution to the conflict, which might require major compromises over East Jerusalem, withdrawal to the 1967 borders and, worst of all from a demographic point of view, a return of some of the Palestinian refugees to their homes in Israel.[45] Israel might face the moment when it would be dictated to, rather than do the dictating. Reflecting the widely held view in senior political and military circles that Sharon's diplomatic inactivity had prompted the Americans to intervene, Ephraim Halevy, the government's former National Security Adviser, warned: "Frankly, there will be those people who say that the time has come to demand of Israel to move quickly to the '67 borders and to make concessions on Jerusalem that will be very difficult for us to make. And we put ourselves into this situation."[46]

By contrast, the principle of unilateral separation embodied in the West Bank wall gave Israel back the initiative. It bypassed the multilateral negotiations at the heart of the Road Map. By definition, the Palestinians were not being asked their opinion; they had been removed from the negotiating table. The only interests that had to be taken into account in a unilateral arrangement were Israel's – as long as the Americans gave their tacit endorsement. This seemed to be Sharon's new guiding vision as he announced at the end of 2003 that Israel would be making a partial disengagement from the occupied territories.

SHARON BECOMES A CONVERT TO DISENGAGEMENT

It was also how Dov Weisglass, the prime minister's main legal "fixer" with Washington on the Road Map, interpreted the advantages of unilateralism. In an interview in *Ha'aretz*, Weisglass noted that Sharon had entered office hoping to drag out the peace process for another 25 years with a series of interim agreements – presumably of the variety that had successfully maintained the occupation for nearly four decades. Rather than the Road Map's three-year timetable to statehood, said Weisglass, "Arik [Sharon] would have preferred that the first stage of the road map go on for three years, the second stage five years and the third stage six years." The outcome of the Road Map, Weisglass insisted, "would be a Palestinian state with terrorism. And all this within quite a short time. Not decades or even years, but a few months." The answer, argued Weisglass, was disengagement:

> It is the bottle of formaldehyde within which you place the president's formula so that it will be preserved for a very lengthy period ... It supplies the

> amount of formaldehyde that's necessary so that there will not be a political process with the Palestinians ... The political process is the establishment of a Palestinian state with all the security risks that entails. The political process is the evacuation of settlements, it's the return of refugees, it's the partition of Jerusalem. And all that has now been frozen.[47]

Weisglass's comments needed careful deciphering. He seemed to be arguing that unilateralism would destroy any chance of Palestinian statehood. However, what he really meant, as would later became clear, was that it would destroy any chance of *viable* Palestinian statehood. Sharon's political calculation was that he could satisfy the letter of the Road Map – though most definitely not its spirit – by ensuring unilaterally that the Palestinian state remained permanently stuck at the "provisional borders" stage. Israel could disengage – in Gaza's case simply by withdrawing, and in the case of the West Bank by building a wall that embraced most of the settlers and the Palestinian land on which they stood – and call the space that was left "a Palestinian state". Unilateral measures would create the form of a Palestinian state but not the substance; it would remove all Palestinian claims to rights in a Jewish state, whether of the refugees or of spouses of Israeli Arabs; and it would continue to allow Israel to shape the fate of the "Palestinian state" through control of the borders, airspace and water resources. By imposing borders on the Palestinians unilaterally, Israel could claim to be creating the Palestinian state demanded by Bush under the Road Map, while crafting it to suit the interests of a Jewish state.

Best of all, Israel might secure American backing for this manoeuvre, legitimising the substantial theft of Palestinian land made over many decades under cover of the settlement enterprise. And just such support came in April 2004, following Sharon's announcement of the planned disengagement from Gaza. In an exchange of letters, President Bush reaffirmed his commitment to a "viable, contiguous, sovereign, and independent" Palestinian state but then dealt a death blow to the Palestinians: "In light of new realities on the ground, including already existing major Israeli population centers, it is unrealistic to expect that the outcome of final status negotiations will be a full and complete return to the armistice lines of 1949."[48] Bush was giving his blessing to Israel's de facto annexation of the major settlements in the West Bank. Implicitly he was giving Israel a green light to impose a state on the Palestinians that would be designed for the benefit of the Jewish state. (In the exchange, Sharon scored another demographic victory: Bush discounted the right of return of Palestinian refugees to their homes in what is now Israel.)

Sharon began revealing his vision of the contours of this "Palestinian state in provisional borders" as far back as March 2003. It was then that he took his cabinet on a tour of the barrier to announce that many sections of it were being moved further from the Green Line and deeper into the West Bank to include more settlements than had been originally assumed. Sharon also dropped, in the words of the Israeli media, "a bombshell": there was to be a second wall, one built on the other side of the West Bank, on its eastern flank, running along the Jordan Valley, and stripping yet more land from the Palestinians.[49] Meanwhile, thousands of Palestinian villagers living between the Green Line and Jewish settlements were expected to be caught on the "wrong side" of the barrier already under construction. They would have to be encircled by separate fences to prevent them from entering Israel, the Defence Ministry announced. When challenged on how tens of thousands of Palestinians would be able to reach their fields or the rest of the West Bank, to get to hospitals, schools and markets, a spokesman replied: "We haven't figured out the logistics of daily life for the Palestinians yet. We'll just have to 'wing it'."[50]

A *Ha'aretz* editorial denounced the changes: "The public's readiness to allocate the necessary funds to build the separation fence should not be exploited by those plotting to move it deep into Palestinian territory and thus create a de facto annexation [of Palestinian land]."[51]

Israeli officials tried to allay critics' fear by claiming that the barrier was a temporary measure. But as estimates of the cost of completing it, manning its watchtowers and patrolling its perimeters climbed into millions, then billions, of dollars it became increasingly hard to believe that was the real intention. "You have to be almost insane to think that somebody uprooted mountains, levelled hills and poured billions here in order to build some temporary security measure," wrote *Yediot Aharonot*'s senior reporter Meron Rappaport.[52]

Supporters of the barrier assumed that it would require the dismantling of a number of settlements, particularly the smaller and remoter ones. They would have to be sacrificed to ensure the principle of separation between Israel and the Palestinians was maintained. The Council for Peace and Security, a body of former senior army and security officers, had proposed a plan for separation based on evacuating a third of the 150 official settlements in the West Bank and most of the 100 or so unofficial ones, known to Israelis as "illegal outposts".[53] But Weisglass suggested that the Americans were privately agreeing to the overwhelming majority of the 230,000 West Bank settlers staying in their homes. "There is an American commitment such as never existed before, with regard to 190,000 settlers," Weisglass crowed.[54] It sounded very similar to the 80 per cent figure hoped for by Barak.

If most of the settlers were remaining in the West Bank, however, that would profoundly complicate the act of disentangling the Jewish and Palestinian populations, particularly in the rural areas close to the Green Line where small Palestinian villages held the title deeds to the land on which many settlements were illegally squatting. Changes to the route of the wall in late 2002 and 2003, and the behaviour of the settlers over the same period, suggested two possible ways Israel hoped to resolve the problem in its favour. Both trends looked suspiciously like they were designed to encourage Palestinians living in isolated rural areas to flee their communities.

First, even though the barrier was officially being erected to protect Israel from Palestinian attacks, its route actually defied the criteria associated with a "defensible border". Wherever the wall departed from the Green Line, as it did often, it twisted and turned through Palestinian farmland, destroying fertile valleys and the lower slopes of hillsides, rather than tracking the higher ground where soldiers would be best able to spot Palestinian incursions. Such a route was "illogical" from a military point of view, as the Israeli human rights group B'Tselem noted, because it offered "inferior lookout points".[55] The barrier's path achieved another objective, however: it laid waste to Palestinian agricultural land, destroying a wide tract of land on each side of the wall for much of the hundreds of kilometres of its length. Some 100,000 olive trees were reportedly uprooted to make way for the barrier. Also, with disturbing regularity, the wall separated Palestinian villages from their outlying farmland and their wells. As many as 400,000 villagers found themselves on one side, [56] and their land on the other, with access becoming entirely dependent on the Israeli army's good will. The effect of the wall was to make insecure the livelihoods of dozens of Palestinian farming communities.

Second, in late 2002 reports surfaced of violent attacks by settlers against isolated Palestinian villages. The most shocking example concerned the tiny, ancient village of Yanun, in the Nablus district of the West Bank. In November of that year it was reported that raiding parties from a particularly militant Jewish settlement, Itimar, had managed to terrorise from their homes all 150 inhabitants of

Yanun. Under the watch of the army, the settlers had beaten village leaders, bulldozed the local olive groves, destroyed the one and only generator, and poisoned the main well.[57] Although Yanun was the most extreme example of such harassment, it was a pattern being repeated across rural areas of the West Bank, particularly as Palestinian villagers tried to collect the olive harvest, their main source of income.[58]

Two Israeli activists, Gadi Algazi and Azmi Bdeir, threw light on what was happening in the West Bank in *Ha'aretz*:

> Transfer isn't necessarily a dramatic moment, a moment when people are expelled and flee their towns or villages. It is not necessarily a planned and well-organized move with buses and trucks loaded with people. [It is] a creeping process that is hidden from view. It is not captured on film, is hardly documented, and it is going on right in front of our eyes. Anyone who is waiting for a dramatic moment is liable to miss it as it happens.

Instead, the pair argued, the government and army were not only turning a blind eye to the settlers but also helping them intimidate and attack Palestinian villages in an attempt to persuade Palestinians to flee their rural areas. "Armed, subsidized and organized, [the settlers] systematically rough up residents of [Palestinian] villages, very much like the paramilitary units employed by hacienda owners in Latin America to inflict a reign of terror on the peasantry. They are above the law."[59] The likely consequence of such attacks was the desertion of isolated rural communities as the inhabitants sought sanctuary in more densely populated areas, particularly nearby towns and cities.

In the view of Algazi, Bdeir and others, Sharon was planning to concentrate the Palestinians in their urban heartlands and take the rest of the West Bank for Israel. That vision of the barrier was suggested by a revelation from Ron Nachman, mayor of the large West Bank settlement Ariel. Looking in May 2003 at a map of the proposed path of Sharon's fence, snaking deep into Palestinian territory to encircle and protect the settlements, Nachman told reporter Meron Rappaport that there was nothing surprising in the route: it had been part of Sharon's thinking for decades. "The map of the fence, the sketch of which you see here, is the same map I saw during every visit Arik [Sharon] made here since 1978," said Nachman. "He told me he's been thinking about it since 1973." According to Nachman, Sharon's defence minister, Shaul Mofaz, had recently come to him "festively" to tell him that Ariel, 15 km from the Green Line, deep inside Palestinian territory, would be on the "Israeli" side of the wall. As Rappaport observed, what would be left of the West Bank after the separation fence had been completed would look more "like a string of Norwegian fjords" than a Palestinian state.[60]

On the other, eastern flank of the West Bank, Sharon apparently had a similar vision of a land grab masquerading as security policy. David Levy, a settler leader in the Jordan Valley, said Sharon had shown him a map of the eastern fence that would annex a 20 km-wide strip of the Jordan Valley to Israel. "Those who try and say that the fence doesn't represent a political line, they don't know what they're talking about. Don't give me that nonsense. Everyone is playing this double game, and it's convenient for everybody. That is why I am in favour of the fence; obviously it will put us inside."[61]

DISCIPLES OF GEN. YIGAL ALLON

Although the international media closely associated the barrier with Sharon, the wall sounded similar to the plans reportedly advanced by both Rabin and Barak. Neither had a chance to build his barrier: Rabin was assassinated before he faced the moment of truth in the Oslo process; and Barak lost office shortly after the collapse of the Camp David talks. Given more time in power, however, there has to be a suspicion that either Rabin or Barak could have ended up being the barrier's architect. It was profoundly mistaken to believe that the policies of disengagement and wall-building stood or fell with Sharon. As Amir Oren, a senior commentator with *Ha'aretz*, observed: "Sharon's personal presence is not essential for the continuation of Sharonism."[62] Opponents of disengagement in Sharon's own Likud party are slowly being won over too, according to recent research. "Even sceptics are bowing to the inevitability of what once would have been considered heretical, and many now accept its political wisdom," concluded the International Crisis Group.[63]

Officially Sharon was considered at the opposite end of the political spectrum from Rabin and Barak, but in practice all three were cut from the same cloth.[64] Raised as "Sabra" Israelis, each was a battle-hardened general with a record of profoundly distrusting Arabs in general and Palestinians in particular, each was considered a *bitkhonist* (security obsessive), and each had meddled deeply in politics before officially taking off his uniform. All, in other words, were products of the military crucible in which most of Israel's statesmen have been forged. The three differed less from each other than from the only other political rival of the period, Binyamin Netanyahu, a technocrat who spoke English in a relaxed American accent rather than the other three's strained Hebrew inflection.

Rabin, Barak and Sharon were also tutored in the army's guiding vision of the West Bank's future, forged long ago by Yigal Allon, a Labor party leader and the former commander of the Palmach, an elite force of the pre-state army that defeated the Palestinians in the 1948 war. When Israel won further substantial territorial gains during the Six-Day War of 1967, Allon was deputy prime minister. He developed a map of the West Bank that would become the blueprint for the settlement drive over the next decades.[65] The Allon Plan carved up the West Bank into two zones, a northern and southern one, surrounded by Israeli-controlled "buffers". Allon had intended that one day Israel would return these two islands of Palestinian-inhabited land – about 60 per cent of the West Bank – to Jordan as part of a negotiated peace deal. But the principle of Israeli colonisation of the West Bank and the cantonisation of Palestinian areas held, as far as the military was concerned, whether the land was to be turned over to Jordan or not. It was at the core of the army's system of isolating and subduing the Palestinian population.

The Allon plan looks remarkably similar to the maps human rights groups like B'Tselem have produced of today's settlement-infested West Bank. The major revision of the Allon map was in the northern West Bank, where in the late 1970s Israel began implanting settlements in territory close to Nablus, including the town of Ariel, home to about 20,000 settlers. Today a wedge of Israeli-controlled land dissects the triangle of Palestinian cities of Nablus, Qalqilya and Ramallah. In practice, then, Allon's plan to create two Palestinian cantons in the West Bank was later adapted to establish three. This appears to be the vision of any future Israeli concession to "Palestinian statehood": three main West Bank cantons, centred on Nablus and Jenin in the north, Salfit and Ramallah in the centre, and Bethlehem and Hebron in the south, separated by wedges of Israeli annexed land that would include the settlement blocs around Ariel in the north and the Ma'ale Adumim "envelope" to the east of Jerusalem. East Jerusalem itself would be cut off from the rest of the West Bank while, on the eastern side of the West Bank, the Jordan Valley would probably be in Israel's control.

From the comments of his fellow cabinet ministers, this appears to be the plan Barak was hoping to sell to the Palestinians at Camp

David. Shlomo Ben Ami, then foreign minister, described the map he was shown by Barak at the start of the negotiations as "a kind of very beefed-up Allon Plan".[66] The Palestinian state "in provisional borders" slowly being shaped by Sharon's fence-cum-wall also appears to have taken the Allon map as its blueprint. In the judgment of the *Jerusalem Post*: "That part of Labor's heritage, the one first presented in 1967 by Yigal Allon, ... has apparently been adopted now by Ariel Sharon."[67]

Following the pullout from Gaza and a handful of isolated settlements near Jenin in the northern tip of the West Bank, Sharon maintained that he would make no further disengagements, but that seemed unlikely. The demographic pressures on Israel had not abated, nor had the diplomatic pressures imposed by the Road Map. Many inhabitants of the remote West Bank settlements that were being abandoned to the Palestinian side of the barrier certainly did not appear to believe him. The "One Home" movement, founded in the wake of the Gaza disengagement, conducted a poll in September 2005 showing more than a third of the settlers on the "wrong" side of the wall were interested in compensation to leave their homes.[68]

According to Sharon's public positions, he is now firmly committed to the establishment of a "Palestinian state" that will satisfy the most basic requirements of the Americans. In an address to the United Nations General Assembly in September 2005, he stated unequivocally: "We respect [the Palestinians] and have no aspirations to rule over them. They are also entitled to freedom and to a national, sovereign existence in a state of their own."[69] Despite Sharon's stated determination to create a Palestinian state, it will be far less sovereign than he claims. His spokesman, Ra'anan Gissin, says the prime minister is planning to establish a state inside "borders that take into consideration realities – demographic realities, economic realities that were created on the ground". Israeli security zones established on the western and eastern flanks of the West Bank, says Gissin, will leave the Palestinians with about 58 per cent of the territory.[70]

If Sharon is creating the semblance of a Palestinian state, it is difficult to believe he will prefer to negotiate the terms with the Palestinians than to continue with his unilateral policies. As a *Ha'aretz* editorial noted, Israeli leaders want "to determine [the state's] border unilaterally, just as the settlements were a unilateral act".[71] Certainly, Sharon's denials about a further disengagement contradict what his senior officials are saying. Ehud Olmert, his staunchest ally in the cabinet, and the man who all but announced the Gaza disengagement a few weeks before Sharon did, insisted that another large-scale unilateral disengagement, this time from the West Bank, would take place. "Israel's interest requires a disengagement on a wider scale than what will happen as part of the current [Gaza] disengagement plan," Olmert said in late December 2004. He added that a "second disengagement" was the only realistic alternative to even larger withdrawals that might be forced on Israel by the Road Map.[72] A month after the Gaza disengagement, three advisers to the prime minister – Aharon Ze'evi, head of Military Intelligence; Eival Gilady, the army's former head of Strategic Planning; and Eyal Arad, Sharon's chief political adviser – suggested separately that there would be further unilateral measures. Gilady told an audience in Tel Aviv: "I believe that in the current reality it is only possible to take unilateral moves and initiatives."[73] At a seminar in Herzliya, Arad said: "We might consider turning the disengagement into an Israeli strategy. Israel would determine [the Palestinian state's] borders independently."[74] Analysts suspected Sharon was testing the waters for the announcement of another unilateral withdrawal, possibly after the next Israeli election, due in late 2006.

The final outline of the "Palestinian state" cannot be known yet: estimates of the amount of land to be left to the Palestinians vary from between 60 and 85 per cent (largely depending on whether Israel tries to annex the Jordan Valley). Few analysts believe such a state, even at the most generous end of the range, would be "viable".[75] The main factors determining the contours of the borders will include: Israel's continuing attempts at the ethnic cleansing of Palestinian farming communities; challenges in the Israeli courts against the barrier's route by human rights groups; and the non-violent struggle by groups of Palestinians and Israelis to protect threatened Palestinian communities, such as Bi'lin, near Jerusalem. Ultimately Israel's success will depend on continuing American support for its unilateral approach. For the moment that does not seem in doubt. In April 2005, Bush invited Sharon to his ranch in Texas to confirm his pledges of a year earlier. A few months later, in September 2005, the departing US ambassador to Israel, Daniel Kurtzer, restated Bush's commitments: "In the context of a final status agreement, the United States will support the retention by Israel of areas [in the West Bank] with a high concentration of Israeli population."[76]

POSSIBLE GOALS OF DISENGAGEMENT

More important than the extent of the "Palestinian state", or the speed with which it is created, is its ultimate purpose. So far Sharon has not given much away politically. "His strength lies in the ambiguity of his goals," suggested a report in April 2005 by the International Crisis Group.[77] But, there are strong clues as to Israel's future direction, as this book has explained. For more than a decade the inspiration for Israel's policies of separation – whether of the negotiated or unilateral varieties – has been demographic. Israel is facing two possible futures: either as a single state, of Israel and the occupied territories, in which there will one day be a majority of Palestinians; or as one of two ethnic states, with an unassailable Jewish majority. Analysts who take as their starting point Israel's demographic priorities have advanced three theories of the Palestinians' future.

The first is a variant of the creeping ethnic cleansing argument set out by Algazi and Bdeir. In this scenario, the Palestinian population, confined to its urban ghettos, will grow poorer and more desperate over time. Starved of resources, land, water, employment and education opportunities, young, middle-class and ambitious Palestinians will seek to emigrate to neighbouring Arab states. This is close to the ethnic cleansing model Prof. Sofer was pondering during my interview with him in late 2001 and which he restated in an interview in 2004:

> Unilateral separation doesn't guarantee "peace" – it guarantees a Zionist-Jewish state with an overwhelming majority of Jews; it guarantees the kind of safety that will return tourists to the country; and it guarantees one other important thing. Between 1948 and 1967, the fence [marking the Green Line] was a fence, and 400,000 people left the West Bank voluntarily. This is what will happen after separation. If a Palestinian cannot come into Tel Aviv for work, he will look in Iraq, or Kuwait, or London. I believe that there will be movement out of the area.[78]

The chief exponent of the second theory is Jeff Halper, director of the Israeli Committee Against House Demolitions. He argues that, once the Palestinians have been persuaded to sign up for their "prison state", Israel will relax its current harsh military regime and replace it with a system of colonial exploitation masquerading as economic development.[79] Such a process, as Halper notes, is already well advanced. With Palestinian cities turned into ghettos and agricultural land largely out of reach, the economies of the West Bank and Gaza have been asphyxiated.[80] A final agreement that pens the Palestinians into their urban heartlands will give Israel ample opportunity to plunder the illusory Palestinian state of what is left of its land and water resources and, more especially, its human pool of cheap labour. Wages can be forced down and Israeli companies invited to build factories, particularly in highly polluting industries, in the territorial enclaves – offering slave labour wages without incurring the costs of meeting health and safety standards enforced inside Israel. Several such Israeli "industrial parks" were built to serve the occupied territories during the Rabin era. Clothing his ideas in humanitarian language, veteran Labor politician Shimon Peres – the upholder of Rabin's legacy – has been proposing for some time the construction of yet more Israeli "industrial parks" for the Palestinians in an attempt to achieve what he terms Palestinian "economic democracy".[81]

The final scenario has been suggested separately by Gary Sussman, a political scientist at Tel Aviv University,[82] and the Israeli journalist Aluf Benn. They argue that the "Jordan is Palestine" option is being dressed up in new clothes. Rather than creating a Palestinian state of two halves, the West Bank and Gaza, Israel is trying to create two separate Palestinian mini-states: an "Eastern Palestine" in the West Bank and a "Western Palestine" in Gaza. This is being achieved by giving the two territories a different status, and by attempts to block political and physical connection between them. Each mini-state will be encouraged instead to identify with its Arab hinterland: in the case of the West Bank with Jordan, and in the case of Gaza with Egypt. Benn states:

> Figures in the Israeli defense establishment speak of their desire to reinstate the pre-1967 situation, when Egypt took care of the Gaza Strip and Jordan took care of the West Bank. They are encouraged by Egypt's willingness to take responsibility for the Philadelphi route [a strip of land separating Gaza from Egypt] and to train the Palestinian defense forces in the Gaza Strip, which would enable Cairo to supervise the area indirectly.[83]

Not all these scenarios are, of course, mutually exclusive. Israel may hope that in the short term it can exploit a trapped Palestinian labour market while in the longer term "thinning out" the Palestinian population by encouraging it to seek a better life abroad and encouraging greater political union between Palestinians and their Arab neighbours. But all these theories ignore parallel developments well under way inside Israel that suggest the political vision of the country's senior political and military leaders presumes a more far-reaching reshaping of the region. The separation Israel has in mind is likely to be far more complete than allowed for in any of the theories described above.

ISRAEL'S VISION IS OF ETHNIC SEPARATION

As we saw in the previous chapter, a wide consensus has developed in Israel since the second intifada not only on the need for a Palestinian state but on the need to end the potential interference by the country's Arab minority in the life of the Jewish state. If Israel is going to concede a Palestinian state, it most certainly is not going to leave a substantial and growing Palestinian minority with influence inside its own final borders. The endgame of the conflict, if it is to work in Israel's favour, requires an ethnic separation of rights as absolute as can be engineered.

That explains the behind-the-scenes work first by Barak and then by Sharon on finding a way to modify Israel's borders so that a narrow sliver of land bordering the West Bank known as the Little Triangle, home to as many as a quarter of the country's one million Arab citizens, can be transferred to a future Palestinian state. At Camp David both Israel and the Palestinians agreed for the first time to the principle of land exchanges, although they disagreed on the ratios.[84] Gemal Helal, a senior adviser to President Clinton at the talks, remembers of the land swap offer: "Israel could annex areas where there are settlement blocs, and in exchange the Palestinians get some territories from Israel proper. Contiguity was an issue. But the Palestinians were willing to go around it conditional on Israeli flexibility – the land had to be equal in size and quality."[85] The Israeli media, as previously noted, reported Barak's interest in swapping the Little Triangle for settlements, though he later recommended government spokesmen "not speak of" such options. After the Herzliya Conference in December 2000, however, talk of transferring the Triangle became a mainstay of Israeli political debate. It was the advice, for example, of Prof. Sofer to the members of the Knesset's influential Foreign Affairs Committee in March 2001.[86] "This isn't expulsion, it's irredentism," he suggested on another occasion.[87]

It was also the preferred option of Sharon, who has been working closely with his legal advisers to find a way to "sell" to the world the transfer of the Triangle to a Palestinian state. Sharon told his confidants: "If we are already exchanging territory [with the Palestinians], why give empty land when we can transfer land with Arabs living on it?" As Israel pushes for consolidation of and sovereignty over its settlement blocs deep in the West Bank – such as Ariel, Ma'ale Adumim and Gush Etzion – it appears likely it will offer up the Triangle, and possibly the Arab neighbourhoods of East Jerusalem,[88] as a bargaining chip "of equal value". Ex-cabinet minister Avigdor Lieberman, a former director-general of the Likud party and of the Prime Minister's Office under Binyamin Netanyahu, has been promoting solutions of this type with Israel's right wing and politicians abroad, including in Moscow and Washington. Such efforts are already winning over important international allies: the *Jerusalem Report* noted in December 2004 that the former US Secretary of State Henry Kissinger was now championing the policy.[89]

That still leaves two more Palestinian heartlands in Israel: the Galilee, home to some 600,000 Arab citizens, and the Negev, with another 150,000, mainly Bedouin, citizens. What future would they have in this arrangement? A little-noticed part of Bush's letter to Sharon in April 2004 touched on this very issue: "We also understand that, in this context [of a two-state solution], Israel believes it is important to bring new opportunities to the Negev and the Galilee."[90] At their meeting a year later in Texas, Bush reiterated the point: "The Prime Minister [Sharon] believes that developing Negev and the Galilee regions is vital to ensuring a vibrant economic future for Israel. I support that goal and we will work together to make his plans a reality."[91] What the two of them meant was not clear until the eve of disengagement, in August 2005, when the Israeli government announced that the Americans had agreed to give an unprecedented extra $2.1 billion in aid, most of it to help "develop" the Galilee and Negev.

These two regions, the country's northern and southern peripheries, have been the subject of decades of fierce state-sponsored programmes of "Judaisation" not unlike the settlement drives in the occupied territories. Judaisation has been designed to tip the balance from an Arab majority to a Jewish one. In the Negev that policy has succeeded: today three out of four inhabitants are Jewish. In the Galilee the population is roughly split between Jews and Arabs. But the long-term trend in both cases is going against Judaisation. The birth rate of Arabs in the Galilee is at least double that of the region's Jews; and in the Negev, where the Arab population is mostly Bedouin, the rate is far higher, maybe four times higher. The government's need to repopulate these two regions with Jews – a further one million, according to Sharon – has been the background to increasingly desperate appeals to Diaspora Jews to migrate to Israel. With most of the world's disadvantaged Jewish populations already in Israel, officials have been turning their attention to well-heeled European and American Jews, trying to attract them by claiming that their communities are threatened by a new wave of anti-Semitism. In a speech in July 2004, Sharon provoked a major diplomatic quarrel by urging French Jews to leave, adding that in France "we see the spread of the wildest anti-Semitism".[92]

Bush's highlighting of the Galilee and the Negev reflected the new priorities of Israeli settlement that had been emerging ever since the second intifada erupted. In July 2003 *Ha'aretz* reported that Sharon had ordered his adviser on settlements, Uzi Keren, to concentrate on settling Jews in these two regions. In what was hailed as the biggest settlement drive inside Israel in 25 years, the Prime Minister's Office demanded the establishment of 30 new towns, mostly in the Negev and Galilee.[93] International Zionist organisations were recruited to join the push. The Jewish Agency announced in late 2002 that it was planning to bring 350,000 Jews to the Galilee and Negev by 2010 to ensure a "Zionist majority" in those areas. At the same time the World Zionist Organisation revealed that it would be building 14 new communities, the first time that it had worked on settlements in Israel rather than the occupied territories since the late 1970s.[94] In January 2003 the government agreed mortgage discounts of up to 90 per cent for recently demobilised soldiers choosing to settle in the Negev,[95] and in November 2004 an "emergency" package worth nearly $4 billion was approved to encourage Jews to live in the Negev and Galilee.[96]

Over the same period, the government confronted what it perceived to be the gravest threat to its Judaisation drive: small "unrecognised" Bedouin farming communities in the Negev that had resisted the state's attempts over several decades to "concentrate" them into seven reservations, known as "planned townships". Unrecognised communities, home to at least 70,000 Bedouin, are deprived by law of all basic services, such as water, electricity, clinics and schools, and their inhabitants' homes are subject to immediate demolition. In April 2003 Sharon announced that the government was allocating millions of dollars over five years to force unrecognised villagers to relocate to the townships, including reclassifying them as "trespassers" on state land.[97] To add to the pressure, from 2002 onwards the Interior

Ministry repeatedly destroyed the crops of the unrecognised Bedouin villages by spraying herbicides over thousands of acres, until the practice was halted by the courts in mid-2004.[98]

The Jewish National Fund, meanwhile, approved plans for a network of more than 30 private farms, similar to Sharon's own Sycamore Ranch, that would control large swaths of the Negev land for Jews only.[99] A ministerial committee overseeing the new Jewish settlements in the Negev agreed that they should be designed to block "Bedouin expansion", according to *Ha'aretz*, though the reporter noted that this terminology would not be used in official documents. "Some things should not be declared out loud," one official said.[100]

All of this activity in Israel's Arab heartlands went unnoticed by the international media. But in truth Israel has been laying the groundwork for the first, and possibly a second, disengagement, clearing the two regions in preparation for enticing most of the Jews living in doomed settlements back into Israel. Before the Gaza pullout, the government announced large sums of extra compensation to settlers who agreed to relocate to the Galilee or Negev, underwritten by the Americans. Moshe Katsav, the Israeli President, called the "absorption" of the settlers "a national task",[101] while writers and intellectuals urged the settlers to redirect their energies to making the Negev bloom as part of their "national mission".[102] A month after the disengagement, Elan Cohen, director of the Prime Minister's Office, revealed a new strategic plan entitled "Negev 2015" to clear the Negev of its "scattered" Bedouin communities through a policy of house demolitions and to replace them with evacuated Jewish settlers.[103] So important was the new task considered that the veteran Labour politician, Shimon Peres, Sharon's vice-premier, chose the government portfolio of minister for developing the Negev and Galilee. Peres argued that Israel was finally "waking up from baseless dreams to a new reality". "We have invested vast funds in the settlements, which were utterly lost. So we are leaving Gaza and building Israel." Peres was in charge of raising some $5 billion to realise the government's plans for the Galilee and Negev, which he characterised as a "battle for the future of the Jewish people".[104]

JUSTIFYING ETHNIC CLEANSING

These government manoeuvres, and others, hint at a dramatic shift in priorities: a preference for Judaisation inside Israel's own borders over settlement in those parts of the occupied territories that will one day have to be abandoned to create a "Palestinian state" . It reflects a decisive scaling back of Israel's territorial ambitions.[105] Instead Israel is returning to the original question faced by its founding fathers: how to protect a Jewish state from the existence of a substantial Arab population? The solutions detailed above, however, can only hope to contain the demographic threat. However much Israel Judaises the Negev and Galilee, it will only be putting off the inevitable: an ever growing number of Arabs whom a Jewish state can never accept as true citizens and who as a result can be expected to push ever harder for real democratic reforms, for a state of all its citizens. In the longer term Israel will have to find a way to separate absolutely from its Palestinian citizens.

It is too early to say precisely how Israel believes it can achieve this goal. From the debates at the Herzliya conferences, we know that Israeli leaders are considering redrawing the Green Line to exclude geographically densely populated Arab areas like the Little Triangle. Severe pressure will be put on Arabs remaining inside Israel's borders to identify with the new Palestinian state. The "carrot and stick" approach advocated by Prof. Sofer will be pursued vigorously. Pressure can be applied using principles similar to those advocated by Moledet: denying Israeli Arabs education and other benefits "until you want to leave".

At the very minimum Israel will require that its remaining Arab citizens sign a loyalty oath and swear allegiance to Israel as a "Jewish and democratic state".[106] More likely, however, they will also be encouraged to reassign their citizenship to the Palestinian state even if they continue living inside Israel. They will become permanent residents, or guest workers, whose national rights – their passports and voting rights – will be exercised inside "Palestine". In this way the threat Israeli Arabs currently pose to the Jewish and democratic state can be nullified. Arabs inside Israel will vote in elections for the Palestinian parliament rather than the Knesset, just as settlers in the occupied territories today vote in the Knesset even though they live outside Israeli sovereign territory. Political activity denying Israel as a Jewish and democratic state, including campaigns for a state of all its citizens, will most definitely not be countenanced. The legislation for this is already in place; only the pretext is needed to enforce it ruthlessly. A "Palestinian state" next door will provide the ideal excuse.

Two aspects of the political debate that surrounds unilateral separation suggest more exactly the future policies Israel will pursue.

In building a series of walls and fences across the West Bank, Israel is trapping a substantial Palestinian population on the "Israeli side". By the time the barrier is finished, there may be as many as a quarter of a million Palestinians living on the wrong side of the wall, incarcerated in their own walled-off ghettos. This aspect of the barrier has baffled most observers as it violates the principle of separation Israel seems to be following. The dovish analyst Yossi Alpher, for example, while approving of the "clearly delineated border" Israel is establishing, which will prevent the country's "demographic slide toward either a binational state or apartheid", notes with concern that there is no "obvious solution for those Palestinians whose villages are included within the new borders [of Israel]".[107] If the barrier is to become a fixed border in a final-status agreement, no one seriously believes Israel will annex this West Bank land and offer its Palestinians Israeli citizenship. Their citizenship rights – however curtailed by the existence of the wall – will continue to be exercised on the other side of the barrier. They will vote in Palestinian, not Israeli, elections; they will hold Palestinian passports; they will use Palestinian schools, hospitals and banks. Palestinians caught on the Israeli side of the border will exercise their political, social, cultural and economic rights on the Palestinian side.

Israel may seek to use this precedent to justify "transferring" the citizenship rights of many of its Arab citizens to the Palestinian state. Certainly that is the fate already being proposed for the quarter of a million of Arab citizens who live in the Little Triangle.[108] It is also likely to apply to a similar number of Palestinians living in East Jerusalem. According to the plans we have already noted, they are likely to have their land and homes assigned to the Palestinian state. They may also find that new sections of the barrier are built around them.

But the same principle could also be extended to the Bedouin in the Negev, Israel's fastest-growing population group. Israel has repeatedly forced the Bedouin off their farming land and into planned urban reservations, using as its legal justification the fact that in most cases the Bedouin have no title deeds to their ancestral territory. Those Bedouin who refuse to be "concentrated" are regularly referred to by the government as "invaders", "criminals" and "squatters". These official pronouncements may offer a clue as to the Bedouin's future after the creation of a "Palestinian state". Israel may argue that the nomadic Bedouin are not indigenous to the Negev but have infiltrated from Sinai and the West Bank – a claim made regularly in the Israeli media. As a consequence it may demand that their citizenship rights be assigned to the new "Palestinian state".

A further debate is being enjoined more tentatively, at least for the time being, but suggests the direction of the new ideological trend. The argument at its simplest is that if Jews are being uprooted from their homes, whether in Gaza or later in the West Bank, why is the same not being proposed for Israel's Palestinian citizens? The most outspoken proponent of this view has been Avigdor Lieberman, a potential power broker on the Israeli right. He observes that the entire region between the Mediterranean and the River Jordan should be reapportioned. "There is no way we will have a Palestinian state that is free of Jews, while Israel becomes a binational state," he says.

> Israeli Arabs must be on this agenda from the beginning, and openly. There is no point to a final status agreement if we don't solve the problem of Israeli Arabs. I don't understand why it's possible to move Jews, and it's impossible to move Arabs.[109]

Similarly another rightwing politician, Michael Kleiner, has argued that the "forceful transfer of Jews" during the Gaza disengagement exposed the world's hypocrisy in rejecting such a solution for Palestinians. "When portions of the Israeli Right proposed a consensual transfer of Palestinian Arabs in the interests of regional peace, they were met with wide criticism, vilification and even attempts at disfranchisement."[110]

Such ideas are taking root and have the power to shape a new Israeli consensus. Moshe Arens, a former hawkish defence minister who vehemently opposed the Gaza disengagement, rejected the new equivalence of transfer, not least because he wanted the settlements saved. But in doing so, he accepted the terms of the debate and that forced eviction might play a role in peacemaking:

> It is high time that Israelis ask themselves whether forcibly evicting Jews from their homes in territories turned over to Palestinian control accords with the norms of a democratic society, or can really be viewed as an essential part of peacemaking in the Middle East.

The observations of Yair Sheleg, a senior commentator in the liberal Israeli media, suggested how rapidly this discourse might gain an intellectual foothold. Following the government's success in imposing its will on the settlers of Gaza, he noted:

> This decision in principle to prefer the national interest to individual rights [of Gaza's settlers] is a justified one. And such a decision can and should have far-reaching implications in a variety of fields, such as the Citizenship Law and the separation fence. For, ... compared with the uprooting of thousands of human beings and the destruction of 25 communities, it is clear that the national interest can justify denying citizenship to people who were never Israeli citizens to begin with [Palestinian spouses of Israeli Arabs], or even impairing the territorial contiguity of lands belonging to Palestinian villages.[111]

What else it might eventually justify has yet to be made clear.

Conclusion
Zionism and the Glass Wall

A partial Jewish State is not the end, but only the beginning.

David Ben Gurion (1937)[1]

I dream of two countries separated by a distinct border. A border that will make clear to each the space in which it exists as a political entity, as a national entity. If there's a border, there is an identity. There is a new living reality in which this identity can begin to heal, to bleed out the poison of illusion.

David Grossman (1993)[2]

In a normal country, the army is responsible for the security of external enemies and the police is supposed to deal with internal conflicts ... but in Israel, we don't know exactly what is internal and what is external, and it's a very unhealthy situation. We have today rabbis who sound like generals and generals who sound like rabbis. Boundaries are necessary that must recognize the limits of military force.

Yaron Ezrahi, professor of political science at Hebrew University, Jerusalem (2003)[3]

On 4 August 2005, a fortnight before Israel's disengagement from Gaza, a young soldier boarded Egged bus number 165 in Haifa and rode it to the end of the line: the Arab town of Shafa'amr. It was the second time 19-year-old Eden Natan Zada had made the journey. The day before he had climbed aboard the bus at the same hour, 5 pm, and pretended to fall asleep. The driver, Michel Bahuth, roused Zada when they reached Shafa'amr's depot, offered him a glass of water and they travelled back together to a point where he could catch another bus home. "The soldier was silent. He had a beard, a kippah, side-locks and was carrying a backpack. He looked calm, not alarmed about being in a strange town," recalled another driver at the depot.[4]

Bahuth apparently noticed the same soldier boarding his bus the next day, even though Israel's public transport system brims with khaki-clad youngsters clutching their rifles. As the bus entered Shafa'amr, say witnesses, Bahuth called out to the young man sitting on the back row to come to the front. Zada walked over to the driver, they exchanged a few words, then Zada lifted up his M-16 rifle and pumped Bahuth's head with bullets. He turned and emptied the magazine into a man sitting directly behind Bahuth, 55-year-old Nader Hayak, and two sisters, Hazar and Dina Turki, aged 23 and 21, on the other side of the gangway. He loaded a second magazine and sprayed the carriage with yet more fire, injuring 12 passengers. Then he walked over to a woman huddling in fear beneath her seat. From point-blank range, he aimed the gun at her head and pulled the trigger. The magazine was empty. As he struggled to reload his weapon with one of the 14 clips stored in his backpack, the woman grabbed the burning barrel of the rifle, scalding her hands, to wrestle it from him. Others joined her and overpowered the soldier. A Druze security guard who arrested Zada on the bus remembers the teenager's reply when asked why he had done it: "All I know is that this is an Arab town. Soon the police will come and it will be OK."[5] Moments later an outraged crowd of bystanders – possibly fearful that, if the police did arrive, everything might be okay for Zada – stormed the bus and beat him to death.[6]

Zada, everyone agreed, had hoped to use his attack to stop the disengagement from Gaza. He belonged to Kach, a far-right movement founded in the 1970s by the late Rabbi Meir Kahane. Kahane's followers, like many other religious Zionists, believe both that Jews are demanded by God to live apart from Gentiles in order to create a pure Jewish culture based on Jewish religious law, *halacha*, and that the creation of Israel heralded the beginning of the Messianic era. Kach distinguishes itself from other religious Zionist groups, however, in the enthusiasm with which it demands the eradication of Arabs from the Promised Land to accelerate the Messiah's coming. Though its platform was outlawed in 1988, support for Kach among young Israelis has traditionally been strong: at its height in the 1980s, it reached as much as 60 per cent in some Jerusalem schools.[7] The movement has also been shown great indulgence by Israel's security services. Despite being part of an outlawed organisation, Kach members are often to be seen abusing and intimidating leftwing demonstrators, and there are regular reports of its activists attacking Palestinians, particularly in Jerusalem.[8] Few are are ever jailed. Members of the youth wing were behind many of the violent blockades of major road intersections in the run-up to the Gaza disengagement, regularly assaulting police who tried to disperse the protests.

Like other Kach activists, Zada had done little to hide his views. Deeply opposed to the disengagement – to returning territory to Arabs – he had recently moved from his parents' home near Tel Aviv to a militant West Bank settlement, Tapuah, to join a group of Kahane's followers. As a conscript, he refused orders to set up the tent encampments used by the soldiers who would be carrying out the disengagement, and eventually he absconded with his gun. His mother repeatedly phoned his commanders and the police to warn them of her son's extremist views and that he was armed. Reportedly, Zada approached police shortly before the attack to hand in his weapon but was turned away.

A JEWISH TERRORIST IS NOT A REAL TERRORIST

In the combustible atmosphere before the disengagement, Prime Minister Ariel Sharon lost no time in denouncing Zada. "This terrorist event was a deliberate attempt to harm the fabric of relations among all Israeli citizens," a statement from his office read.[9] That line dominated the next day's coverage. But few observers noticed the story's epilogue. Israeli victims of terrorist attacks are entitled to government compensation under the 1970 Law for Victims of Hostile Acts. Anyone killed or wounded by "a member of an organization hostile to Israel" is given the status of "terror victim". But the welfare authorities soon notified the families of Zada's victims that they would not be eligible for payments under the scheme. A short time later the decision was confirmed by a ministerial committee, which pointed out that Zada was a soldier and therefore could not be considered a member of an enemy organisation.[10] Nazia Hayak, brother of Nader Hayak, retorted bitterly: "What kind of message does this send to the public, especially to those who think like Eden Natan Zada? That killing Arabs is not considered terror?"[11]

Several failed attempts had been made to include victims of "Jewish terror" in the law. In 1994, in the wake of the massacre by an Israeli army physician, Baruch Goldstein, of 29 Muslim worshippers in Hebron, an amendment to compensate all victims of nationalist attacks was rejected by the Knesset. Another attempt was made following the October 2000 events, when the families of the 13 Arabs killed by the police in the Galilee filed for compensation. Their case was rejected too. It seemed that in a Jewish state only the actions of Arabs could be considered terror.

A few days before Zada's attack, several leading Israeli Arab intellectuals were interviewed by the *Ha'aretz* newspaper about the country's future after disengagement. Like other Israelis, they had noticed the preponderance of orange ribbons – the insignia of those who opposed disengagement – fluttering from car aerials across the country rather than the blue ribbons of disengagement's supporters. They had watched the nightly Hebrew television news describing in excruciating detail the trauma of the settlers who would have to leave Gaza. They had heard the Jewish public referring to the evacuation as the Catastrophe, suggesting that most had no idea that the word was already loaded with another, far more tragic association for Arab citizens.[12] They had heard rabbis telling their followers in the army to refuse orders. They had seen Jewish settlers being treated with kid gloves as they blocked intersections, placed nails on roads, poured glue into the locks of government buildings, attacked police officers, and on a few occasions committed arson. And all the while they had listened to the endless incitement from politicians, rabbis, settlers and media against "Arabs".

Dr Adel Manna, a historian at Hebrew University, Jerusalem, observed:

> I see how the settlers, who used to be referred to as obstacles to peace, now receive empathy and a measure of support in their chauvinist and fascist discourse. And I think to myself that if this is already happening now, what will happen when they have to dismantle Beit El [a religious settlement in the West Bank]? Into what psychosis will Israeli society fall then? I feel less Israeli than ever before. For me, it's a simple equation: The more they concede to the Palestinians, the more Jewish Israel will be, and I will be left further outside.

In a disturbingly prescient comment, Lutfi Mashour, editor of the Arab weekly newspaper *As-Sinara*, hinted at the inevitability of Zada's attack: "When the settlers come back inside the Green Line, we will be their Palestinians. The internal conflict with the Arabs in Israel will only be aggravated." There was little reason to celebrate the withdrawal from Gaza, according to Mashour.

> If the disengagement process will in fact be extended to other territories, the result will be that you will finally establish the Jewish, the truly Jewish, state. I have no doubt that that is the plan ... People are already talking now – not by chance – about moving Umm al-Fahm to the Palestinian state, and that is

> only the beginning. And when this real Jewish state is established, alongside, perhaps, the Palestinian state, they will say to me: 'Go there, or go to hell.' I have no doubt that that is what they will say. So what sort of good news does the disengagement have for me?[13]

As he watched the protests against the Gaza withdrawal on Israeli television, seeing young settlers hitting and kicking soldiers and police, Mashour said it made him think back to October 2000. How would these clashes between settlers and soldiers have ended were the protesters Arabs rather than Jews?[14]

AN ARAB ISRAELI IS NOT A REAL ISRAELI

Although Israeli commentators roundly condemned Zada as a "rotten apple", he was far from the exceptional figure they liked to suppose. Zada's attempt to foil the disengagement by massacring Israeli Arabs was inspired by many of the same distorted assumptions that led the state to use lethal repression in October 2000. Both Zada and the state believed that Israeli Arabs were as much part of the regional conflict as the Palestinians of the West Bank and Gaza. Israeli Arabs and Palestinians were seen as posing an equal threat to the Jewish state. Both Zada and the state accepted that, in a conflict of interest between the Jewish majority and the Arab minority, the interests of the Jews took precedence unconditionally; equality of citizenship, they understood, was meaningless inside a Jewish state. And both rejected the principle that the Green Line made a difference: Arabs were Arabs, whether they were to be found in Nablus or Nazareth, Hebron or Haifa.

There was another similarity. Zada's view of the Arab, the Other, determined his understanding of what it meant to be a true Israeli. Like other hardcore religious Zionists – more than one in ten of the Jewish population[15] – Zada believed that Jews, the Chosen People, were under a divine obligation to settle the whole of Greater Israel. Whatever international law said, religious Zionists believed that Jews living in Gaza and Hebron, Ariel and Ma'ale Adumim were no more occupiers than Jews living in Tel Aviv, Haifa and Be'ersheva. How could it be a crime to live on the lands now called Gilo or Tapuah, occupied in 1967, if it was not also a crime to live on the lands now called Netanya and Ashkelon, occupied in 1948? The only difference was a date. In the view of the religious camp, Jews had the title deeds to Greater Israel from God. As Emuna Elon, a settler leader and the wife of the former far-right cabinet minister Benny Elon, observed ironically: "If we invaded their national home, why should they agree to a 'compromise' in which we continue to live in their house while generously offering to 'return' their porch?"[16] For Elon, like Zada, there could be no question that the Jews stole the land: it had been promised by God thousands of years ago.

In truth, the religious Zionists were only taking to its ruthless conclusion the commonly expressed view of Israeli leaders since the birth of the Jewish state. It was Sharon who affirmed in 2002 that Netzarim, a tiny, isolated settlement in Gaza, was no different from Tel Aviv.[17] And much earlier, in 1969, it was Moshe Dayan who reminded young students at the Technion technical university in Haifa that they should not judge harshly the West Bank settlers, who were making choices identical to those made by the students' parents in 1948.

> Jewish villages arose in the place of Arab villages. You do not even know the names [of the villages] and I do not blame you, because those geography books no longer exist. Not only do the books not exist, the Arab villages are not there either. Nahlal arose in the place of Mahlul, Gvat in the place of Jibta, Sarid in the place of Haneifis, and Kfar Yehoshua in the place of Tal Shaman. There is not one single place built in this country that did not have a former Arab population.[18]

In terms of territorial aspirations and Jewish chauvinism, the respective ideologies of religious and secular Zionists were not so far apart. On the religious view, the Green Line was non-existent, an all too human, fallible distraction from God's will; on the secular view, the Green Line was infinitely adaptable, limited only by the power of Jews to shape it in their interests. In Zada's mind and Dayan's, Jews were the rightful and only owners of the Jewish state. And, conversely, Arabs were at best unwelcome guests, at worst invaders or the enemy.

The Zionist movement, Baruch Kimmerling has argued, was bound to become a religious project the moment its leaders reimagined Palestine as the sacred Land of Israel.

> The essence of this society and state's right and reason to exist is embedded in symbols, ideas, and religious scriptures – even if there has been an attempt to give them a secular reinterpretation and context. Indeed, [Zionism] was made captive from the beginning by its choice of a target-territory for

> immigration and a place for its nation-building. For then, neither the nation nor its culture could be built successfully apart from its religious context, even when its prophets, priests, builders, and fighters saw themselves as completely secular.[19]

In other words, one did not need to be a religious Zionist to be infected with its assumptions. Some 68 per cent of Israeli Jews, noted Kimmerling, believed they were the Chosen People, and 39 per cent believed in the coming of the Messiah.[20]

SECULAR–RELIGIOUS DIVIDE REPLACES POLITICAL DIVIDE

Until the outbreak of the second intifada, the central fracture line in Israeli Jewish society was political: between the left, largely affiliated with Labor, and the right, identified with Likud. The two parties' respective visions could be easily summarised: Labor wanted the maximum amount of land with the minimum number of Arabs; Likud, in the tradition of Jabotinsky, wanted the maximum amount of land, period. As the power of the settlers grew in the 1980s and 1990s, so did the success of Likud, a party whose platform could comfortably accommodate – even if it did not entirely reflect – the settlers' messianic dream of a Greater Israel. The land-hungry, expansionist policies of Likud could neatly run hand in hand with the zealotry of the religious Zionists.

That pact was threatened with dissolution only as the right's natural leader, Sharon, was finally persuaded of the need for territorial separation, the policy of the Labor party and many of the faceless security bureaucrats who head the army, police, Shin Bet and National Security Council. Bowing to the demographic realities of the region, Sharon agreed to begin partitioning of the land. Abandoning the traditional absolutist positions of Likud, he occupied the centre ground and started the long struggle to forge a Jewish Zionist consensus. That will entail many traumatic consequences Israel's leaders have avoided confronting for a generation or more: fixing the final borders of the Jewish state; defining who is included as a citizen; and finally trying to resolve the deep internal fractures within Israeli Jewish society.

If Sharon's term has heralded the beginning of the end of left and right as relevant political categories, it has, however, widened another fault line in Jewish society: between the secular and religious Zionists. As a secular consensus forms around the policy of unilateralism, a potentially dangerous rift could open up with the religious Zionists.[21] So far the ideological standoff has been at its most acute, even if only briefly, over the Gaza disengagement. But it is in danger of reaching crisis point if significant withdrawals are made from the West Bank, which has far more religious significance to the settlers. The battle now, in the words of the historian Tom Segev, is between the ideologues of the State of Israel and those of the Land of Israel,[22] between those who swear loyalty to a Jewish state and those who swear loyalty to a Jewish God.

The consequences of such a clash could be severe, not least because since the 1970s the settlers have been encouraging their offspring to serve in the army, with many reaching senior ranks. Where once military commanders were the children of the kibbutz, whose ultimate loyalty was to the state created inside its 1948 borders, today the settlers' children predominate, helping to shape and reinforce the army's commitment to the settlement project. Young religious Zionists, according to two seasoned observers, have been educated "to adopt the military profession as a religious duty, to join the combat and elite units of the army and to become officers".[23] Many serve close to their settlements and after conscription continue "to behave like soldiers on leave or in the reserves, pursuing Palestinians with weapons that the army gave them and taught them how to use".[24] Today, religious men account for nearly 50 per cent of the graduates of platoon commanders' courses, 40 per cent of officers' courses and 30 per cent of company commanders.[25]

MOVES TO AVOID CIVIL WAR AMONG JEWS

The hijacking of large parts of the army by the settlers possibly inspired the worried comments Sharon made as the date of the Gaza disengagement approached. "The tension here, the atmosphere here looks like the eve of the civil war," he told NBC television shortly before a meeting with President Bush in April 2005.[26] At the time Sharon was facing death threats from rabbis, not unlike the crescendo of incitement that prompted a young religious settler to kill Yitzhak Rabin in 1995 in an attempt to sabotage the Oslo process. Other senior religious figures, including the former chief rabbi Avraham Shapira, commanded religious soldiers to refuse orders to evacuate the settlements. Another former chief rabbi, Mordechai Eliahu, damned the disengagement as "a curse from heaven".[27] And a handful of Gaza rabbis orchestrated the violence against the army as it came to clear the settlements in August 2005, one of them even overseeing a group of youngsters who threw caustic soda in soldiers' faces.

Nonetheless, there are grounds for suspecting that if the state dismantles the small number of West Bank settlements needed to establish the final, expanded borders of Israel, the settlers will seek a compromise rather than a showdown. An early indication of this was the images of soldiers and settlers tearfully hugging each other as Gaza's settlements were vacated. Since the disengagement, the rabbis who incited against the government have quickly made peace. In an interview with the *Jerusalem Post* Rabbi Eliahu told religious Zionists to remain loyal to the state, urging all Jews to seek "love and unity".[28] Likewise, settler leader Israel Harel counselled: "The national religious public absolutely must not disengage [from the state]."[29] Religious Zionists understand where ultimately the source of their power lies: in the secular state of Israel, its institutions and its arsenal.

The trauma of disengagement will nevertheless have profound effects on the future of religious Zionism. Analysts have speculated about which direction disillusioned members of the religious camp might choose next. The options include: adopting the anti-Zionism of the ultra-Orthodox, thereby turning their backs on settlement as a goal; returning towards the more consensual, non-Messianic positions of the religious camp before the Six-Day War; and moving further towards the racism and confrontation of Kach. Moshe Halbertal, a philosopher at Hebrew University, suggests that most of his fellow religious Zionists will "not break the bond with mainstream Israel". A critical mass of religious Zionists, he believes, will put Jewish unity before any other consideration.[30] How the religious camp might attempt this has been suggested by Rabbi Dan Be'eri. He called on the religious Zionists to seek ways to infiltrate the country's political and economic elites in the same way they had penetrated the army. "Just as our public sent its sons to the army and to the officer corps and brought about a quantitative change in the army landscape, so we ... have to prepare our finest youth to reach the true centers of power."[31] Instead of moving towards Israel's middle ground, the religious camp might try to bring the middle ground towards the settlers.

Secular commentators have found such scenarios disturbing. Avraham Tal of *Ha'aretz* warns: "Jewish democratic Israel is facing a double threat: as a Jewish state from those who favor a 'state of all its citizens'; as a democratic state from those who favor a State of the Faithful. It is hard to decide which threat is more serious."[32]

In the equation of Jewish versus democratic, however, there can be no doubt which group – religious Zionists or Arabs – is the most vulnerable. The challenge for Sharon and those who come after him will be how to transform the political consensus behind partition of the land into an ethnic consensus; how to consolidate the Jewish state from a physical act into an ideological act that encompasses both secular and religious Jews. And as Dr Adel Manna and Lutfi Mashour suggest, the damaging consequences of such consolidation will be felt most acutely by the country's Arab citizens. They will not be invited to join the consensus because the consensus will reject them from the outset. As former cabinet minister Natan Sharansky observed: "The civil war [over disengagement] that wasn't teaches us that we are all in the same camp."[33] He was referring, of course, to Jews, not to Israelis.

THE 'FAMILY' AGAINST THE ARAB INTRUDER

"This family-type feeling is what ensures that it will be possible for the state to carry out the required surgery of partitioning the country without civil war," noted Prof. Alexander Jacobson of Hebrew University, adding as an afterthought: "It should be asked, however, where all this Jewish family solidarity leaves non-Jewish Israelis."[34] At least one rabbi had the answer, telling television viewers that if Palestinians, including Israeli Arabs, refused to leave the Land of Israel they would "pay the price".

Veteran peace activist Uri Avnery wonders whether the popularity of Kahanism among young settlers may hint at where Israeli society will head next.

> Kahane publicly preached what many of the settlers, and perhaps most of them, say in private: that God not only promised us this country, but also commanded us (in the Book of Joshua) to eradicate the non-Jewish inhabitants. They have no place here. If they cannot be terrorized into leaving by themselves ("voluntary transfer"), they must be eliminated.[35]

If secular and religious Jews are to unite, it will be around the principle that the Other, the enemy, is the Arab. As Zada and the police understood, a Jewish state ultimately knows the Arab only by what he is not: he is not Jewish. He is the unwelcome guest, the intruder, the saboteur, the terrorist. And therefore he must be the one to leave, or made to leave. The Israeli writer Sefi Rachlevsky observed that Zada's massacre in Shafa'amr had been possible only because *halacha* (Jewish religious law) regarded the harming of "non-Jews" with relative equanimity. Rachlevsky predicted that "an escalation of racism" toward Arabs would offer religious Zionists the "compensation" necessary to win their grudging approval for partition. The Shafa'amr killings, he noted, are "apparently only the beginning".[36]

Sharon, like Barak before him, understands the importance of religious ideas and symbols in the battle to build a Jewish consensus that embraces both the religious and secular. At the centre of such a struggle is the Temple Mount, the raised section of land in Jerusalem's Old City where Israel is quietly trying to wrestle historic sovereignty away from the Palestinians. This is where Barak, as he prepared for negotiations with the Palestinians at Camp David, found his secular faith and converted the Temple Mount into "the Holy of Holies". It is also where Sharon began his election campaign, winning his almost-sacred mandate to reshape the Promised Land. And it is where the ultimate national and religious symbol will be found to unite all Jews as they fight for their pure state. Their Jewish fortress.

Appendix
"We're Like Visitors in Our Own Country"

An interview with Nazareth teenagers, aged 17 and 18, conducted on 1 December 2001, about the October 2000 events in which 13 unarmed Palestinian citizens were shot dead by the Israeli police.

Why did you go out to protest in October 2000?

Nur: Look at the streets here, and then go to our "Jewish neighbours" in Upper Nazareth or Haifa and see the difference: the pavements, houses, street lights, public gardens. We assume the government wants public money to go to Jewish areas and not to us.

Ashraf: We weren't there just to stand by the Palestinians. We were angry about how Israel took away our land. We lived here first but we are treated like visitors in our own country. What we saw on TV – Muhammad al-Durra being shot dead [a 12-year-old Palestinian killed in the crossfire of Israeli soldiers in Gaza] – was just the straw that broke the camel's back. What made us angry in the first place were social conditions, the lack of equality between Jews and Arabs. It needed to come out.

Do you think your parents and grandparents feel the same way?

Nur: Of course, they raised us that way.

Ashraf: Most of us on the streets were teenagers who are attracted to a Western way of life. Our parents' generation were preoccupied with the political struggle to keep their historic lands, and expended all their energies on protecting a traditional way of life. But the young people are fighting literally to protect their family homes. That is all we have left. It's not just about having fields to grow crops but about whether you are allowed to have a home, a roof over your head. It's much clearer to us what we must fight for.

Abid: Look at Upper Nazareth [a Jewish town built in 1957 on a bluff of land confiscated from Nazareth]. They are always building up on the top of hills as though they need to keep a watch on us. Like we can't be trusted.

Ashraf: Ben Gurion [Israel's first prime minister] said you can spot an Arab in the bread queue because of how backward he is. And that is how they want us to be. The driving instructors even take us up to [Jewish] Upper Nazareth for lessons because the roads here are such a mess. It's like they want us to be left behind, to be left in the dark ages.

Why do you think Israel wants you to be left behind?

Nur: They worry that if we are educated and modern we will start to build our own organisations. Then we will have the ability to fight for our rights and our lands. Uneducated people don't have the ability to understand how state policies are interconnected, so they don't know how to oppose them.

Abid: They don't want us to know about our history or about how our rights were taken from us.

Did October 2000 make a difference?

Ashraf: Until October 2000 Israelis thought we would go to the street, make some noise, and then go home. This time we stayed there and refused to budge. But October was a little thing, not a revolution. We weren't trying to change the thinking of the Jews overnight. We were just showing them how angry we are.

Nur: Things have only got worse. It's worse than ever because they are more afraid of us than ever.

Do you still have Jewish friends?

Rami: After October 2000, my Jewish friends stopped talking to me. I think they found it easy to break contact – their parents taught them to distrust us, that we are dangerous, and now they think we have proved their parents right.

Ashraf: I don't blame the Jews. The problem is with their state and its ideas. It's Zionism that gets in the way of us being friends.

Nur: Even before October, there were limits on friendships. We could never talk politics with them.

What did you think when the police started shooting at you?

Nur: I thought we were all going to die. I thought after the first murder in Umm al-Fahm, "Now they will stop it". But they just kept shooting. The government didn't make any attempt to stop it. They just got better at shooting us.

Nur: Our deaths were acceptable to them.

Ashraf: They stopped because we stopped. We realised the violence would carry on unless we gave up and went home.

What do you want for the future?

Nur: I want to live in a free country. I want Nazareth to be a small town with no connections to Israel. Just our town.

Ashraf: We have to go to the streets again.

Nur: We can improve things by negotiation.

Ashraf: We were forced to stop in October because every father got scared that he would lose his son. We stopped because if they kept killing us there was going to be no one left. But we will find another way.

Abid: We need the international community on our side.

Ashraf: But the same thing could happen again. We can't keep hoping that one day we will have a democracy in Israel.

Given the choice, would you rather live in Israel or a future Palestinian state?

Nur: I want to live in Nazareth. I would not move to Palestine. [The others agree.]

But what if you stayed put and Nazareth could either remain inside Israel or become part of a future Palestinian state. Would you want the borders moved?

Abid: I'd rather stay in Israel. Our problem is not about whether we are Palestinian or Israeli but about being equal.

Nur: If there's peace I'd choose to stay but I don't think Sharon wants peace. The Palestinian people think we are Jewish and the Jews think we are Palestinian. We are trapped between them and don't know where we can go.

Ashraf: I'm not against the idea of being part of Palestine. But I would only accept Nazareth becoming part of Palestine if Israel was prepared to return all the towns and villages it has stolen from the Palestinians. But if it did that it would have no land left at all.

Do you see yourselves as Palestinian Arabs?

Ashraf: I would say I am an Israeli Palestinian Arab but I wouldn't say I am an Israeli or even a citizen. A citizen gets his rights. The only thing Israeli about me is my identity card.

Rami: I don't see any of us as Israelis – we just live here.

Nur: After October 2000 the Palestinians' idea of us changed. Now we must make sure we fight to be recognised by Jews as Palestinians living in Israel. Our parents wanted that but they failed to make things change.

Ashraf: Our parents didn't fight hard enough. You have to want it badly enough to make it happen.

Notes

NOTES TO THE INTRODUCTION, pp. 1–30

1. "The paradox of Jerusalem", *Ha'aretz*, 9 June 2005.
2. The land needed for the settlements, military installations and roads was estimated to include as much as 40 per cent of the Strip's territory. The settlers were 0.006 per cent of Gaza's population.
3. George W Bush, "President Addresses American Society of Newspaper Editors Convention", Washington, 14 April 2005, accessed on 26 August 2005: http://www.whitehouse.gov/news/releases/2005/04/20050414-4.html.
4. "Israel to seal off Gaza with underwater wall", *Guardian*, 18 June 2005.
5. American civil rights activist Lenni Brenner has exposed the support of many leading Revisionists for European Fascism in the 1930s.
6. Avi Shlaim, *The Iron Wall*, p. 14.
7. Today the term "Israeli Arab" is used in a confusing and inconsistent manner. Originally it referred to those Palestinians given Israeli citizenship as an outcome of the 1948 war. Nowadays, it usually also includes the Palestinians of East Jerusalem, who were annexed to Israel in 1967. Most, however, have never accepted Israeli citizenship and remain "permanent residents". The figure citing 1.3 million Israeli Arabs, from the Central Bureau of Statistics, includes these 250,000 East Jerusalemites.
8. In the Israeli context, the idea has an interesting antecedent in the glass booth that protected the Nazi war criminal Adolf Eichmann during his trial in Jerusalem.
9. Noam Chomsky, foreword to Sabri Jiryis, *The Arabs in Israel*, p. vii.
10. "Or panel rethinks public sessions", *Ha'aretz*, 26 March 2001.
11. "Glass wall to protect Or panel hearings", *Ha'aretz*, 4 April 2001.
12. For accounts of this period, see Fouzi el-Asmar, *To be an Arab in Israel*, and Jiryis, *The Arabs in Israel*.
13. "When B-G told the cabinet about the Kfar Kassem massacre", *Ha'aretz*, 28 March 2001.
14. David Hirst, *The Gun and the Olive Branch*, p. 312.
15. For accounts of this incident see Nur Masalha, *A Land without People*, pp. 21–33, and Shira Robinson, 'Occupied Citizens in a Liberal State' (PhD diss., Stanford University, 2005).
16. See two recent articles: "The spirit of '76", *Jerusalem Post*, 2 April 2001; "An Interview with Fr Shehadeh Shehadeh on the First Yum El-Ard Protest", *Adalah's Newsletter*, Vol. 11, March 2005.
17. "An Israeli learns some are more Israeli than others", *New York Times*, 1 March 1998.
18. Recording from Israeli radio by the Adalah legal centre, quoted in my "Email from Baqa", *Guardian*, 18 March 2002.

19. According to the statistics of the National Insurance Institute in 2002, nearly half of all Arab families with children lived below the poverty line compared with 11 per cent of Jewish families. Between 1990 and 2002 poverty rates increased for Arab families while declining for Jewish families. Furthermore, after state benefits and taxes were included in the calculations, poverty rates remained unchanged for most Arab families while being cut by nearly two-thirds for Jewish families. Asad Ghanem (ed.), *Civic Developments among the Palestinian-Arab Minority in Israel*, First Annual Report 2004 of Ibn Khaldun (June 2004), pp. 105–6.
20. Disingenuously, Israel sometimes claims it has established seven Bedouin towns in the Negev. However, these communities were created on already-existing Bedouin villages the state had previously refused to recognise in an attempt to "concentrate" tens of thousands of other Bedouin living in "unrecognised" villages.
21. Bishara was not the originator of this idea. In *A Land Without a People*, Nur Masalha notes a parliamentary vote in 1985 overwhelmingly rejecting a proposed amendment to the Knesset election law declaring Israel as a "Jewish state and the state of all its citizens" (p. 155).
22. The "state of all its citizens" mantra was largely misunderstood. It was clear Bishara meant that, as well as guaranteeing individual rights, such a state should ensure national minority rights for Israeli Arabs similar to the group rights enjoyed by Jews. However, this was not how the term was popularly understood. For a discussion of these problems, see Raef Zreik, "Themes of Justice and Power: The Palestinians in Israel", *Journal of Palestine Studies*, Vol. 33 No. 1, Fall 2003.
23. David Shipler, *Arab and Jew: Wounded Spirits in a Promised Land*, pp. 437–8.
24. Rashid Khalidi, "The Palestinians and 1948: the underlying causes of failure", in Rogan and Shlaim (eds), *The War for Palestine*, p. 14.
25. Dan Rabinowitz, "The Palestinian citizens of Israel, the concept of trapped minority and the discourse of transnationalism in anthropology", *Ethnic and Racial Studies*, Vol. 24 No. 1, January 2001.
26. Majid al-Haj, *Education Empowerment and Control*, p. 121.
27. Such divisions were not simply sectarian. Many members of Hadash/Jabha and of Bishara's nationalist Tajamu party are Muslim. But for Christians these parties were the main political vehicles available to them for countering the advance of the Islamic Movement.
28. "Umm al-Fahm prefers Israel", *Ha'aretz*, 1 August 2000.
29. Alan Dowty, "Is Israel Democratic? Substance and Semantics in the 'Ethnic Democracy' Debate", *Israel Studies*, Vol. 4 No. 2, Fall 1999, pp. 1–15.
30. Ruth Gavison, "The Jews' Right to Statehood: A Defense", *Azure*, Summer 2003.
31. The leading exponent of the "ethnic democracy" model in Israel was Sammy Smooha, a sociologist from Haifa University. See, for example, his "The Model of Ethnic Democracy", *ECMI Working Paper No. 13*, October 2001.

32. Oren Yiftachel, "'Ethnocracy': The Politics of Judaizing Israel/Palestine", *Constellations*, Vol. 6, No. 3, 1999, p. 365. Two other Israeli academics, both Arab, As'ad Ghanem and Nadim Rouhana, also developed the ethnocracy model.
33. "A respresentative of Israel's Arab minority experiences the harsh reality of Zionism", *Daily Star* (Beirut), 29 November 2001.
34. "A Double Responsibility: Palestinian Citizens of Israel and the Intifada", *Middle East Report* No. 217, Winter 2000.
35. A conference comparing the treatment of different indigenous peoples was held at Ben Gurion University in Be'ersheva on 16–18 June 2004.
36. "Democratic towards Jews and Jewish towards Arabs", *Bitterlemons*, Edition 24 Vol. 2, 24 June 2004.
37. For a fuller exposition of these ideas, see my article "Amnon Rubinstein's lazy – and misleading – math", *Electronic Intifada*, 11 March 2003.
38. Marwan Dalal, "Imagined Citizenship", *Adalah's Newsletter*, Vol. 12, April 2005.
39. Whereas it is clearly not possible to naturalise as a Jew, there are routes to naturalising as an Israeli, although they are fearsomely difficult (see Chapter 3).
40. Baruch Kimmerling, "Religion, Nationalism and Democracy in Israel", *Constellations*, Vol. 6 No. 3, 1999, p. 340.
41. "So this Jew, Arab, Georgian and Samaritan go to court", *Ha'aretz*, 28 December 2003.
42. Dalal, "Imagined Citizenship".
43. From a Knesset debate on 22 July 2002, cited in Nimer Sultany (ed.), *Israel and the Palestinian Minority 2004*, p. 191.
44. Hassan Jabareen, "Collective Rights and Reconciliation in the Constitutional Process: The Case of Israel", *Adalah's Newsletter*, Vol. 12, April 2005.
45. Laqueur and Rubin (eds), *The Israel–Arab Reader*, p. 81.
46. That said, a Knesset committee has been working on drafting a constitution since early 2003. Azmi Bishara, the sole Arab committee member, withdrew after he was denied the right to argue that the constitution should not include the words "Jewish and democratic". See my "Israeli Constitutional Committee Faces Double Bind", *Middle East Report* No. 234, Summer 2004.
47. Adalah, *Institutionalised Discrimination against Palestinian Citizens of Israel*, August/September 2001, p. 8.
48. Nimr Sultany, *Citizens without Citizenship*, p. 57; Sultany (ed.), *Israel and the Palestinian Minority 2004*, p. 34.
49. "A state in emergency", *Ha'aretz*, 19 June 2005.
50. Observation made by Dr Michael Karayanni of Hebrew University at the Second International Academic Conference on Collective Rights in Nazareth, organised by Mada, 26 June 2004.
51. During the 1990s, typically 98 per cent of the Ministry's budget was reserved for religious services available to the Jewish population. Adalah, *Institutionalised Discrimination*, pp. 67–72.

52. "Report: Haredi school spending twice as much per pupil as state schools", *Ha'aretz*, 6 August 2004.
53. The Law of Return allows anyone with one Jewish grandparent to claim immediate Israeli citizenship and bring their spouse. At least 280,000 immigrants from the former Soviet Union qualified under this legislation but fell foul of the rabbinate's stricter definition of a Jew: i.e., someone born to a Jewish mother. As a result, many have no official religion. "Quarter of a million Israelis cannot marry or get a divorce", *Ha'aretz*, 17 May 2005.
54. "Israel recognises consular divorces for the time", *Ha'aretz*, 5 May 2005.
55. The Jewish majority is far from homogeneous, and sharp differences of income and privileges exist. The major groups are Jews of European origin (Ashkenazim), those of Mediterranean or Middle Eastern origin (Sephardim or Mizrahim), the small community of Falashmura from Ethiopia, the one million recent arrivals from the former Soviet Union, and the 700,000 ultra-Orthodox, who resist modern innovations. The settlers in the occupied territories, particularly of the national-religious variety, constitute another distinct grouping. Nonetheless, by far the biggest division in social, economic, political and cultural terms is between the Jewish and Arab populations.
56. In consequence there has been a substantial exodus of Christian Arabs. This and their low birth rates have been reflected in figures showing that, while in 1955 they comprised 22 per cent of Israel's Palestinian population, today they are slightly less than half that. The 1955 figure is from Jiryis, *The Arabs in Israel*, p. 291.
57. Known as Hadash in Hebrew and Jabha in Arabic, as well as the English acronym DFPE (Democratic Front for Peace and Equality). The party is an offshoot of the country's Communist movement. Over the years the party has lost most Jewish supporters, though some officials are Jewish, and has become an Arab party in all but name. In the 2003 election, three Hadash MKs were elected, all of them Arab.
58. The term "symbolic" was used by the Israeli Arab political scientist As'ad Ghanem when describing Arab participation in Israeli politics, cited in Susan Nathan, *The Other Side of Israel*, p. 246.
59. Israeli leaders have found themselves in a quandary over referendums determining borders. Given profound divisions in Jewish society, the outcome would hinge on the vote of Israeli Arabs. Both Ehud Barak and Ariel Sharon were reluctant to hold referendums – Barak on ending the occupation of the Golan, and Sharon on disengagement from Gaza – for precisely these reasons.
60. "Livnat questions legitimacy of bill passed by Arab MKs' vote", *Ha'aretz*, 9 February 2005.
61. The Law of Political Parties (1992) bars the registration of any party whose goals directly or indirectly deny "the existence of Israel as a Jewish and democratic state". The law was made stricter after an amendment in 2002. The Central Election Committee, a body comprising representatives from the major political parties, oversees

which parties and candidates can stand for election based on their interpretation of this legislation.

62. Kimmerling, "Religion, Nationalism and Democracy in Israel", p. 360.
63. For more on these investigations, and on physical assaults by soldiers and policemen on Arab MKs, see Jonathan Cook and Alexander Key, *Silencing Dissent*, Arab Association for Human Rights, October 2002.
64. Bishara's party is also known as Tajamu in Arabic and Balad in Hebrew.
65. In late 2001 Bishara was charged over a trip he made to Syria, for which he had diplomatic immunity, and a speech in which he suggested Palestinians under occupation could learn from Hizbullah's resistance to the occupation of South Lebanon. One charge was dropped and judgment in the other apparently postponed indefinitely. Salah, arrested in May 2003, faced an array of charges that he had funded terrorist organisations in the occupied territories. During his lengthy trial almost all of the charges were dropped and the state arranged a plea bargain. Salah admitted funnelling funds to organisations proscribed by Israel, mainly Islamic charities helping orphans and widows. Salah, however, maintains that he had authorisation from the security services for the donations he made.
66. Anthropologist Dan Rabinowitz's book *Overlooking Nazareth* explores the connection between proximity to the Other and racism. He spent a year in Upper Nazareth, a Jewish town built next to the Arab town of Nazareth. He concludes that Upper Nazareth inhabitants' well-known racism reflects the fact that they have more frequent contact with Arabs, and more opportunity to express their racism. Jews in Tel Aviv are no less racist: they just rarely meet an Arab.
67. "Umm el-Fahm, Palestine", *Jerusalem Post*, 11 March 2004.
68. "Camp David and After: An Exchange (1. An Interview with Ehud Barak)", *New York Review of Books*, 13 June 2002.
69. Ibid.
70. "Three Strikes and You're Out", *Ha'aretz*, 16 September 2003.
71. "Shame of the Jews – & Arabs", *Jerusalem Post*, 11 August 2005.
72. "Israel's disengaged establishment", *Jerusalem Post*, 22 September 2005.
73. David Grossman, *Sleeping on a Wire*; Jacob Landau, *The Arab Minority in Israel*; Elie Rekhess (ed.), *Arab Politics in Israel at a Crossroads*; Sammy Smooha, *Arabs and Jews in Israel, Vols 1 & 2*; Nadim Rouhana, *Palestinian Citizens in an Ethnic Jewish State*.
74. See, for example, "The Democracy Index: Major Findings 2003", Israel Democracy Institute, accessed on 26 August 2005: http://www.idi.org.il/english/article.asp?id=1466.
75. "Sharon's South African strategy", *Ha'aretz*, 18 September 2002.

NOTES TO CHAPTER 1, pp. 31–61

1. From his diary entry for 1 January 1948, cited in Noam Chomsky, *The Fateful Triangle*, p. 182.

2. From an article in *Ma'ariv*, 2 November 1973, cited in David Hirst, *The Gun and the Olive Branch*, p. 183.
3. Quote from Martin van Crefeld, professor of military history at Jerusalem's Hebrew University, cited in Hirst, *The Gun and the Olive Branch*, p. 119.
4. The complex reasons for the ban include the fact that rabbis do not know the location of the temple and therefore fear that Jews could unwittingly step on an area known as the "Holy of Holies", an inner sanctum where only the High Priest, after he had been ritually purified, was allowed to enter. However, since 1967 some rabbis have been arguing that access to the Temple Mount is allowed. See "Leading rabbis rule Temple Mount is off-limits to Jews", *Ha'aretz*, 18 January 2005.
5. See, for example, "Yatom: Jews nearly succeeded in 1984 Temple Mt bomb plot", *Ha'aretz*, 25 July 2004.
6. The Christian Zionists, esssentially anti-Semites, are reported to number in the tens of millions in the United States. Their involvement in American politics is nevertheless extremely helpful to Israel. They believe that the Jews must return to the Promised Land to bring about the Second Coming. Any Jews who have not converted to Christianity before the Messiah's arrival will perish in the Battle of Armageddon. See Gershom Gorenberg, *The End of Days*.
7. Clayton E Swisher, *The Truth About Camp David*, p. 321.
8. Amirav observed: "The first Zionist leader to insist on the Temple Mount, interestingly, was Ehud Barak. He referred to the 'Holy of Holies'... Barak applied this term to the entire plaza, including the mosques ... When it came time to discuss the Temple Mount, he decided to blow up the entire negotiations over this issue." "Barak began referring to the 'Holy of Holies'", *Ha'aretz*, 9 December 2002.
9. Belatedly Barak admitted Sharon's visit was "directed against me, not the Palestinians, to show that the Likud cared more about Jerusalem than I did." "Camp David and After: An Exchange (1. An Interview with Ehud Barak)", *New York Review of Books*, 13 June 2002.
10. Yossi Beilin, *The Path to Geneva*, p. 189, cited in Swisher, *The Truth About Camp David*, p. 382.
11. From the Or Commission and Mitchell Reports, cited in Marwan Dalal, *October 2000*, p. 17.
12. Many sources put the death toll at seven, but the figure cited here is from the conservative estimate of the US special envoy to the Middle East, George Mitchell. "Sharm el-Sheikh Fact-Finding Committee Final Report", 30 April 2001, accessed on 20 August 2005: http://usinfo.state.gov/mena/Archive_Index/Sharm_ElSheikh_FactFinding_Committee_Final_Report.html.
13. "Bloodbath at the Dome of the Rock", *Independent*, 30 September 2000.
14. B'Tselem, *Illusions of Restraint*, December 2000.
15. Human Rights Watch, *Erased in a Moment: Suicide Bombing Attacks against Israeli Civilians*, October 2002.

16. See, for example, "How West Bank fighters had planned 'war' a year before", *The Observer*, 19 November 2000.
17. "Camp David and After", *New York Review of Books*.
18. See, for example, "Camp David: The Tragedy of Errors", *The New York Review of Books*, 9 August 2001.
19. "Popular misconceptions", *Ha'aretz*, 11 June 2004.
20. "Following the stretch from concept to axiom to dogma", *Ha'aretz*, 13 June 2004.
21. "Imperial Misconceptions", *Challenge*, July–August 2004.
22. "The stronger side creates reality", *Ha'aretz*, 16 June 2004.
23. "More than a million bullets", *Ha'aretz*, 30 June 2004.
24. Adalah news update, "Barak and Ben Ami shirk responsibility for the events of October 2000", 9 December 2001.
25. "Barak sure police followed orders to show restraint", *Jerusalem Post*, 20 August 2002.
26. "Border cops contradict each other's testimony", *Ha'aretz*, 20 February 2001.
27. "The enemy within", *Ha'aretz*, 30 August 2002.
28. Rhoda Kanaaneh, 'Embattled identities: Palestinian soldiers in the Israeli military", *Journal of Palestine Studies*, Vol. 32 No. 3, Spring 2003.
29. "The quiet revolution after October 2000", *Ha'aretz*, 13 January 2002.
30. Ibid.
31. "It crossed the Green Line", *Ha'aretz*, 6 July 2001.
32. Muhammad Jabareen, 24, was killed in Umm al-Fahm on 1 October. Another two victims shot that day, Ahmad Jabareen, 18, and Rami Jarra, 21, died the next morning.
33. The full list is Iyad Lawabny, 26, in Nazareth; Aseel Asleh, 17, and Ala Nassar, 22, in Arrabe; Imad Ghanem, 25, and Waleed Abu Saleh, 21, in Sakhnin; and Misleh Abu Jarad, 19, from Gaza, who was killed in Umm al-Fahm.
34. Ramez Bushnaq, 25, in Kafr Manda, and Muhammad Humaysa, 21, in Kafr Kana.
35. "Israeli Arab leaders renew general strike threat", *Jerusalem Post*, 11 October 2000.
36. "Summary of events", *Ha'aretz online*, undated, accessed on 5 September 2005: http://www.haaretzdaily.com/hasen/pages/ShArt.jhtml?itemNo=96428&contrassID=3&subContrassID=1&sbSubContrassID=0&listSrc=Y.
37. "Autopsies prove that police fired live ammo at Israeli Arabs", *Ha'aretz*, 13 March 2001.
38. "Black flag order", *Ha'aretz*, 2 March 2001.
39. Dr Nakhleh Bishara in Nazareth estimated that 800 people sought treatment at Arab hospitals and from local doctors.
40. Dr Afu Ajabaria of Umm al-Fahm, for example, refused to hand over a list of patients, saying many had asked for anonymity, fearing police retribution. "'MDA told us that police should stay out of Umm al-Fahm'", *Ha'aretz*, 22 February 2001.

41. Ibid.
42. "More than an inquiry into riots", *Ha'aretz*, 27 February 2001.
43. "Or panel gets report on police racism", *Ha'aretz*, 2 May 2001.
44. Several witnesses from Nazareth recalled seeing many coaches parked nearby and surmised that many of the Jews threatening Nazareth had been bussed in. Nazareth, the capital of the Israeli Arab population, would be the obvious target for organised retaliatory strikes, if they took place.
45. "Police: Arabs were killed by fellow demonstrators", *Ha'aretz*, 10 November 2000.
46. "Or panel slams police's own inquiry of Nazareth slayings", *Ha'aretz*, 22 August 2001.
47. See, for example, "Or panel hears of Nazareth riot", *Jerusalem Post*, 17 July 2001.
48. Interview with Dr Nakhleh Bishara in Nazareth on 21 February 2002.
49. "Or panel, lacks clear-cut evidence trail", *Ha'aretz*, 10 June 2001.
50. See, for example, "The Israeli Arab grievance: Inequality", *Jerusalem Post*, 6 October 2000.
51. "Only through force", *Ha'aretz*, 8 October 2000.
52. See, for example, "Those who refuse to call a spade a spade", *Ha'aretz*, 22 November 2001.
53. "Jewish rights on the Temple Mount", *Jerusalem Post*, 3 October 2000.
54. See Barak's testimony to the Or Commission in August 2002, and his interview in the *New York Review of Books*.
55. "Don't blame the Israeli Arabs", *Jerusalem Post*, 11 October 2000.
56. "Good Fences for a Bad Neighbour: The Case for Unilateral Israeli Disengagement", *Middle East Insight*, April–May 2001.
57. "The pessimists were right", *Ha'aretz*, 6 October 2000.
58. Ever since, those deaths have been commemorated annually on 30 March by Palestinians around the world as Land Day.
59. "Not by hummus and za'atar alone", *Ha'aretz*, 13 October 2000.
60. See, for example, the testimony to the Or Commission of Dov Lutzky in "October's Arab riots felt like Yom Kippur War, Or panel told", *Jerusalem Post*, 29 August 2001.
61. Editorial, "A proper investigation", *Ha'aretz*, 12 October 2000.
62. "They must choose between Israel and the enemy", *Ha'aretz*, 22 February 2001.
63. Benny Morris, *Righteous Victims*, p. 661.
64. Many of the videos were presented by the Adalah legal centre to the Or Commission.
65. "The New Israeli Arab", *Ha'aretz*, 6 October 2000.
66. "Gov't panel to probe events in Arab towns", *Ha'aretz*, 4 October 2000.
67. "Or panel hears evidence the gov't knew of sniper use early in riots", *Ha'aretz*, 16 January 2002.
68. Email from Maha Qupty, "13 Palestinian citizens of Israel killed since Sunday October 1 2000", dated 10 October 2000.

69. "Police shot to kill in Nazareth riots", *Jerusalem Post*, 11 July 2001.
70. "Adalah's correspondence with the Police Investigation Unit (Mahash) and the Attorney General since October 2000", accessed on 20 August 2005: http://www.adalah.org/eng/index.php.
71. Interview with Dr Amr Ramadan at his surgery in Nazareth on 13 March 2002.
72. "Police invented Molotov cocktail story to justify shootings, Or hears", *Ha'aretz*, 27 June 2001.
73. "Police shot to kill in Nazareth riots", *Jerusalem Post*.
74. "Police officer admits 'shoot-to-kill' order against Arab car", *Ha'aretz*, 13 June 2001.
75. "Camp David and After", *New York Review of Books*.
76. For similarities in Barak and Sharon's thinking, see Tanya Reinhart, *Israel/Palestine: How to End the War of 1948*, ch. 4.
77. "Ehud Barak", *London Review of Books*, 25 January 2001.
78. "Barak testifies that severity of October riots was unexpected", *Israel Insider*, 22 November 2001.
79. "Barak: I did not order opening of roads 'by any means' during riots", *Ha'aretz*, 21 August 2002.
80. In one of those ironies to which Israeli politics are especially prone, Barak in effect destroyed his own hopes of re-election by terminally alienating Arab voters and by persuading Jewish voters that there was no Palestinian peace partner. Jews concluded that they needed a hawk like Sharon instead.
81. For details of the 4 bn shekel plan, see Shuli Dichter and As'ad Ghanem (eds), *The Sikkuy Report 2001–2002*, July 2002.
82. Swisher, *The Truth about Camp David*, p. 403.
83. The Saville inquiry was established in 1998 after the discrediting of the original British government inquiry led by Lord Widgery.
84. "Commission gets new Israeli Arab judge", *Ha'aretz*, 13 June 2001. Although the official grounds for replacing Jarah were medical, rumours suggested problems between him and Or.
85. Adalah press release, "Adalah Challenges the Legality of the Mandate of the Newly Appointed Commission of Inquiry", 12 November 2000.
86. Ibid.
87. "Barak snubbed by bereaved Arab families", *Ha'aretz*, 31 December 2000.
88. "Ending the game of citizenship", *Al-Ahram Weekly*, 8–14 February 2001.
89. "PM sorry for death of 13 Israeli Arabs", *Ha'aretz*, 5 February 2001.
90. Mossawa, *Election report*, February 2001.
91. "Some Arab Israeli leaders insist on a total vote boycott as the only option", *Ha'aretz*, 10 January 2001.
92. See my "The skeletons in Israel's closet", *Al-Ahram Weekly*, 3–9 May 2001. A Health Ministry spokeswoman called the phrase "Enemy operation" on hospital reports a "technicality". "The road to reconciliation", *Jerusalem Post*, 16 October 2000.

NOTES TO CHAPTER 2, pp. 62–96

1. Theodor Herzl, *The Jewish State* (1896), quoted in Laqueur and Rubin (eds), *The Israel–Arab Reader*, p. 5.
2. David Grossman, *Death as a Way of Life*, p. 2.
3. Yaron Ezrahi, *Rubber Bullets*, p. 277.
4. Adalah, *1999 Annual Report*, p. 19.
5. Adalah press release, "Adalah to Attorney General: Cancel Registrar of Associations' Decision to Appoint an Investigator into Adalah's Activities", 13 August 2002.
6. "A commission of inquiry under suspicion", *Ha'aretz*, 1 May 2002,
7. "Israeli Arabs slam Landau on Or inquiry", *Jerusalem Post*, 18 April 2001.
8. "Battered badge", *Jerusalem Post*, 1 June 2001.
9. "Attempts to influence an investigation", *Ha'aretz*, 10 September 2001.
10. "Ron: Lacking reinforcements, I had to use marksmen", *Jerusalem Post*, 5 September 2001.
11. "Israeli Arabs demand Or Commission hear injured protesters", *Jerusalem Post*, 21 March 2001.
12. "Or inquiry assailed by victims' distrust", *Ha'aretz*, 20 February 2001.
13. "Trust the inquiry commission", *Ha'aretz*, 26 March 2001.
14. "Border cops contradict each other's testimony", *Ha'aretz*, 20 February 2001.
15. "'Inexperienced cops' blamed for bloody October clashes", *Ha'aretz*, 21 March 2001.
16. "Border police tell Or Commission: 'We fired live ammo'", *Ha'aretz*, 14 March 2001.
17. "Border cop tells Or panel, officers fired 'like in war'", *Ha'aretz*, 14 June 2001.
18. "Or: Police officer's replies are 'untrue'", *Ha'aretz*, 15 June 2001.
19. Ibid.
20. "Much mumbling from the police force", *Ha'aretz*, 1 August 2001.
21. "They didn't see, they didn't hear, they don't remember", *Ha'aretz*, 2 July 2001.
22. "In the valley of death", *Jerusalem Report*, 7 March 2001.
23. Ibid.
24. "Document shows PID okayed burial of four Arab riot victims without autopsy", *Ha'aretz*, 20 September 2005.
25. "In the valley of death", *Jerusalem Report*.
26. "Or panel learns about peace activist's death", *Ha'aretz*, 6 June 2001.
27. "Or Commission witness: Police murdered my son", *Jerusalem Post*, 6 June 2001.
28. "Police disagree in Or Commission testimony", *Jerusalem Post*, 3 August 2001.
29. Ibid.
30. "Or Commission fails to discover who killed Arrabe youth", *Ha'aretz*, 7 June 2001.

31. Uniquely, Shimoni refused to take a polygraph test. "Document shows PID okayed burial of four Arab riot victims without autopsy", *Ha'aretz*, 20 September 2005.
32. "Police disagree in Or Commission testimony", *Jerusalem Post*, 3 August 2001.
33. "Senior cop says 'police cannot afford growing damage to public image'", *Ha'aretz*, 12 March 2001.
34. "'Alik Ron ordered protesters shot,' police snipers testify", *Ha'aretz*, 23 February 2001.
35. "Police officers okayed shots at people they couldn't see", *Ha'aretz*, 23 August 2001.
36. "Snipers admit they fired live bullets during Nazareth riots", *Ha'aretz*, 4 July 2001.
37. Ibid.
38. Ibid.
39. "Gov't panel to probe events in Arab towns", *Ha'aretz*, 4 October 2000.
40. Some Negev Bedouin involved in weapons smuggling from Egypt were also armed. They too did not use their guns during the October 2000 events.
41. "Or hearings told of 'success' in ending Negev clashes in October", *Ha'aretz*, 20 June 2001.
42. "Barak backs police, gov't over October 2000 riots", *Ha'aretz*, 21 November 2001.
43. "Israel's Palestinians and the Politics of Law and Order", *Middle East Report PIN 31*, 23 September 2000.
44. Adalah press release, "Adalah Submitted a File Documenting Alik Ron's Abuse of Authority to the Or Commission", 30 August 2001.
45. Umm al-Fahm has been a stronghold of the least co-optable elements of the northern Islamic Movement for many years, a reason why Israeli security services dislike the town. The northern wing boycotts parliamentary elections and has created a network of charities for residents. It also funds Islamic charities in the occupied territories, particularly those working with orphans, which led to the arrest and trial of Sheikh Raed Salah, the Movement's leader, in May 2003.
46. "Israeli Islamics 'Exploiting Democracy'", *Ha'aretz*, 23 September 1999.
47. Adalah press release, "Adalah Submitted a File Documenting Alik Ron's Abuse of Authority", 30 August 2001.
48. Ibid.
49. "Ben-Ami meets with Hadash MKs", *Jerusalem Post*, 12 May 2000.
50. "A-G approves investigation of MK Barakei", *Jerusalem Post*, 14 September 2000.
51. "Police accuse Hadash MK of incitement", *Jerusalem Post*, 13 September 2000.
52. "Smoke but no fire", *Al-Ahram Weekly*, 21–27 September 2000.
53. "Israeli Arab cells uncovered", *Arutz Sheva*, 13 September 2000.
54. "Police accuse Hadash MK of incitement", *Jerusalem Post*, 13 September 2000.

55. "Smoke but no fire", *Al-Ahram Weekly*.
56. "A-G approves investigation of MK Barakei", *Jerusalem Post*.
57. Ibid.
58. Contrary to the impression created by Ron, organised terrorism by the Palestinian minority has been almost unheard of. Two exceptions, extensively covered by the media, were a double car bombing in Tiberias and Haifa in September 1999, in which only the organisers were killed, and a suicide bombing in Nahariya in September 2001. Hamas had recruited the bombers. Other Israeli Arabs reported to have assisted in Palestinian attacks usually did so unwittingly: several Israeli Arab taxi drivers – like Jewish drivers – transported Palestinian bombers into Israel, assuming they were illegal workers. Israel labelled the Arab drivers (though not the Jewish drivers) as terrorists' accomplices.
59. Torture was outlawed by the Israeli Supreme Court in 1999, except in exceptional "ticking bomb" cases, where the suspect may have information the authorities need urgently to save lives. However, the Public Committee Against Torture in Israel found that 58 per cent of Palestinian detainees had been beaten or physically abused during the second intifada.
60. Defence of Children International, "Israel recruits Palestinian children to collaborate", *Electronic Intifada*, 13 June 2005.
61. "Whose freedom is it anyway?", *Ha'aretz*, 30 April 2004.
62. Interview with Ilan Pappe, Haifa University, 30 October 2001.
63. "Former northern police chief: I didn't consult over snipers", *Ha'aretz*, 4 September 2001.
64. "October riots were 'apocalyptic dream'", *Jerusalem Post*, 4 September 2001.
65. Ibid.
66. Adalah news update, "Barak and Ben Ami shirk responsibility for the events of October 2000", 9 December 2001.
67. "Ron defends use of live bullets", *Jerusalem Post*, 23 July 2002.
68. Bernard Wasserstein, *Divided Jerusalem*, pp. 341–2.
69. "The battles will begin in the streets", *Ma'ariv*, 25 September 1998.
70. "Minority report", *Jerusalem Post*, 4 September 2003.
71. Marwan Dalal, *October 2000*, p. 21.
72. Adalah news update, "Barak and Ben Ami shirk responsibility".
73. "Police had trained for riots in Galilee", *Ha'aretz*, 6 October 2000.
74. Dalal, *October 2000*, p. 22.
75. "The skeletons in Israel's closet", *Al-Ahram Weekly*, 3–9 May 2001.
76. "Or panel slams National Police HQ deputy commander", *Ha'aretz*, 13 September 2001.
77. "Ministerial responsibility", *Jerusalem Post*, 23 November 2001.
78. "Public Security Minister wanted police disarmed during Oct riots", *Ha'aretz*, 10 October 2001; "Ben Ami says he asked to remove northern police commander", *Ha'aretz*, 20 November 2001.
79. "Cop says police in riots ignored PM's orders", *Ha'aretz*, 17 October 2001.
80. "Nowhere man", *Ha'aretz*, 23 November 2001.
81. Adalah news update, "Barak and Ben Ami shirk responsibility".

82. Dalal, *October 2000*, p. 22.
83. "Or panel hears evidence the gov't knew of sniper use early in riots", *Ha'aretz*, 16 January 2002.
84. Dalal, *October 2000*, p. 27.
85. "October's Arab riots last October felt like Yom Kippur War, Or panel told", *Jerusalem Post*, 29 August 2001.
86. "Unacceptable norms", *Ha'aretz*, 26 September 2004.
87. "Ben Ami tells Or inquiry he asked for Alik Ron's removal", *Ha'aretz*, 21 November 2001.
88. "Ben Ami says he asked to remove northern commander", *Ha'aretz*.
89. "Wilk defends police, contradicts Ron in testimony to Or panel", *Ha'aretz*, 25 October 2001.
90. Dalal, *October 2000*, p. 21.
91. Adalah news update, "Barak and Ben Ami shirk responsibility".
92. "Barak: intelligence failure preceded riots", *Ha'aretz*, 21 November 2001.
93. "We accuse", *Ha'aretz*, 22 January 2001.
94. "A grave report, tepid conclusions", *Ha'aretz*, 2 September 2003.
95. All Or Commission Report quotes are from the official summary in English published on the *Ha'aretz* website, accessed on 5 September 2005: http://www.haaretz.com/hasen/pages/ShArt.jhtml?itemNo=335594.
96. "Report cites failures in Barak's performance", *Ha'aretz*, 2 September 2003.
97. "Or report won't affect Barak's comeback plan", *Ha'aretz*, 2 September 2003.
98. Ibid.
99. "Borovsky rejects Or recommendation to dismiss Waldman", *Ha'aretz*, 3 October 2003.
100. "Officer promoted despite Or findings", *Jerusalem Post*, 20 October 2004.
101. "Angered by report, Arabs demand justice", *Jerusalem Post*, 1 September 2003.
102. "PID investigated only two policemen immediately after October 2000 riots", *Ha'aretz*, 22 September 2005.
103. Telephone interview with Marwan Dalal, 7 September 2003.
104. "Or else", *Jerusalem Post*, 28 Aug 2003.
105. "Police Investigations Unit begins inquiries after Or Commission report", *Jerusalem Post*, 2 September 2003.
106. "Barak testifies that severity of October riots was unexpected", *Israel Insider*, 22 November 2001.
107. "No officers to face charges for October riots as ministry closes investigations", *Ha'aretz*, 19 September 2005.
108. "Or panel member slams police probe into 2000 riots", *Ha'aretz*, 21 September 2005; "Shamir: failure to prosecute disgraceful", *Jerusalem Post*, 19 September 2005.
109. Adalah press release, "The truth about the bodies of the victims of October 2000", 20 September 2005.
110. "Or else", *Jerusalem Post*.

111. "Barak backs police, gov't over October 2000 riots", *Ha'aretz*, 21 November 2001.
112. "Minority report", *Jerusalem Post*; "Report leaves police force reeling", *Ha'aretz*, 2 September 2003.
113. "Ministerial panel on Or Commission issues recommendations", *Ha'aretz*, 3 June 2004.
114. "There's a tiger in the basement", *Ha'aretz*, 13 June 2004.
115. "Or: Not enough done after 2000 clashes", *Ha'aretz*, 22 June 2005.

NOTES TO CHAPTER 3, pp. 97–133

1. From diary entry 12 June 1895, cited in Benny Morris, *Righteous Victims*, pp. 21–2.
2. From diary entry 20 December 1940, cited in Benny Morris, *The Birth of the Palestine Refugee Problem*, p. 27.
3. Speech at the 2003 Herzliya Conference, cited in "Lapid lambasts 'barbaric settlers'", *Ha'aretz*, 19 December 2003.
4. The Nationality Law is the government's translation of the law's Hebrew title. It is sometimes referred to as the Citizenship Law.
5. Not all Israelis were equally affected. Jewish settlers had unhindered access to much of the West Bank – or at least the 60 per cent under Israeli security control.
6. For a discussion of the effects of Israel's nationality laws on the rights of Palestinians, see Victor Kattan, "The Nationality of Denationalized Palestinians", *Nordic Journal of International Law*, Vol. 74, 2005.
7. B'Tselem press release, "The Knesset: Enshrining Racism in Law", 18 June 2003, accessed on 23 September 2005: http://www.btselem.org/english/press_releases/20030618.asp
8. Human Rights Watch, "Israel: Joint letter to the members of the Internal Affairs Committee of the Knesset", 27 July 2003, accessed on 23 September 2005: http://hrw.org/press/2003/07/israel072703-ltr.htm.
9. "Knesset forbids citizenship to Palestinians who marry Israelis", *Ha'aretz*, 18 June 2003.
10. "Israel denies Palestinians citizenship", Agence France Presse, 31 July 2003.
11. "The existing laws suffice", *Ha'aretz*, 31 July 2003.
12. Joanne Mariner, "Israel's New Citizenship Law: A Separation Wall Through the Heart", *FindLaw's Legal Commentary*, 11 August 2003.
13. "PM defends tighter immigration laws", *Ha'aretz*, 23 May 2005.
14. "PM extends law meant to maintain Jewish demographic edge", *Ha'aretz*, 4 April 2005.
15. "'Israel must remain Jewish'", *Ynet*, 4 April 2005.
16. "Legislation seeks to hinder citizenship for Palestinians, non-Jews", *Ha'aretz*, 5 April 2005.
17. "Gov't mulls severe new immigration, citizenship policy", *Ha'aretz*, 11 May 2005.
18. To be precise, Sharon announced an intention to make a unilateral disengagement at the Herzliya Conference in December 2003. He

specified that the disengagement would be mostly from Gaza two months later. "PM: I gave order to plan evacuation of 17 Gaza settlements", *Ha'aretz*, 2 February 2004.

19. "Sharon tells settlers to 'Run, grab hills'", *Jerusalem Post*, 16 November 1998.
20. Sharon faced other pressures. First, he was being investigated over a string of corruption allegations. Second, he needed an alternative to the Geneva Initiative, a draft agreement signed in October 2003 by Israelis and Palestinians. The Initiative showed negotiations with the Palestinians were possible.
21. There were other hoped-for benefits. First, protection of the settlers in Gaza was a huge drain on the defence budget. Second, the painful nature of the withdrawal – the digging up of cemeteries, the scenes of settlers fighting soldiers – might make the Americans wary of repeating the exercise in the West Bank. Third, evacuation freed Israel's hands for future reprisals against the Strip.
22. As of 2005, there were estimated to be 1.3 million Gazans, 1.1 million Palestinian citizens of Israel, 250,000 East Jerusalemite Palestinians and 2.3 million Palestinians in the West Bank, making the total Palestinian population "between the Mediterranean and the River Jordan" about 4.95 million.
23. UN Special Committee to Investigate Israeli Practices Affecting the Human Rights of the Palestinian People and Other Arabs of the Occupied Territories, "Report on the Period 27 August to 30 November 1992", 16 April 1993, accessed on 23 September 2005: http://domino.un.org/UNISPAL.NSF/0/cddd1705ade209ec852568c000698a56?OpenDocument.
24. "Anglican church hardens its stance on investment in Israel", *The Times*, 25 June 2005; "Threat to Divest Is Church Tool in Israeli Fight", *New York Times*, 6 August 2005.
25. "Lecturers vote to boycott Israeli universities", *Guardian*, 23 April 2005.
26. Many Zionist Jews in Europe understood the danger too. See, for example, David Aaronovitch, "Peace will prevail", *Observer*, 27 February 2005: "Israel cannot remain both a democracy and a Jewish state if it chooses to rule over an area in which resides a non-Jewish majority. So it must withdraw or it must become a new apartheid state."
27. "The Israeli public is ready for radical compromise", *Bitterlemons*, 21 January 2002.
28. This position equated apartheid with a simple numbers game. Whites in apartheid South Africa, however, manipulated the law and borders – rather than elections – to legitimise their racist agenda. Blacks had the vote, but only inside their own sham homelands, the Bantustans.
29. The figure of 5.2 million Jews did not include nearly 300,000 immigrants from the former Soviet Union whose Jewishness was rejected by rabbis. Many were non-Jews married to a Jewish immigrant. If their numbers were added to those of the Palestinians, demographers warned, non-Jews were already in a majority. "For first time, Jews are no longer a majority between the Jordan and the sea", *Ha'aretz*, 11 August 2005.

30. One of the more conservative demographic gurus, Sergio della Pergola, believed that date would be reached by 2020.
31. "Maximum Jews, minimum Palestinians", *Ha'aretz*, 13 November 2003.
32. "It's the demography, stupid", *Jerusalem Post*, 20 May 2004.
33. Some commentators suggested Sharon reverse Israel's illegal annexation of East Jerusalem, so another 250,000 Palestinians could be lost. "Does Israel want to exist?", *Ha'aretz*, 13 May 2005.
34. "It's demographic security, stupid", *Bitterlemons*, 4 July 2005.
35. "Sharon's speech on Gaza disengagement", *BBC News online*, 15 August 2005.
36. "Disengagement and ethnic cleansing", *Guardian*, 16 August 2005.
37. Some ministers took an even more purist position, wanting to prevent the non-Jewish spouse of a Jew immigrating under the Law of Return from gaining citizenship as well. "The right to marriage", *Ha'aretz*, 15 July 2005.
38. "Either country or family", *Ha'aretz*, 19 May 2005.
39. See As'ad Ghanem, "Zionism, Post-Zionism and Anti-Zionism: Jews and Arabs in the Conflict over the Nature of the State", in Ephraim Nimni (ed.), *The Challenge of Post-Zionism*.
40. "The Democracy Index: Major Findings 2003", Israel Democracy Institute, accessed on 26 August 2005: http://www.idi.org.il/english/article.asp?id=1466.
41. Arnon Sofer, *Israel, Demography 2000–2020*, p. 35.
42. "A new exodus from the Middle East?", *Guardian*, 3 October 2002.
43. "Survival of the fittest", *Ha'aretz*, 9 January 2004.
44. "Minister to his subordinates", *Yediot Aharonot*, 15 October 2004, cited in Nimr Sultany (ed.), *Israel and the Palestinian Minority 2004*, p. 87.
45. "The enemy within", *Ha'aretz*, 30 August 2002.
46. Baruch Kimmerling, *Politicide*, p. 166.
47. "Parting shots", *Ha'aretz*, 2 June 2005.
48. "Netanyahu: Israel's Arabs are the real demographic threat", *Ha'aretz*, 18 December 2003.
49. "Fortress Israel", *London Review of Books*, Vol. 27 No. 10, 19 May 2005.
50. Fouzi el-Asmar, *Through the Hebrew Looking-Glass*, p. 13.
51. Nur Masalha, *A Land without a People*, pp. 61–2.
52. El-Asmar, *Through the Hebrew Looking-Glass*, p. 20.
53. Under the 1947 plan, the Jewish state received 54 per cent of Palestine, the Arab state 45 per cent, and Jerusalem was an internationally administered zone. The Arab state's population was 807,000 Palestinians and 10,000 Jews; and the Jewish state's 500,000 Jews and 400,000 Palestinians. The Jerusalem zone was to contain 105,000 Palestinians and 100,000 Jews.
54. Ilan Pappe, *A History of Modern Palestine*, p. 125.
55. Simha Flapan, "The Palestinian exodus of 1948", *Journal of Palestine Studies*, Vol. 16 No. 4, Summer 1987, p. 16. In 1995 Yitzkak Rabin raised the percentage, presumably reflecting his commitment to holding on to East Jerusalem: "The red line for Arabs is 20% of the population; that

must never be gone over." Quoted in Kanaaneh, *Birthing the Nation*, p. 50.

56. Israeli anthropologist Uri Davis observes that, even were this latter claim true, it would not justify the refusal to let Palestinians return. See my report on the first Right of Return conference held in Israel: "Palestinian right of return: history still in the making", *Daily Star* (Beirut), 1 April 2004.
57. "Survival of the fittest", *Ha'aretz*.
58. Nur Masalha's books detail these expulsion policies.
59. Masalha, *A Land without a People*, pp. 9–13; Penny Maddrell, *The Beduin of the Negev*, p. 6.
60. Masalha, *A Land without a People*, pp. 21–35.
61. "Book: Rabin backed transfer of Arabs in '56", *Ha'aretz*, 1 July 2005.
62. Masalha, *A Land without a People*, p. 33.
63. Simha Flapan, "The Palestinian exodus of 1948", p. 17.
64. Originally, a Jew was defined under the law as anyone born to a Jewish mother. In 1970 the definition was widened to include anyone with one Jewish grandparent.
65. Jewish Agency website, accessed on 23 September 2005: http://www.jafi.org.il/aliyah1/.
66. The 1949 and 1970 figures are from Sabri Jiryis, *The Arabs in Israel*, p. 289.
67. Masalha, *A Land without a People*, p. 144.
68. David Ben Gurion, *Israel: A Personal History* (New English Library, 1972), p. 839, cited in Jacqueline Rose, *The Question of Zion*, p. 51.
69. Reinhard Wiemer, "Zionism and the Arabs after the Establishment of the State of Israel", in Alexander Scholch (ed.), *Palestinians over the Green Line*, cited in Kanaaneh, *Birthing the Nation*, p. 35.
70. "Birth of a nation", *Ha'aretz*, 1 November 2002.
71. Kanaaneh, *Birthing the Nation*, p. 36.
72. Ibid, p. 38.
73. Ibid, p. 36.
74. Ibid, p. 37.
75. "Sharon wants 1m new Jews for Israel", *Guardian*, 7 November 2001; "Sharon aims to get 1 million Jews to move to Israel in next few years", *Ha'aretz*, 12 March 2004.
76. "Address by Sharon at the Fourth Herzliya Conference", 18 December 2003, accessed on 23 September 2005: http://www.mfa.gov.il/MFA/Government/Speeches+by+Israeli+leaders/2003/Address+by+PM+Ariel+Sharon+at+the+Fourth+Herzliya.htm.
77. "A very moving scenario", *Ha'aretz*, 23 March 2001.
78. "Special Document: The Herzliya Conference on the Balance of National Strength and Security in Israel", *Journal of Palestine Studies*, Vol. 31 No. 1, Autumn 2001, p. 53.
79. Ibid, p. 52.
80. Cited in Rabinowitz and Abu Baker, *Coffins on our Shoulders*, p. 148.
81. "Special Document: The Herzliya Conference", p. 54.
82. Ibid, p. 54.
83. "A very moving scenario", *Ha'aretz*.

84. "Camp David and After: An Exchange (1. An Interview with Ehud Barak)", *New York Review of Books*, 13 June 2002.
85. "Umm al-Fahm prefers Israel", *Ha'aretz*, 1 August 2000.
86. Ibid.
87. "Sharon considers placing some Arab-Israelis under PA control", *Jerusalem Post*, 3 February 2004.
88. "Sharon plans to swap towns", *Mail and Guardian online*, 4 February 2004, accessed on 23 September 2005: http://www.miftah.org/Display.cfm?DocId=3075&CategoryId=14.
89. "PM nixes moving Israeli Arab villages to a Palestinian state", *Ha'aretz*, 25 February 2004.
90. Sultany (ed.), *Israel and the Palestinian Minority 2004*, pp. 122–3.
91. "A Jewish demographic state", *Ha'aretz*, 28 June 2002.
92. See, for example, "Is Jordan Palestine?", *Commentary*, October 1988.
93. "'Racist' bills move to the Knesset", *Ha'aretz*, 18 February 2002.
94. "Lost freedoms of Israel", *Le Monde Diplomatique*, February 2004.
95. "Boim: Is Palestinian terror caused by a genetic defect?", *Ha'aretz*, 24 February 2004.
96. "We must stop their illegal invasion of state land by all means possible. The Bedouins have no regard for our laws", cited in Oren Yiftachel, "The shrinking space of citizenship", *Middle East Report*, No. 223, Summer 2002.
97. "Lieberman presents to Russia plan to expel 'disloyal' Arabs'", *Ha'aretz*, 30 May 2004.
98. "Dear God, this is Effi", *Ha'aretz*, 23 March 2002.
99. Masalha, *Imperial Israel and the Palestinians*, pp. 177–8.
100. "The transfer legacy", *Ha'aretz*, 8 October 2002.
101. "Knesset establishes commemoration of Ze'evi", *Jerusalem Post*, 12 July 2005.
102. "Weekly Review of the Arabic Press in Israel", Arab Association for Human Rights, No. 230, 8–15 July 2005.
103. "Elon gets in hot water over 'transfer' campaign", *Ha'aretz*, 3 February 2002.
104. "Moledet Party promoting Israeli Arab emigration", *Jerusalem Post*, 26 March 2002.
105. "A shame for the government", *Ha'aretz*, 3 February 2002.
106. "Legitimising anti-Arab racism", *Ha'aretz*, 21 February 2002.
107. "MK Elon lobbies US legislators for voluntary transfer plan", *Jerusalem Post*, 27 June 2002.
108. "Rubinstein doesn't get involved in racism", *Ha'aretz*, 21 February 2002.
109. "Poll: Most Israeli Jews favour emigration of Israeli Arabs", *Ha'aretz*, 4 April 2005.
110. Human Rights Watch press release, "Cuts in Child Allowance Discriminate Against Palestinian Arab Children", 7 June 2002.
111. Most Muslims, who comprise 80 per cent of the Israeli Arab population, are excluded by law from the military draft. Christians can volunteer, as can the Bedouin. Only Druze men are required to serve under an agreement with their leaders in 1956.

112. Kretzmer, *The Legal Status of Arabs in Israel*, ch. 7.
113. "Worst-ever poverty report shows one-third of children below poverty line", *Ha'aretz*, 9 August 2005.
114. "An alternative to child allowances", *Ha'aretz*, 2 March 2005.
115. Ibid.
116. "Arab birthrate drops for first time in years", *Ha'aretz*, 24 January 2005.
117. "A more effective birth control", *Ha'aretz*, 1 February 2005.
118. "Birth of a nation", *Ha'aretz*.
119. "Benizri reconvenes long-dormant council on demography today", *Ha'aretz*, 3 September 2002.
120. See, for example, "Foreign workers, Israeli corruption", *Ha'aretz*, 3 October 2002.
121. "A state-sponsored racist campaign", *Ha'aretz*, 11 November 2002.
122. "'I never saw such fear'", *Guardian*, 21 February 2005.
123. *On the Verge of Slave Labour*, Kav La'Oved, February 2002; *Migrant Workers in Israel – A Contemporary Form of Slavery*, International Federation for Human Rights, October 2003.
124. "100,000 illegal aliens deported under police operation", *Ha'aretz*, 21 April 2004.
125. "Returning" Jews are not regarded as immigrants but as *olim* (ascendants), making *aliyah* (ascent) to Israel, reflecting the idea that in coming to Israel Jews are honouring a contract with God. Supreme Court judge Elyakim Rubinstein, explained this point: "The nation's character is that of a 'nation of aliyah' – that is, a nation of return, rather than immigration." Immigration, he added, "is not in keeping with the unique Israeli experience and the Zionist vision". "A nation of return, not immigration", *Ha'aretz*, 3 July 2005.
126. For example, Baqa al-Gharbiyya and Baqa al-Sharkiyya (Western and Eastern Baqa respectively), and Ba'arta al-Gharbiyya and Ba'arta al-Sharkiyya.
127. The technical distinction in this case between the Law of Return and the Nationality Law was significant. The Law of Return allows a Jew "returning" to Israel to bring a spouse, the couple's children and spouses, and the couple's grandchildren and spouses – all of whom additionally qualify for citizenship even if they are not considered Jewish in *halacha* (religious law). But an Israeli Jew who marries a non-Jew while in Israel cannot use the Law of Return and must apply for the spouse's naturalisation using the Nationality Law. Although the 1999 ruling forced the state to treat all applications for citizenship under the Nationality Law equally, whether submitted by a Jewish or Arab citizen, the government tightened the rules for the non-Jewish spouse of a Jew rather than liberalise them for the Palestinian spouse of an Arab citizen. Adalah, *Institutionalised Discrimination against Palestinian Citizens of Israel*, August/September 2001, pp. 12–14.
128. "Yishai seeks to cut non-Jewish citizenship", *Ha'aretz*, 8 March 2002.
129. "Gov't approves freeze on reunification of Arab families", *Ha'aretz*, 13 May 2002.
130. "A 16,000-person discrepancy", *Ha'aretz*, 22 September 2005.

131. "Reviewing immigration laws", *Jerusalem Post,* 11 July 2005.
132. "Yishai: Let's restrict citizenship for Arab spouses", *Ha'aretz,* 10 January 2002.
133. B'Tselem, *Forbidden Families,* January 2004.
134. "New law for Israeli-Palestinian couples", Associated Press, 31 July 2003.
135. "Racism reinforced", *Al-Ahram Weekly,* 7–13 August 2003.
136. "Extension of family reunification ban advances", *Jerusalem Post,* 26 May 2005; "Family unification pared down for Palestinian spouses", *Ha'aretz,* 28 July 2005.
137. Adalah news update, "Adalah to Supreme Court: Freeze Implementation of Ban on Family Unification", 4 August 2005.
138. "ACRI slams Interior Min for human rights violations", *Ha'aretz,* 6 December 2004.
139. "No longer keeper of the gate", *Ha'aretz,* 28 May 2004.
140. This scathing series by Shahar Ilan prompted a *Ha'aretz* editorial bemoaning "the intolerable maltreatment on the part of Population Administration officials of any non-Jew trying to become a resident of the state". "Wanted: A humane immigration policy", *Ha'aretz,* 20 June 2005.
141. "Legislation seeks to hinder citizenship for Palestinians, non-Jews", *Ha'aretz,* 5 April 2005.
142. "Eiland proposes citizenship limitations for Palestinians", *Ha'aretz,* 3 March 2005.
143. "Shocken's mistakes", *Ma'ariv,* 8 May 2005 (Hebrew).
144. "There is no 'right' of return", *Jerusalem Post,* 15 March 2005.
145. "From Discrimination to the Denial of Basic Freedoms", *Adalah's Newsletter,* Vol. 13, May 2005; article originally published in *Ha'aretz* on 18 May 2005.
146. All comments made by Prof. Yoav Peled were recorded at the Mada conference, "The Relationship between Israel and the Palestinian Minority: Present and Future", in Haifa on 26 July 2005.

NOTES TO CHAPTER 4, pp. 134–168

1. Noam Chomsky, "Middle East Diplomacy: Continuities and Change", *Z Magazine,* December 1991.
2. "Iceman", *Ha'aretz,* 15 June 2001.
3. "Sharon repeats call for French Jews to immigrate to Israel", *Ha'aretz,* 29 July 2005.
4. For true zealots, Greater Israel includes large tracts of neighbouring Arab states, including the East Bank of the Jordan River, South Lebanon, parts of Syria and Egypt.
5. Bernard Wasserstein, *Divided Jerusalem,* p. 205.
6. Michael Prior, *Zionism and the State of Israel,* p. 84.
7. Chomsky, "Middle East Diplomacy: Continuities and Change".
8. "The One-Fence Solution", *New York Times Magazine,* 3 August 2003.
9. "Golda speaking from Bush's mouth", *Ha'aretz,* 18 April 2004.

10. B'Tselem, *Land Grab: Israel's Settlement Policy in the West Bank*, May 2002.
11. "Lords of the manor", *Ha'aretz*, 7 March 2002; "Settlers enjoyed NIS 130M in income tax benefits last year", *Ha'aretz*, 6 November 2002; "Every settler a king", *Ha'aretz*, 1 February 2002.
12. "Defensible borders", *Jerusalem Letter/Viewpoints*, 15 June–1 July 2003.
13. Rabin's demographic concerns were also evident in the decision not to include an Israeli Arab in his delegation to Washington to sign the Declaration of Principles, even though the group was intended to reflect the diversity of Israeli society. Asked his reasons, Rabin replied: "Because we are going to sign a peace treaty between Jewish Israel and the PLO." "Covert support", *Ha'aretz*, 25 August 2005.
14. "The Missing Peace: The Inside Story of the Fight for Middle East Peace", a meeting at the Council on Foreign Relations in New York on 13 September 2004, accessed on 2 October 2005: http://www3.cfr.org/pub7355/thomas_l_friedman_dennis_b_ross/the_missing_peace_the_inside_story_of_the_fight_for_middle_east_peace.php.
15. "Iceman", *Ha'aretz*.
16. "Separation means economic punishment", *Ha'aretz*, 23 October 2000.
17. "Israel's closure policy: An effective strategy of containment and repression", *Journal of Palestine Studies*, Vol. 31 No. 2, Spring 2002.
18. This slogan closely echoed that of Rehava'am Ze'evi's Moledet party, which, as noted in the previous chapter, led the demand for expulsion of the Palestinians from the occupied territories.
19. B'Tselem, *Land Grab*.
20. Tanya Reinhart, *Israel/Palestine: How to End the War of 1948*, p. 193; Baruch Kimmerling, *Politicide*, pp. 123, 127.
21. Dan Schueftan, "Good Fences for a Bad Neighbour: The Case for Unilateral Israeli Disengagement", *Middle East Insight*, April–May 2001.
22. Clayton E Swisher, *The Truth About Camp David*, p. 256.
23. Charles Enderlin, *Shattered Dreams*, pp. 145–6, cited in Swisher, *The Truth About Camp David*, p. 198.
24. "End of a journey", *Ha'aretz*, 14 September 2001.
25. "Why we need to withdraw unilaterally", *Jerusalem Report*, 6 May 2002.
26. Israel's predilection for unilateralism, as Meron Benvenisti observes, dates back even further. Following the Arab rebellion in the 1930s, Arthur Ruppin, a leftwing Zionist leader, concluded: "What we can get is not what we need, and what we need we cannot get." "90 years of unilateralism", *Ha'aretz*, 28 July 2005.
27. Speech at the Washington institute of Near East Policy, 15 December 2003, cited in Swisher, *The Truth About Camp David*, p. 222.
28. "It would bring about a terrible response", *Bitterlemons*, 4 February 2002.
29. "Building a wall against terror", *New York Times*, 24 May 2001.
30. "For a Jewish border", *Jerusalem Post*, 19 July 2002.

31. "Destroy terror and disengage", *Jewish Telegraphic Agency*, 13 June 2002.
32. "Defensible borders for Israel", *Jerusalem Letter/Viewpoints*.
33. "Destroy terror and disengage", *Jewish Telegraphic Agency*.
34. "Disengagement the only choice", *Jerusalem Post*, 14 February 2002.
35. "Destroy terror and disengage", *Jewish Telegraphic Agency*.
36. "No to unilateral disengagement", *Jerusalem Post*, 21 August 2001.
37. "The fence: stakes in the heart of the settlers' dream", *Ha'aretz*, 18 June 2002.
38. "Finally getting off the fence", *Jerusalem Post*, 13 June 2002.
39. "Defense ministry wants fence moved deeper into West Bank", *Ha'aretz*, 23 March 2003.
40. "Defense Minister Ben-Eliezer: Delaying fence would invite terror", *Jerusalem Post*, 17 June 2002.
41. "A Wall in the Heart", *Yediot Aharonot*, 23 May 2003 (Hebrew).
42. "The fight of Sharon's life: His place in history", *Ha'aretz*, 28 May 2003. Sharon later retracted the statement, after advisers warned that the admission would make it difficult for Israel to justify its refusal to apply international law to the occupied territories.
43. Accessed on 2 October 2005: http://www.state.gov/r/pa/prs/ps/2003/20062.htm.
44. This idea had first been floated by Bush on 24 June 2002.
45. Reservation Six insisted on demographic references to "Israel's right to exist as a Jewish state and to the waiver of any right to return for Palestinian refugees to the State of Israel".
46. "The spy who went into the cold", *Jerusalem Post*, 31 December 2004.
47. "The big freeze", *Ha'aretz*, 8 October 2004.
48. "Exchange of letters between PM Sharon and President Bush", accessed on 2 October 2005: http://www.mfa.gov.il/MFA/Peace+Process/Reference+Documents/Exchange+of+letters+Sharon-Bush+14-Apr-2004.htm.
49. "The fence: stakes in the heart of the settlers' dream", *Ha'aretz*.
50. "Making right of way", *Jerusalem Post*, 3 October 2002.
51. "Deviation from the principle of separation", *Ha'aretz*, 24 March 2003.
52. "A Wall in the Heart", *Yediot Aharonot*.
53. "The semiotics of 'fence'", *Ha'aretz*, 17 June 2002.
54. "The big freeze", *Ha'aretz*.
55. B'Tselem, *The Separation Barrier: Position Paper*, September 2002.
56. Norman Finkelstein, *Beyond Chutzpah*, pp. 201–2.
57. "Alone with the settlers", *Al-Ahram Weekly*, 21–27 November 2002; "It's the pits", *Ha'aretz*, 25 October 2002.
58. There was widespread coverage of this phenomenon in late 2002 and 2003.
59. "Transfer's real nightmare", *Ha'aretz*, 16 November 2002.
60. "A Wall in the Heart", *Yediot Aharonot*.
61. Ibid.
62. "Sharonism without Sharon", *Ha'aretz*, 2 September 2005.

63. ICG, *Disengagement and After: Where Next for Sharon and the Likud?*, 1 March 2005.
64. Sharon's ideological inheritance is discussed in "Is Sharon really a Trojan horse?", *Ha'aretz*, 16 August 2005.
65. Maps of the Allon Plan can be viewed at: http://www.jewishvirtuallibrary.org/jsource/History/allonplan.html.
66. "End of a journey", *Ha'aretz*.
67. "Labor's last chance", *Jerusalem Post*, 4 September 2005.
68. "Settlers on 'wrong' side of the fence seek gov't aid to evacuate", *Jerusalem Post*, 30 September 2005.
69. "Verbatim: Ariel Sharon's UN speech", *Jersualem Post*, 18 September 2005.
70. "Editor's notes: His master's (very loud) voice", *Jerusalem Post*, 6 January 2005.
71. "The year of the turnabout", *Ha'aretz*, 3 October 2005.
72. "Sharon: Only one unilateral pullout", *Jerusalem Post*, 30 December 2004.
73. "Sharon reaffirms pledge to road map", *Jerusalem Post*, 29 September 2005.
74. "PM denies plan for 'Disengagement II'", *Ha'aretz*, 29 September 2005.
75. The Israeli Committee Against House Demolitions makes a telling analogy. If a prison gives its inmates full control over all of the building apart from 5 per cent – the walls, barred windows and doors – they are still imprisoned.
76. "Outgoing ambassador Kurtzer: US will support retention of some settlements", *Ha'aretz*, 19 September 2005.
77. ICG, *Disengagement and After*.
78. "It's the demography, stupid", *Jerusalem Post*, 20 May 2004.
79. This view was advanced by Halper during a tour of East Jerusalem on 21 April 2005.
80. It is startling the extent to which Israeli policies in the West Bank mimick earlier policies used against Israel's Arab minority. The purpose of the military government of 1948–66 was not primarily about ethnic cleansing but about the subjugation of the Palestinian population on Israeli terms, through the erasing of their Palestinian identity to make them more suitable for exploitation. Israeli Arabs were isolated from neighbouring Palestinian population groups; their traditional agricultural way of life was destroyed; and they were refashioned as a casual labour force.
81. The Peres Center for Peace has been at the forefront of attempts to establish "industrial parks" since the early days of the Oslo process.
82. "Ariel Sharon and the Jordan Option", *Middle East Report online*, March 2005, accessed on 2 October 2005: http://www.merip.org/mero/interventions/sussman_interv.html.
83. "The new partition plan", *Ha'aretz*, 2 September 2005.
84. Swisher, *The Truth about Camp David*, pp. 200–1, 287–8.
85. Ibid, p. 325.
86. "Squaring the triangle", *Al-Ahram Weekly*, 11–17 October 2001.

87. "A Jewish demographic state", *Ha'aretz*, 28 June 2002.
88. The 250,000 Palestinians of East Jerusalem mostly do not have Israeli citizenship. Because of their inferior legal status, Israel's room for manoeuvre is far greater.
89. "Will peace moves breathe new life into land-swap plan?", *Jerusalem Report*, 27 December 2004
90. "Exchange of letters between PM Sharon and President Bush".
91. White House press release, "President and Prime Minister Sharon Discuss Economy, Middle East", 11 April 2005.
92. "French Jews 'must move to Israel'", *BBC online*, 18 July 2004.
93. "PMO issues rush order for 30 new towns in Negev, Galilee", *Ha'aretz*, 20 July 2003.
94. "Jewish Agency readies plan to foster a 'Zionist majority'", *Ha'aretz*, 28 October 2002.
95. "Come settle the Negev", *Ha'aretz*, 1 June 2004.
96. "Emergency plan to boost Negev, Galilee formulated", *Ma'ariv*, 17 November 2004.
97. For background to the Negev plan, see my "Bedouin in the Negev Face New Transfer", *Middle East Report online*, 10 May 2003, accessed on 2 October 2005: http://www.merip.org/mero/mero051003.html.
98. "Beduin claim crop spraying aims to drive them from land", *Jerusalem Post*, 29 January 2004.
99. "Fencing out the Bedouin", *Ha'aretz*, 1 July 2003.
100. "Jewish communities planned to 'block Bedouin expansion'", *Ha'aretz*, 5 June 2004.
101. "Katsav: Absorbing evacuees is a 'national task'", *Ha'aretz*, 29 August 2005.
102. See, for example, Avrum Ehrlich, "Now, can we make the Negev bloom?", *Jerusalem Post*, 25 August 2005.
103. "Weekly Review of the Arabic Press in Israel", Arab Association for Human Rights, No. 240, 16–23 September 2005.
104. "Peres Asking US Jewry To Push Aid For Galilee", *Forward*, 5 August 2005.
105. Plans concentrated on "consolidating" the West Bank settlement blocs, particularly Ma'ale Adumim and Ariel.
106. Several citizenship loyalty schemes have been proposed, including by Avigdor Lieberman and Uzi Landau, both former government ministers.
107. "It's time for a serious public debate", *Bitterlemons*, 4 February 2002.
108. This region is unique in being the only part of Israel not conquered in the 1948 war. It was handed over by Jordan in 1949 during the armistice negotiations. Israel may use this irregularity as a legal pretext for treating the area's inhabitants in the same way as West Bank Palestinians on the "wrong side" of the barrier.
109. "A party, and everyone's invited", *Ha'aretz*, 2 September 2005.
110. "Encourage Arab emigration", *Jerusalem Post*, 20 September 2005.
111. "National interest vs human rights", *Ha'aretz*, 5 September 2005.

NOTES TO CONCLUSION, pp. 169–179

1. "Back to a coalition of pragmatism", *Ha'aretz*, 5 September 2002.
2. "Suddenly human contact", *Death as a Way of Life*, p. 6.
3. Talk at University of Toronto: "Israeli professor sees a way out of Palestine conflict", 20 March 2003, accessed on 10 October 2005: http://www.thevarsity.ca/media/paper285/news/2003/03/20/News/Israeli.Professor.Sees.A.Way.Out.Of.Palestine.Conflict-396923.shtml.
4. "A day before, the driver gave the killer a drink of water", *Ha'aretz*, 7 August 2005.
5. Telephone interview with Hussam Elayan, 11 August 2005.
6. This account draws on my own interviews and testimonies from the Arab Association for Human Rights' report *One Killer, Many to Blame*, October 2005.
7. Nur Masalha, *Imperial Israel and the Palestinians*, pp. 202–3.
8. See, for example, "The child hour", *Ha'aretz*, 20 January 2005.
9. "PM Sharon's statement following the terrorist attack in Shfaram", 4 August 2005, accessed on 10 October 2005: http://www.mfa.gov.il/MFA/Government/Communiques/2005/PM+Sharons+statement+following+the+terrorist+attack+in+Shfaram+4-Aug-2005.htm.
10. "Shfaram victims won't be recognised by terror law", *Ha'aretz*, 30 August 2005.
11. "One law for all terror victims", *Ha'aretz*, 2 September 2005.
12. The Catastrophe, "al-Nakba", is how Palestinians refer to the loss of their homeland in the 1948 war.
13. "This isn't my story", *Ha'aretz*, 27 July 2005.
14. Ibid.
15. Israel Shahak and Norton Mezvinsky, *Jewish Fundamentalism in Israel*, p. 8. A similar number of Jews, about 13 per cent, are religious but not Zionist. The ultra-Orthodox, or Haredim, cite the Talmud's injunction on Jews not to emigrate in large numbers to the Promised Land before the coming of the Messiah as justification for their anti-Zionism. In contrast, a majority of religious Zionists, though not all, believe they are living at the beginning of the Messianic age.
16. "The dangers of seeing Netzarim as Tel Aviv", *Ha'aretz*, 6 May 2002.
17. Ibid.
18. From *Ha'aretz*, 4 April 1969, cited in Nur Masalha, *A Land without a People*, p. 100.
19. Baruch Kimmerling, "Religion, Nationalism and Democracy in Israel", *Constellations*, Vol. 6 No. 3, 1999, pp. 342, 358.
20. Shahak and Mezvinsky, *Jewish Fundamentalism*, p. 75.
21. Many religious Zionists live inside Israel but subscribe to the same views as the religious settlers. A majority of the 450,000 settlers are not religious; they are economic settlers, attracted by the financial benefits of living in the occupied territories.
22. "Leaving Gaza – The sky did not fall down", *Ha'aretz*, 12 September 2005.
23. Shahak and Mezvinsky, *Jewish Fundamentalism*, p. 90.
24. "Agony and ecstasy", *Ha'aretz*, 26 August 2005.

25. "Time of Reckoning", *Ha'aretz*, 26 September 2005.
26. "Sharon expects violence during Gaza pullout", *NBC online*, 11 April 2005.
27. "Rabbi Eliahu changes mind on refusal", *Jerusalem Post*, 23 September 2005.
28. Ibid.
29. "Don't disengage from the state", *Ha'aretz*, 6 October 2005.
30. "Religious Zionism's identity crisis", *Jerusalem Report*, 5 September 2005.
31. "A decade of dreams down the drain", *Ha'aretz*, 29 September 2005.
32. "The faith connection", *Ha'aretz*, 5 August 2005.
33. "The civil war that wasn't", *Jerusalem Post*, 10 September 2005.
34. "Who is part of the family?", *Ha'aretz*, 7 September 2005.
35. "March of the Orange Shirts", Gush Shalom, 24 July 2005.
36. "There are no wild weeds here", *Ha'aretz*, 31 August 2005.

Select Bibliography

BOOKS

Abu Hussein, Hussein, and Fiona McKay, *Access Denied* (London: Zed Books, 2003)

Al-Haj, Majid, *Education, Empowerment and Control* (Albany: SUNY, 1995)

Amnesty International, *Broken Lives* (London: Amnesty International, 2001)

Benvenisti, Meron, *Sacred Landscape* (Berkeley: University of California Press, 2000)

Bishara, Marwan, *Palestine/Israel: Peace or Apartheid* (London: Zed Books, 2002)

Carey, Roane et al. (eds), *The Other Israel: Voices of Refusal and Dissent* (New York: The New Press, 2002)

Chomsky, Noam, *The Fateful Triangle: The United States, Israel and the Palestinians* (London: Pluto Books, 1999)

Dalal, Marwan, *October 2000: Law and Politics before the Or Commission of Inquiry* (Shafa'amr: Adalah, 2003)

Davis, Uri, *Apartheid Israel* (London: Zed Books, 2003)

El-Asmar, Fouzi, *To be an Arab in Israel* (London: Frances Pinter, 1975)

—— *Through the Hebrew Looking-Glass* (Vermont: Amana Books, 1986)

Ezrahi, Yaron, *Rubber Bullets: Power and Conscience in Modern Israel* (Berkeley: University of California Press, 1998)

Finkelstein, Norman, *Image and Reality of the Israel–Palestine Conflict* (London: Verso, 2001)

—— *Beyond Chutzpah: On the Misuse of Anti-Semitism and the Abuse of History* (Berkeley: University of California Press, 2005)

Ghanem, As'ad, *The Palestinian-Arab Minority in Israel, 1948–2000* (Albany: SUNY, 2001)

Gorenberg, Gershom, *The End of Days* (New York: Oxford University Press, 2002)

Grossman, David, *Sleeping on a Wire* (New York: Farrar, Straus and Giroux, 1993)

—— *Death as a Way of Life* (London: Bloomsbury, 2003)

Hirst, David, *The Gun and the Olive Branch* (London: Faber & Faber, 2003)

Jiryis, Sabri, *The Arabs in Israel* (New York: Monthly Review Press, 1976)

Kanaaneh, Rhoda Ann, *Birthing the Nation* (Berkeley: University of California Press, 2002)

Kimmerling, Baruch, *Politicide* (London: Verso, 2003)

Kimmerling, Baruch, and Joel Migdal, *The Palestinian People* (Cambridge, MA: Harvard University Press, 2003)

Kretzmer, David, *The Legal Status of the Arabs in Israel* (Boulder: Westview Press, 1990)

—— *The Occupation of Justice* (New York: SUNY, 2002)

Landau, Jacob, *The Arab Minority in Israel, 1967–1991* (Oxford: Clarendon Press, 1993)

Laqueur, Walter, and Barry Rubin (eds), *The Israel–Arab Reader* (New York: Penguin Books, 2001)
Lustick, Ian, *Arabs in the Jewish State* (Austin: University of Texas Press, 1980)
Maddrell, Penny, *The Beduin of the Negev* (London: Minority Rights Group, 1990)
Masalha, Nur, *A Land without a People* (London: Faber & Faber, 1997)
—— *Imperial Israel and the Palestinians* (London: Pluto Press, 2000)
—— (ed.), *Catastrophe Remembered* (London: Zed Books, 2005)
Morris, Benny, *The Birth of the Palestine Refugee Problem* (New York: Cambridge University Press, 1988; 2nd edn, 2004)
—— *Righteous Victims* (New York: Vintage, 2001)
Nathan, Susan, *The Other Side of Israel* (London: HarperCollins, 2005)
Nimni, Ephraim (ed.), *The Challenge of Post-Zionism* (London: Zed Books, 2003)
Pappe, Ilan, *A History of Modern Palestine* (Cambridge: Cambridge University Press, 2004)
Prior, Michael, *Zionism and the State of Israel* (London: Routledge, 1999)
Rabinowitz, Dan, *Overlooking Nazareth* (Cambridge: Cambridge University Press, 1997)
Rabinowitz, Dan, and Khawla Abu Baker, *Coffins on our Shoulders* (Berkeley: University of California Press, 2005)
Reinhart, Tanya, *Israel/Palestine: How to End the War of 1948* (New York: Seven Stories Press, 2002)
Rekhess, Elie (ed.), *Arab Politics in Israel at a Crossroads* (Tel Aviv: Moshe Dayan Centre, 1996)
Rogan, Eugene, and Avi Shlaim (eds), *The War for Palestine* (Cambridge: Cambridge University Press, 2001)
Rose, Jacqueline, *The Question of Zion* (Princeton: Princeton University Press, 2005)
Rouhana, Nadim, *Palestinian Citizens in an Ethnic Jewish State: Identities in Conflict* (New Haven: Yale University Press, 1997)
Said, Edward, *Peace and its Discontents* (New York: Vintage, 1996)
—— *The End of the Peace Process* (London: Granta, 2001)
Shahak, Israel, *Jewish History, Jewish Religion* (London: Pluto Press, 1994)
Shahak, Israel, and Norton Mezvinsky, *Jewish Fundamenstalism in Israel* (London: Pluto Press, 1999)
Shipler, David, *Arab and Jew* (New York: Penguin Books, 1987)
Shlaim, Avi, *The Iron Wall* (London: Penguin Books, 2000)
Slyomovics, Susan, *The Object of Memory* (Philadelphia: University of Pennsylvania Press, 1998)
Smooha, Sammy, *Arabs and Jews in Israel, Volume 1* (Boulder: Westview Press, 1989)
Sofer, Arnon, *Israel, Demography 2000–2020: Dangers and Opportunities* (Haifa: University of Haifa, 2001)
Sultany, Nimr, *Citizens without Citizenship* (Haifa: Mada, 2003)
—— (ed.), *Israel and the Palestinian Minority 2003* (Haifa: Mada, 2004)
—— (ed.), *Israel and the Palestinian Minority 2004* (Haifa: Mada, 2005)

Swisher, Clayton E, *The Truth About Camp David* (New York: Nation Books, 2004)
Wasserstein, Bernard, *Divided Jerusalem* (London: Profile Books, 2002)
Zureik, Elia, *The Palestinians in Israel: A Study in Internal Colonialism* (London: Routledge and Kegan Paul, 1979)

REPORTS

ACRI, Adalah and HRA, *Fatal Force* (December 2000)
Adalah, *Institutionalized Discrimination against Palestinian Citizens of Israel* (August/September 2001)
Amnesty International, *Israel and the Occupied Territories: Excessive Use of Lethal Force* (October 2000)
Arab Association for Human Rights, *The Palestinian Minority in Israel* (Nazareth: HRA, 1998)
—— *Silencing Dissent* (October 2002)
—— *By All Means Possible* (July 2004)
Ibn Khaldun, *Civic Developments among the Palestinian-Arab Minority in Israel* (June 2004)
International Crisis Group, *Identity Crisis: Israel and its Arab Citizens* (March 2004)
—— *Disengagement and After: Where Next for Sharon and the Likud* (1 March 2005)
Mossawa, *The Arab Citizens of Israel* (2003)
—— *Israel's Citizenship and Family Unification Law* (January 2004)
Physicians for Human Rights, *Medicine under Fire* (November 2000)
Rabinowitz, Dan, et al., *After the Rift* (November 2000)
Sikkuy, *The Sikkuy Report 2001–2002* (July 2002)

Index

Printed and bound by CPI Group (UK) Ltd, Croydon, CR0 4YY

13/04/2025

14656488-0001